Thirteen Sick Tasteless Classics, Part V

Thirteen Sick Tasteless Classics, Part V

By

Jay Dubya

Published by
Bookstand Publishing
Morgan Hill, CA 95037
4216_3

Copyright © 2014 by Jay Dubya
All rights reserved. No part of this publication may be reproduced or transmitted in any form or by any means, electronic or mechanical, including photocopy, recording, or any information storage and retrieval system, without permission in writing from the copyright owner.

ISBN 978-1-63498-018-0

Printed in the United States of America

Other Books by Jay Dubya
Adult Fiction

Black Leather and Blue Denim, A '50s Novel
The Great Teen Fruit War, A 1960' Novel
Ron Coyote, Man of La Mangia
Frat' Brats, A '60s Novel
Pieces of Eight
Pieces of Eight, Part II
Pieces of Eight, Part III
Pieces of Eight, Part IV
The Wholly Book of Genesis
The Wholly Book of Exodus
Thirteen Sick Tasteless Classics
Thirteen Sick Tasteless Classics, Part II
Thirteen Sick Tasteless Classics, Part IV
So Ya' Wanna' Be A Teacher!
Mauled Maimed Mangled Mutilated Mythology
Fractured Frazzled Folk Fables & Fairy Farces
FFFF & FF, Part II
Nine New Novellas
Nine New Novellas, Part II
Nine New Novellas, Part III
Nine New Novellas, Part IV
One Baker's Dozen
Two Baker's Dozen
Random Articles and Manuscripts
Time Travel Tales
Modern Mythology
UFO: Utterly Fantastic Occurrences
Prime-Time Crime Time
Snake Eyes and Boxcars
The Psychic Dimension
The Psychic Dimension, Part II

Young Adult Fantasy Novels and Stories

Pot of Gold
Enchanta
Space Bugs, Earth Invasion
The Eighteen Story Gingerbread House

Contents

"Rip Van Winkle" 1

"The Mark of the Beast" 19

"King Midas" 37

"Dr. Tarr and Professor Fether" 47

"The Rocking Horse Winner" 59

"To Build a Fire" 73

"The Notorious Sleeping Beauty" 85

"Excerpt: The Wholly Book of Exodus" 97

"The Green Door" 105

"Punch, Brothers, Punch" 115

"The Gay Tailor Who Became King" 125

"All's Well That Ends Well" 137

"Dr. Heidegger's Experiment" 211

"Rip Van Winkle"

Whoever has made a pleasurable boat voyage up the Hudson River will automatically be impressed with the Catskill Mountains, especially if the observer previously and exclusively believed and thought that cats kill mice. The Catskills are a segment of the great Appalachian Mountain Chain, and yes, as everyone who studies American geography is quite aware, the Appalachians are parallel to the equally magnificent Peachalachians. And in truth, the magical hues characteristic of the Catskills change from season to season, and the promiscuous wives of elderly impotent male residents are perfect weather barometers, even though few of these sex-crazed nymphomaniacs have any lethal measure of mercury in their un-prudish-but-fully-covered hourglass bodies.

When the daily air and wind pattern is fair and tolerable, the Catskills are cloaked in a majestic blue and purple haze, but when the sky is remarkably sunny and cloudless, the wondrous mountains will accumulate a hood of gray mist around their loftiest summits, a peculiar vapor that simply mystifies (mistifies) the casual observers randomly taking peeks at the peaks, making the apexes appear to be akin to the stellar gleaming of the Crown Jewels of England.

At the base of these fairy (but not gay) fabled mountains, the visitor could on a clear autumn day notice smoke billows swirling-up from various chimneys situated throughout the somnolent village, a hamlet of great antiquity, having been founded by conscientious early Dutch colonists. The houses themselves had been built of small yellow bricks that had been carefully imported across the *Atlantic* from the Netherlands, the construction materials never ever passing through the famous Holland Tunnel. The mediocre village homes featured latticed windows, gabled fronts and un-circumcised weathercocks adorning the roofs used for the sole purpose of gauging wind direction.

Within this aforementioned nondescript village existed a certain dwelling that was rather shabby and weatherworn, and inside the hideous-looking eyesore lived a lazy indolent asshole named Rip Van Winkle. Several decades before the "Great Revolutionary War", un-industrious Van Winkle resided in the grotesque-looking abode with his shrewd shrew of a wife, Dame Van Winkle, along with his toddler daughter Judith and seemingly comatose infant son Rip Junior.

As for lethargic Rip Van Winkle, the unmotivated bumpkin claimed to be a direct descendant of the noble Van Winkles of yore, a noteworthy clan that had audaciously battled against savage and peaceful Indians alike in the chivalrous days of valiant Peter Stuyvesant, the last Dutch Governor of New Netherland, before the province became New York under notorious British dominion.

But poor Rip Van Winkle was neither a fighter nor a wife lover. And much to his nasty spouse's chagrin, Rip was beloved by the lackadaisical men and horny women of the commonplace village', despite the fact that even Rip's listless donkey was a totally lazy ass also. So whenever Van Winkle either tilled his potato garden or disked his small field to plant assorted summer and fall vegetables, it was indeed a *harrowing* experience for the pleasant peasant to endure.

But popular Rip Van Winkle was a kind and humble neighbor and an obedient henpecked husband, who obviously never had ever read and comprehended William Shakespeare's supreme masterpiece "The Taming of the Shrew," for Van Winkle was illiterate and never even learned the twenty-six letters of the standard alphabet.

Despite these rather glaring shortcomings, the benevolent man possessed an enormous penis that remained erect for hours on end, several centuries before Viagra, Cialis and Levitra were ever commercially produced by greedy drug companies and then vastly distributed by avaricious left-wing liberal pharmacies along with immoral profit-minded apothecaries.

And without a doubt, the good kinky adulterous village wives, all of whom were infatuated with Rip Van Winkle's superb perpetual erection, unanimously sided with the Pauper's "accursed position" against the frequent railing of his dominant shrew, and their abundant gossip always laid the ultimate blame for any one-sided family dispute squarely on sharp-tongued Dame Van Winkle.

"Poor Rip! If only his nasty-tempered wife knew what the hell she was missing," the village wives would marvel and chatter during afternoon quilting bees, "but unfortunately, she's a reprehensible frigid bitch who absolutely hates her own damned cunt! God! Rip's eight-inch-long tongue is almost as delightful as his fantastic foot-long pussy stuffer! How the hell that venomous bellicose frigid witch ever had two kids I'll never know!"

And psychologically defeated Rip often assisted the younger village boys in making miniature outhouses and massive dildos, and also flying kites exhibiting artistically-drawn nude women, and the innovative experimenter occasionally demonstrated to the hamlet's youth the proper manner in which to be licking wet pink hairy pussy, how to be shooting square marbles in the thick mud, along with proficiently exploding large quantities of putrid sperm juice into the lower atmosphere.

And finally, Van Winkle was proudly adept at telling the more superstitious male urchins all about dangerous Iroquois Indians, about weird witches possessing three hairy-crack slits, and also about vile pedophile ghosts that ironically raped and tortured unprepared priests, ministers, bishops, parsons, imams, popes and rabbis. So naturally, when Rip was preoccupied napping or slumbering under a secluded tree, the inspired acne-faced juvenile delinquents would obsessively masturbate each other when they weren't privately jerking-off inside their family's smelly wooden outhouses.

But truly benign Rip positively despised any form of toil or labor for himself, or more specifically, for his own monetary advancement, but the good-natured loser would gladly help any of his neighbors plow their fields, and as a wonderful reward, the appreciative farmers would allow Van Winkle to sexually service their nympho' wives when they themselves were too pooped to pop their already overworked weasels. And when the accommodating fellow wasn't intensively porking the kinky neighborhood sluts, wily Rip would carry his foul fowling piece upon his shoulder into the local woods and shoot squirrels, foxes, rabbits, lemmings, cockroaches and even pet pigeons named Walter.

But regrettably, Rip farted around so much that there was a tremendous gaping gash in the crotch part of his very baggy pants. Van Winkle's favorite attire was a pair of ancient galligaskins, similar to the oddball garb that the first Hudson River Dutch settlers had worn in the early 1700s. And formidable Dame Van Winkle's persistent oral tirades made Rip think, 'My wife's uncouth mouth is too big even to suck on my gigantic dick! If she were any respectable ordinary woman,' Van Winkle sadly considered, 'my wife could administer a superior blow-job much more adequately than any sex-skilled whore, harlot or hussy residing in the entire Hudson Valley!'

Rip's truest domestic friend was his sole canine Wolf, who also feared Dame Van Winkle's wrathful diatribes much more than the trained predator was intimidated by hostile area Indian tribes. However, Wolf was a ferocious attacker of docile pet dogs, often behaving like a fierce cannibalistic sadist, habitually biting-off little puppies' wieners as well as those belonging to wildly bullying bulldogs, compelling the vanquished victims into licking their own disgusting-looking mangy-furred peckers, which were shaped sort of like lengthy Z-formed lightning bolts. And in regard to his psycho' dog, grateful Rip earned many a shilling having Wolf lick various old men's dicks, especially those limp danglers attached to elderly geezers who hadn't enjoyed either an erection or a decent ejaculation for several decades.

As years of difficult matrimony rolled by, Rip became extremely disenchanted with Dame Van Winkle's perpetual litany of threatening remarks. 'She's got the only adult pussy in the village that I've never both licked and screwed on the same night,' Van Winkle lamented in reference to his lambasting partner for life. 'I think I'll head over to the village inn and see what the fuck my loyal buddies Nicholas Vedder and Derrick Van Bummel are bullshitting about. We three assholes really relish sitting together in the shade around and beneath the hanging sign of His Majesty King George the Third. At least the cozy tavern is one placid spot for me' to relax and escape my cruel woman's chronic ridiculing.'

Nicholas Vedder was the inn's revered proprietor, whose favorite St. Bernard Barf-thalamew would always vomit whenever all-too-aggressive Wolf was busy patrolling and prowling the immediate vicinity. Rip's thoroughly obnoxious mutt would (without warning) deliberately stick his pecker into a bowl full of vinegar and then force poor Barf-thalamew to lick the sour taste off. This was particularly humiliating to Vedder's exploited pooch, because Barf-thalamew happened to be the only Muslim animal in the entire Christian hamlet, and the abused cur secretly desired celebrating Ramadan year-round without licking any sour meat.

Erudite Derrick Van Bummel was the sagacious village schoolmaster who had the distinct reputation during every school day of teaching his illiterate students a boring classic that would make the class sick. Each sultry summer and fall afternoon Vedder, Van Bummel, Van Winkle along with three of their undistinguished cronies would sit on the splintery circular bench constructed around a tall oak tree and loudly gossip about local news and current politics, and to make their physical existence more comfortable, there were six square holes hollowed-out upon the rudely fabricated rickety round bench, each senile man sitting upon a separate one, so that if anyone had to take a serious crap during an intriguing group dialogue, the aged fellow in question, not wanting to miss any important conversation being exchanged, quite fortuitously, the curious gent didn't have to rise and stroll over to the inn's rear outhouse, but instead, just made a fecal deposit right then-and-there in front of the inn while sitting upon his own private hopper.

And flamboyant Van Bummel would daily fascinate his proletarian audience of five morons from early June until late September, adroitly and impressively employing his enviable vocabulary, articulating certain significant dictionary words like "cunnilingus," "pornography," "copulation," "ejaculation," "fellatio," and incredibly, the perverted schoolmaster's mesmerized listeners really never fully fathomed one iota of what the fuck the knowledgeable pedagogue was adroitly orating.

"You know Nicholas," garrulous Van Bummel prefaced, his skinny ass seated upon his square hopper hole located beneath the really tremendous oak, "you preposterously verbalize your mediocre pedestrian concepts like you're a combination of a contemporary Sophist and a sacrilegious Pharisee-turned-Sadducee."

And then next a rather bewildered Nicholas Vedder indignantly answered, "Derrick, speak normal Swahili so that maybe I could fuckin' understand your dull dumb-ass bullshit better!"

"Nicholas, don't you know what the esoteric nomenclature 'coitus' means?" Van Bummel deliberately asked his very flabbergasted inn acquaintance.

"Yes, I happen to have a bad case of *colitis* and have to pass gas every time I hear you speak your totally ridiculous drivel," Vedder all-too-honestly replied, just as the zany innkeeper loudly propelled a large amount of fecal matter down into the wide square hole his fat ass had been hovering over, much to the general amusement of the five other Dutchmen. "I lack the intestinal *fart*itude to comprehend or endure any of your fucked-up insane gibberish. Every time I listen to your lingo Van Bummel, I nearly shit my brains out!"

Just then an enraged Dame Van Winkle showed-up in front of the inn, lifted an embarrassed Rip Van Winkle up from his familiar bench, furiously kicked her appalled husband in the testicles three times, and then after dropping her humiliated spouse into the nearby high weeds, grabbed both Nicholas Vedder and Derrick Van Bummel by their exposed necks, hoisted the surprised nitwits up off their square thrones and then violently plunged their heads precisely into their two pungent square shitholes, whose never-cleaned storage drums were situated directly beneath.

Then without any evident hesitation, the incensed hag latched onto her already-stunned husband's right ear and forcefully yanked

Rip out of the high weeds, dragging him off the friendly premises, cursing and screaming vehemently during the whole bizarre enterprise.

* * * * * * * * * * * *

On a most excellent autumn afternoon, seldom motivated Rip Van Winkle, accompanied by his faithful companion Wolf, initiated an arduous ramble high-up into the interior of the scenic Catskill Mountains, the challenging excursion occurring immediately after petulant Dame Van Winkle had brutally scolded her husband, telling Rip to "Take a long hike off a short crag!"

The crestfallen Dutchman reckoned that he should scramble as far away from oppressive "Petticoat Tyranny" as the persecuted soul possibly could wander. 'I dare not lie down here,' the disconsolate trekker realistically thought, 'or else Wolf will certainly piss on my face as is the nasty scoundrel's distasteful habit. My neurotic mutt must have some sort of major urinary or kidney problem. I just gotta' maintain my spunk and keep ascending. Too damned bad I'm not ascending up into Heaven instead of up from that raunchy village below! Oh well. I suppose this rugged mountain just has to satisfy my weary emotional needs for the time being!'

From a narrow opening positioned amidst the dense tree growth Rip's eyes again detected the sleepy village far below, and his keen pupils also perceived the incomparable Hudson River glittering like a silver stream off in the distance, shining from the bright sunlight's weakening reflection. Several small fishing boats (that had learned how to catch pike and shad all by themselves) were recognizable to the south, the vessels obviously heading towards New Amsterdam (New York) where the ambitious fishermen would sell their daily catches at market.

To Rip's immediate right was an ordinary mountain glen, with steep ridges, and now the overhead crags were gloomily shading that part of the lofty ravine from the fearful adventurer's eyes. 'I hope I can shoot a squirrel or two with my trusty fowling gun,' Rip wished and prayed. 'I gotta' remember to string those fur-babies over my shoulder and conceal them underneath my tawdry wool jacket or else Wolf will wolf-down those luscious suckers before I could ever say 'That gay faggot Attila the Hun' just once.'

As bedraggled Van Winkle was about to reluctantly descend the precarious incline his cold ears detected a squeaky voice hallooing from a distance, "Rip Van Winkle! Rip Van Winkle!" Thirty seconds later Rip's surprised eyes discerned a freakish-looking midget of sorts, the queer-looking bloke struggling to carry a heavy cask through a tunnel that nature had (over the eons) carved through *that* remote side of the picturesque mountain.

'That little twerp in desperate need of help is wearing a jerkin that the short piss-head more than likely wears when jerkin'-off!' Rip mused and smiled. 'And what's with the wild grizzled beard and the shabby galligaskins the puny asshole is wearing, quite similar to the ones I have on my bony rear-end right this minute; yes, they're just like the tarnished ones I had inherited from my great-great-great grandfather! Maybe this gay-looking son-of-a-bitch elf is really masquerading as a fucked-up female transvestite in disguise.'

The diminutive wrinkle-faced dwarf gestured for Rip to approach and assist him in enacting and completing *his* seemingly difficult task. Thinking that he might earn a cup of rum or gin as a reward for his solicited cask-transport employment, Rip readily complied with the strange imp's tacit hand-signal. The unusual pair clambered onward with their difficult burden, laboring up a narrow shadowy gully, and as the encumbered duo awkwardly ventured on, Van Winkle heard certain long rolling peals of thunder originating a mile or so up the desolate rustic trail.

'That peculiar noise sounds a lot like people playing a game of ninepins!' Rip recollected. 'I have no money so I hope I can participate in their merry gambol without having to gamble! Come to think of it,' Rip nostalgically reminisced, 'bowling's definitely up my alley! But even without a map, I'm aware that we're perilously climbing just east of Tarrytown! We're certainly not anywhere near friggin' Bowling Green, Ohio!'

Soon the un-dynamic twosome emerged from the thin dark tunnel and next ventured into a second hollow that was surrounded by high precipices along with towering coniferous trees that understandably shrouded the glaring sun and made all visibility almost opaque. 'This little asshole companion of mine must have a mild case of laryngitis because the wimpy knucklehead hasn't spoken a damned word since he first beckoned my name! How did the little jerk-off know my full name to begin with?' Rip wondered. 'Oh, now I get it!' Van Winkle comprehended, his inquisitive mind swiftly shifting gears. 'Another name for being a bowler is *kegler*, and now I've been helping this annoying mute pipsqueak deliver this keg of liquor to some sort of mysterious mountain party! Shit! I hope they have plenty of marijuana and drunken whores there too!'

The exhausted transporters slowly entered a natural pristine environment that handsomely formed a remarkable sylvan forest amphitheater, and in the center of the surreal phenomenon stood a company of odd-looking serious-faced miniature gentlemen actively playing an intense game of ninepins. The extraordinary chaps were dressed in the quaint-but-ancient fashion of revered Dutch fellows who had lived several centuries before, all sporting behemoth-sized breeches having decorative rows of buttons down each pant side. 'Those idiotic jerk-offs are wearing jerkins just like my anonymous guide. Holy Hades! I now feel just like Alex in Fantasyland!'

The tiny corpulent 'Dutch leprechauns' all possessed stone-cold melancholy expressions upon their visages, suggesting that they were fundamentally bored and unhappy with life and with living, and if the oddball phantoms were indeed three centuries old as it initially seemed, one could easily sympathize with their remarkably tired plight.

A stout little gray-haired asshole sporting a short shiny sword dangling from his waistband appeared to be the contingent's supreme commander. And the entire astonishing assemblage reminded Rip of smaller versions of characters in an old Flemish painting he had once viewed while touring a prominent New Amsterdam museum, and when the speechless festooned personages began coughing-up and spitting disgusting green lungers all over the damned verdant meadow, alert Van Winkle accurately concluded that the diminutive repugnant freaks were indeed 'phlegmish.'

'Those portly Lilliputian Dutchmen must all bathe their cats in vinegar because they're all showing sour-pusses exactly where natural human smiles oughta' be displayed upon their faces!' Rip creatively imagined. 'These frightening petite ghouls oughta' have been dead two hundred years ago! At least that's what my inferior education is tellin' me!'

Suddenly, upon noticing the arrival of their impoverished native human guest, the pint-sized ancient Dutchmen ceased their bowling activities and then concentrated their full attention upon incredulous Van Winkle, whose eyelids immediately began to neurotically flap and winkle. The alien celebrators then emptied the contents of the heavy keg into a sturdy flagon, and next the eccentric group gestured for Rip to wait upon and serve the designated alcohol to them, and upon clumsily completing the obliging servant's duty, the sad-faced entourage motioned to Van Winkle to indulge in sampling the potent beverage himself.

Rip was delighted to acknowledge that the wonderful drink tasted exactly like the Holland gin that old tavern owner Nicholas Vedder secretly kept as 'inn's treasure' down inside his cobweb-infested 'wine cellar'. But being extremely thirsty, Rip 'Let it rip!' and promptly gulped-down two additional cups of the abominable intoxicant, and soon thereafter, the dizzy and giddy imbiber's sensibilities had been egregiously conquered, and a few seconds later, victimized Van Winkle's body collapsed upon the wet soggy turf, and soon poor Rip's vulnerable mind drifted-off into a deep intoxicated sleep.

* * * * * * * * * * *

Upon waking-up from his extended drunken siesta, Rip found himself' lying upon a damp knoll, strangely enough, the exact spot where he had first observed the old hobbled dwarf carrying the heavy wooden cask upon his shoulder. Birds were busily hopping, chirping and twittering around the tangled bushes with several rude sparrows zooming-down from tall pine trees and then prodigiously crapping upon Van Winkle's exposed scruffy head.

'Surely I have not accidentally slept here for a full night!' Rip's fuzzy mind evaluated. 'Dame Van Winkle will barbarically castrate me and gladly feed my shriveled-up testicles to hungry Wolf, who will surely voraciously devour them without any particular regret. Say, where the hell is old Wolf anyway? I hope my mutt hasn't run-off with some dominant Doberman bitch. Perhaps he's been attacked and eaten by those ravenous black hawks from Chicago that migrate here to the gorgeous gorges every autumn.'

Then the awoken sleeper speculated for a moment. 'How could I ever again say 'Fleas Navidad' to my psychotic dog on Christmas if Wolf's permanently abandoned me up here in the Catskills? Oh that flagon! That certainly was a terribly lethal vat of Holland gin!' Rip remorsefully remembered. Without any more pondering, confused Van Winkle moved his hand down inside his tattered galligaskins. 'Thank goodness I still seem to have my dependable balls and scrotum sac somewhat intact!'

Lying flat on the ground, Rip anxiously rummaged around and soon frantically searched the immediate proximity for his well-oiled fowling gun but instead, the anxious fellow discovered a rusty old firelock that had apparently experienced better times. Van Winkle now suspected that the reveling roisters who had been partying the night before had cast a mischievous black magic spell upon him and that the inane rascals had cleverly traded the well-maintained fowling piece for the "useless piece of junk" he now held in his hands.

"Woe is me!" the beleaguered man exclaimed to his apathetic surroundings. "Woe is me!" Van Winkle repeated to the empty and uncaring forest. "I had been sleeping on cruddy algae and upon slimy ferns, but at least I wasn't resting on my goddamned laurels!"

After weakly rising from his former prone situation, the disenchanted explorer noticed that his aching back was suffering from severe rheumatism! 'This raunchy pain is absolutely excruciating!' Van Winkle thought, successfully utilizing an academic word he had learned from all-too-vociferous Derrick Van Bummel. 'Holy shit! I've lost my formerly reliable hard-on! Now only if my flaccid dick can get stiff again from my new-found advanced arthritis condition. In truth,' Van Winkle fearfully conjectured, 'my shrew of a spouse won't give a flying shit about this exceptional deficient predicament of mine, because we never now have oral, kinky or even standard straight sex. To this very day I don't know how the hell we ever had two repulsive biological children. But I don't know if the horny town wives and the equally horny village kids will be able to adjust to and appreciate me suddenly becoming Mr. Softy!'

Cautiously descending from a series of treacherous mountain slopes, Rip next slipped, tripped and tumbled several times among birch-wood and sassafras trees, and after slowly rising to his feet, moments later the confused wanderer trampled through random dense growths of witch hazel and poison oak. Wild grapevines also impeded Van Winkle's downward progress, the dense brush abruptly interrupting one rollicking downhill roll, but still the stubborn perplexed fellow stumbled, and his frame again rotated round and round in another prolonged frenzied descent.

After eventually smashing into an enormous elm tree, and now fearing the looming prospect of starvation, the famished squirrel hunter courageously persevered and doggedly (without Wolf) continued pursuing his ill-fated destination. 'I can't die up here in the middle of nowhere!' the troubled trekker worriedly assessed. 'I need to visit Nicholas Vedder's wife's fucked-up erotic tattoo and body mutilation parlor at least one more time before I fuckin' die!'

After finally locating the huge mountain's base, a half-hour later the encumbered ambler approached the *outskirts* of the village, which was easily identifiable since all of the gay-looking hamlet homosexuals were appropriately dressed in short red kilts with accompanying matching pink brassieres.

'Shit!' Rip instinctively hypothesized. 'I know just about every straight and homo' asshole cavorting around the whole countryside and yet, I can't recognize a single one of these nauseous degenerate jerk-offs, who are all staring at me like a gaggle of homos' as if I'm some sort of LBTG ghost! If this is an innocent dream, it's rapidly transforming into an intolerable nightmare!'

And then the busy-body village residents followed the new arrival's path in what actually constituted an improvised parade. One of the Village People, a goofy goon named "Tonto from Toronto", was elaborately dressed as a savage Indian warrior, and another outstanding faggot wearing tight black leather was indeed a modified backwoodsman, while a third village personage was in the costume of a city policeman, and upon Rip's baffled scrutiny, the fourth associated fruitcake (prancing around within the unorthodox singing group) voluntarily described his totally naked presence to Van Winkle as attributable to *him* essentially being an out-of-the-closet British Redcoat "going full-musket bare-ass naked."

The abnormal un-religious procession eventually reached the village center, and not one friendly dog or unfriendly child pretended to know who the hell the formerly notorious Rip Van Winkle was. But the returning lazy farmer imagined that he was a victorious General leading a triumphant phalanx of soldiers into ancient Rome, but then on second thought, the strange new homes, the unfamiliar names painted upon overhead shingles, along with the fully indecipherable new-town scenario further addled Rip's already-disoriented thought processes.

And upon managing to rub his grimy cold right hand under his chaffed chin, flustered Rip Van Winkle made a rather startling discovery. 'Holy tits' flying all-around in Satan's Hell! My beard's grown a foot! Thank the Lord it's a foot without five or more fucked-up tocs!'

Indeed, the new arrival was under mental duress and his now-anemic mind was rapidly encountering a wicked identity crisis. Rip's deteriorating brain was indeed thoroughly disheveled.

'Who the fuck am I?' the groggy refugee futilely guessed and self-interrogated. 'I feel horribly bewitched without my witch of a wife ever being involved! Of all the lousy fucked-up negative luck! Why couldn't damned Dame Van Winkle take-up squirrel hunting and get herself lost up in the alluring Catskills, instead of poor old me?'

* * * * * * * * * *'

The still-restless vagabond gradually made his journey to his treasured home, but much to his mounting apprehension, Van Winkle observed an abode existing in abject decay with the windows shattered, the doors unhinged and the roof and shingles half caved-in. An ugly cur that somewhat resembled Wolf (but having protruding rib bones) skulked around, wagging its ruffled mangy tail between its hind legs, growling incessantly from misery while moving among the knee-deep weeds, and then the despicable beast very pathetically managed leaving the greatly neglected front yard. "My very dog finds me quite avoidable!" Rip softly muttered. "Even without the aid of a mirror, come to think of it, I do smell like shit in addition to probably looking like shit too!"

Upon very deliberately stepping into the ramshackle house, Van Winkle instantly determined that the hideous place was far beyond repair. Staggering through the dilapidated shack's most accessible zone, Rip called-out for his wife and children, but only morbid echoes could be heard bouncing off the decrepit walls and then ringing like ghostly whistles throughout the more distant chambers.

The frustrated fellow next exited his former modest bungalow and made his way to the prior scene of Nicholas Vedder's Inn, which now displayed a unique shingle reading, "The Union Hotel Owned by the Honorable Mr. Jonathan Doolittle."

"Jonathan Doolittle," whispered Rip to himself. "He sounds like a worthless indolent asshole, just like I am and was. We oughta' get along famously, he and I."

And then Rip perceptively noticed a shoddy flagpole and the attendant banner atop seemed rather alien to his vague memory, the fluttering cloth characterized by a circle of stars and supplemented with thirteen alternating red and white horizontal stripes. "What the hell's that weird eyesore?" Van Winkle yelled to a crowd of pedestrian bystanders.

"Why that's the Flag of the States!" shouted back an astounded citizen. "Where the fuck have you' been hiding your ass? In fuckin' Siberia?"

And next Rip peered at the overhead portrait of King George, who was no longer garnished in a bright red aristocratic jacket but now was proudly wearing a blue coat with buff trim, and instead of a scepter in the monarch's palm, the impressive military figure now held a gleaming sword. "Who's that strange soldier portrayed up there?" Rip hollered-out. "Who the hell is this new guy General Washington, as that alien sign up there reads?"

"Why it's George Washington of course! He was instrumental in inspiring the American Continental Army in defeating the dreaded British at Yorktown in the last battle of the Revolutionary War!" a local politician rather boisterously bellowed. "You musta' slept through the entire major conflict, you dumb old fuck Geezer! And by the way, are you trying to lead some kind of local revolt here with that rusty old piece of shit you're toting, and are you mischievously leading a disorganized rabble of rebel women and children at your heels? Tell me, Old Codger. Are you a Federal or a Democrat?"

"I think this senile jerk-off is a riot, even with his mob of women and children!" a Second Politician arrogantly boomed as everyone else hardily laughed aloud. "I'm willing to wager that this near-dead Methuselah's real name is Arthur Wrightis! Ha, ha, ha!"

Meanwhile, throughout the entire stranger-than-fiction spectacle, a third egocentric politician, a laconic African named Maliko Akimbo, stood there reticent in the middle of the clamorous throng, and quickly flashing a broad grin, the gaunt Kenyan, indiscriminately wearing tight leotards, was deftly standing semi-erect with his left arm akimbo and with his right hand leaning against a long silvery cane.

"Alas assembled Ladies and Gentlemen," cried-out Rip in a timid and dismayed tone of voice. "I'm a simple poor quiet asshole, and yes, a foolish native of this fucked-up place, and quite confidentially, I must admit that I'm also a loyal disciple and a true-blue bona fide subject of His Majesty, King George. God bless his mortal soul!"

"The crazed nutcase intruder is a bleepin' Tory!" a male voice in the crowd screamed. "This senile Old Fart is a contemptible Tory, a spy, a despised British supporter! Let's lynch his wrinkled ass from the tall oak tree right here and now!"

"Yes indeed, the reprehensible King had all of the Tories on his side except one," the opinionated First Politician loudly yelled above the din. "And that asshole's name was Vic Tory! Ha, ha, ha!"

"Folks, truly I mean no-one any harm," Rip all-too-candidly testified. "I merely came here to the center of town looking for some old friends that I used to bullshit with."

"Well then, who the hell are these imaginary chums of your?" snobbishly demanded the cocky Second Politician. "I hope that your old pals aren't fucked-up hangable Tories too!"

"Where's my good buddy Nicholas Vedder?"

After a moment's silence, an elderly curmudgeon stepped forward and replied in a shrill piping voice, "Holy fuck! Nicholas Vedder! That gabby shithead's been deceased and buried these last eighteen years. A wooden tombstone that's now rotted away in the graveyard told of his date of birth and also of his date of death! But," the pencil-necked geek qualified, "Nicholas Vedder's very shrewd wife still operates the extremely profitable tattoo and body mutilation shop on the corner, and she's even selling myriad volumes of immoral pornography down in Mr. Doolittle's dank cellar, which used to be her perverted husband's personal sex and sadism clinic that most people thought was a mere gin storage area!"

"Well then," apologetically continued Rip, "where the hell's my favorite drinking crony, Brom Dutcher?"

"Brom Dutcher!" exclaimed a fairly delirious woman standing in the raucous crowd. "Why he was killed in the great siege that had been fought at the base of Antony's Nose! Old Brom was shot in the face by a musket ball and instantly lost both his enlarged nostrils. The poor bastard couldn't breathe anymore and his lungs soon expired from a lack of air!"

"Well then, where's my old talkative pal Derrick Van Bummel, the wise-assed schoolmaster who knew more impractical educated bullshit than either Miguel Shakespeare or William Cervantes?"

"Derrick Van Bummel?" yelled-out an old destitute prostitute who could no longer hump and pump upon either a soft or hard mattress. "That imbecile jerk-off went off to fight in the war, became a fabulous general, and now the disliked windbag is incompetently serving in Congress way down south in Washington."

Rip's puzzled mind was swimming in sheer quandary with the amount of new complicated terminology being divulged and delivered to his oversized dirt-laden ears: Revolutionary War, General Washington, Stony Point, Antony's Nose, Congress, along with the vague allusions 'Federal and Democrat'. "Does nobody here know an unfortunate hen-pecked fella' named Rip Van Winkle?"

"Rip Van Winkle!" hooted a loud-mouthed lesbian standing in the volatile mob. "Why that's Rip Van Winkle leaning against that tree over yonder. Yes, the detestable dolt is as idle as a sleeping turtle! This unbelievable tale you're spouting Old Man can only be described as the bullshit of all bullshits!"

Rip turned his head and gingerly glanced to his right. His bloodshot eyes beheld an acne-faced punk frenetically scratching his testicles and then alternating to vigorously rubbing his scrawny ass in public. The ragged wretch was indeed as lazy and as phlegmatic as his obedient biological father had always been.

"Hey Old Fuck!" the First Politician haughtily commanded. "Who the hell are *you* anyway? Tell us your legitimate name or else I'll summon the town constable and have your butt mercilessly tossed into the clinker!"

"God only knows who the hell I am," Rip complained with an indication of genuine concern. "I'm at the limit of my wits, to be sure. I'm somebody else other than who I thought I was. No, that's me screwing around scratching my ass over yonder, but no, that juvenile delinquent is somebody else that's gotten into my shoes."

Rip then felt compelled to look-down at his feet and with a degree of worry, confirmed to everyone in his doubting audience the fact that he was now barefooted. "I had been my old happy-go-lucky self just last night but soon I fell fast asleep very fast, and those little trouble-making morons evilly switched my gun, and the naughty creeps also stole my splendid dog, and now everything's radically changed for the worse. I mean," Rip lamented, "I'm changed, and now to be perfectly honest, I can't tell who the fuck I am!"

* * * * * * * * * * *

The still somewhat-interested village witnesses now began looking at each other, impulsively demonstrating a variety of winks and nods, the aggregate of folks simultaneously circling their index fingers around the sides of their foreheads. Some of the more suspicious inhabitants even schemed to secure the rusty gun by wrestling it away from the itinerant old codger, who then unpersuasively prattled-on with his erratic narrative.

At that most critical juncture an attractive young lady frenetically pushed her way through the jabbering crowd, simply to obtain a better peep at the bizarre bearded newcomer. The young female was holding a chubby baby in her arms, the alarmed infant crying at the sight of the aged man inadvertently possessing "the rough gray crocodile skin." "Hush Rip! Hush you little whimperer! The old hysterical asshole won't harm you one bit!"

The child's singular name along with the air of the mother's voice magically caught Rip Van Winkle's attention. "Who might you be my Fair Woman?" the undesirable-looking village visitor nervously inquired. "What is your formal married name?"

"Judith Gardener," the young mother stammered. "I'm as good as divorced right now from my irresponsible husband. But on the positive side of things, I do own and operate a small town landscaping business titled: 'Do your gardening with Gardener'."

"Do you also have a nursery?" Rip inquired.

"Yes," Judith eagerly answered. "That's the back room in my house where I breast-feed my infant son!"

"And your father's name?"

"Ah, the poor bad-luck slug; Rip Van Winkle was his name. But it's been twenty years since the frivolous fool marched-up into the mountains with his dog and gun," Judith sadly disclosed. "His pooch Wolf returned home the following morning without him. Some gossipers say that my pop had been shot by a tribe of inebriated Indians from Cleveland or Braves from Atlanta. But I was only a naïve little girl at the time, excitedly looking forward to experiencing the highly anticipated glory of entering puberty and getting violently raped and laid!"

Rip then sighed heavily, for the distraught geezer wanted his parched tongue and dry lips to produce one more salient question. "Where's your mother?"

"Oh, she had died several years back," Judith divulged without any sign of sorrow. "She broke a blood vessel in her throat while excessively yelling at a traveling peddler from Boston."

'What a marvelous *stroke* of luck!' Rip automatically thought. And then the sentimental codger couldn't control his rampant emotions any longer. Van Winkle aggressively grabbed and gathered his daughter and her shrieking offspring into his grimy arms and boldly announced, "I *am* your derelict father! Young Rip Van Winkle once! Old Rip Van Winkle now! Does nobody here in this fucked-up lesbian and gay community remember Rip Van Winkle?"

A debilitated hoary old whore nonchalantly stepped forward and raised her withered hand up to her brow, her movement quite closely and methodically surveying and inspecting the old hunter's haggard-looking countenance. The gruesome-looking wench paused for a pregnant moment and then succinctly proclaimed, "Sure enough, it is truly Rip Van Winkle! Don't you recall? You had screwed me three times in your stenchy outhouse and twice more upon a neighbor's haystack, all in the same day!"

Rip's implausible story was told and retold a plethora of times, for amazingly, the whole two decades being fast asleep had been to Van Winkle as but one crazy sinister night. Virtually every settlement along the Hudson from Tarrytown to Albany knew the exotic tale by heart, and soon Rip gracefully evolved into an overnight sensation, lecturing at esteemed, prestigious colleges and universities such as West Point, Harvard, Princeton and Yale, quixotic safe havens where the new savant's inimitable oratorical presentations were much in demand and coincidentally, immensely received and savored.

But the authentic and highly-regarded village historian, one venerated Peter Vanderdunk, who was renowned for dipping doughnuts into huge cups of gin-spiked tea concocted by irascible Nicholas Vedder, was well-versed in the various Dutch fables and legends that were prevalent throughout the resplendent Hudson River Valley. Peter immediately collaborated and confirmed the validity of Rip's totally spectacular tale.

"Every twenty years," dementia-suffering Vanderdunk commenced his recitation, "noble explorer Henry Hudson and his crew of tiny sailors come up the river and together the disgruntled immortal assholes haunt the royal Catskills. Their ship is still called the *Half Moon*, meaning that Henry Hudson and his goofball mariners were, at best, only half-assed sea-goers. In fact," Peter loquaciously communicated, "my delusional father once came upon the four-foot-tall zany shitheads playing ninepins up in the mountains, and the disturbing noise of their balls crashing into bowling pins resulted in frightening blasts of thunder radiating throughout the indigenous ravines and valley passes. I mean," Peter proceeded with his' informative exposition, "nobody's ever goin' to roll *my* friggin' balls down a fuckin' rocky ravine, that's for goddamned sure! How the fuck could I ever have a wild and miraculous orgasm screwing some receptive tramp at age ninety-nine without any goddamned testicles merrily bouncing around inside *my* shriveled-up scrotum?"

Eventually the tragic anachronism affectionately known as "Rip Van Winkle" was able to reunite with several of his old inn companions, and most of them (including a rejuvenated Rip) could still respectively achieve super erections and consequently squirt sticky sperm juice all over the round wooden outhouse table still-situated in front of Mr. Doolittle's totally ghetto hotel.

And Rip was unanimously accepted as the principal patriarch of the now-bustling town, ingeniously chronicling certain hazy-minded events that had occurred in the Hudson River vicinity years before the all-important American Revolutionary War had evolved.

Despite his now-honored regional reputation, Rip Van Winkle could never fully fathom how he was presently a free citizen of the United States, but in reality, *that* new-found special liberty meant little to his ultra-sensitive psyche. Losing twenty years of a person's life' while still aging *that* length of time would certainly represent a massive dilemma in anyone's general mental and emotional development.

The abusive dictatorship of King George the Third of England was truly diminished in Rip's scattered mind when in essence, the onerous debacle, when compared to the vicious "Petticoat Tyranny" of the all-too-diabolical Dame Van Winkle, was of minimal significance to the now-eminent Van Winkle. And whenever the vengeful shrew's awful name was incidentally mentioned outside Mr. Doolittle's Hotel, Rip's contemporary cronies would all reflexively piss their pants soaking wet, and likewise, amused Van Winkle would concurrently crap a mammoth load directly into his two-century-old galligaskins.

Washington Irving (1783-1859)

Named after George Washington, author Washington Irving was America's first internationally recognized literary figure. Irving started-out as a lawyer, but from the very beginning of his career the man fully resented the monotony of his chosen profession.

In addition to authoring his first huge success titled *Knickerbocker's History of New York,* Washington Irving later achieved tremendous popularity with the publishing of *The Sketch Book*, which included his classic American stories "Rip Van Winkle" and "The Legend of Sleepy Hollow."

In later years Washington Irving had built a beautiful mansion on the Hudson just below Tarrytown, the estate being named *Sunnyside*. The famous writer also is credited with creating the still-used cliché, "the almighty dollar."

"The Mark of the Beast"

East of the Suez Canal, which is just north of the bloody Root Canal, the direct authority of the British Empire ends and widespread lawlessness prevails. Especially in many sections of bad-ass India, so-called "modern civilization" experiences organized political control neutralized by the superstitious belief in the power of pagan gods and wicked demons, whom the "gullible natives" both revere and fear respectively.

And even in the case of supposedly sophisticated British government men assigned to represent the Empire in the unruly regions, the distant Church of England exercises only meager control over Great Britain's tough resilient soldiers and over the glut of crazed demented pioneer lunatics who insanely call the hellish zones their new home. My incredible story only affirms *this* strange tale's opening narrative.

Several years ago my closest friend was Strickland, a loyal officer of the frontier police establishment, a competent investigator who was more of an expert on the customs and behavior of the native population than I ever was. Yes, even if only mildly interrogated, all-too-honest and objective Strickland, an avowed celibate who never gets laid or jerks-off because he simply desires to preserve his vital reproductive juices *inside* his body, will candidly testify to the astounding veracity of my totally surreal story.

Then there was "by-the-book" Dr. Damien Dumoise, a perverted French physician, who also exactly observed the crazy shit both Strickland and I had each endured. But Dumoise's hypothetical medical evaluations (principally based upon fallacious Western Science) were in the end entirely erroneous, founded exclusively on materialism, on legal and illegal drugs, and also on that charlatan Sigmund Freud's rather suspect psychology theories.

Dumoise, who obsessively consumed and digested an abundance of peanuts, pecans and cashews morning, noon and night, had died suddenly last October in a very peculiar manner, having six huge hemorrhoids that had piled-up inside his fat asshole, all exploding simultaneously.

Finally, a maniac acquaintance named Fleete had arrived in India last spring with intentions of opening a new deli, but the impractical imbecile owned no property, and the bipolar dolt had accumulated little money all throughout his rather lackluster life. But much to Fleete's personal satisfaction, a deranged uncle had died of a combination of malaria and leprosy, leaving his sole beneficiary an inferior estate near Dharmsala, situated and isolated in the perilous foot-hills of the grand Himalayas.

This unpredictable British transplant Fleete was a portly, overweight and seemingly harmless settler that absolutely despised the area's indigenous dark-skinned natives, whose language and temperament the sometimes belligerent homesteader completely misunderstood, relentlessly complaining to apathetic associates that both the sick Sikh inhabitants along with their erratic jargon were "extraordinarily primitive" and "obviously quite antediluvian."

"The ugly bastards should take their turbans and all their shoddy possessions and migrate to a safer place like Pakistan, where the prehistoric freaks could play hide and Sikh all the fuckin' time," Fleete more than once vehemently expressed to Strickland, Dumoise and to myself'.

That particular New Year's Day this lunatic Fleete had ridden his feeble stallion into town all the way from his dilapidated cottage high-up in the forbidden hills, coming into town for the purpose of partying with us other three Limeys at the local police station where Strickland had been the chief official. In fact, according to prearranged plans, Fleete was to stay the night at the head cop's apartment located overtop a popular nearby illegal bordello. And in substitution for paying the evening's lodging, Fleete agreed to administer to Strickland three lengthy enemas at six hour intervals, just as he had often done with the now-deceased ass-scratching Dr. Dumoise.

That night there was an enormous buffet provided at the "Police Club" to celebrate the birth of the New Year. Plenty of drinking was the standard pattern (and the accepted tradition) of the raucous nocturnal "Old Country Beefeaters Fraternity." Certainly when Englishmen of all diverse occupations gather from the farthest regions of the province, the prospect of wild revelry is normally quite inevitable.

From the remote wilderness arrived a posse of "Catch-'em-Alive-O's," adventurous bounty hunters and overzealous deputies that hadn't seen other white faces since last year's January 1st shindig bash. These audacious reckless cowboys would ride fifteen miles at a clip from village to village risking being shot, stabbed or butchered by hostile ethnocentric Indian scumbags, all of whom egregiously hated our guts, our semi-colons and also our ultra-sensitive colons.

Before entering the mediocre police station, the clamorous Catch-'em-Alive-O's played an amusing game of polo along the side field, innovatively using a curled-up half-dead hedgehog they had found lying in the weeds as their official game ball. And then, imaginatively employing their long rifles as improvised hitting sticks, the merry boys' teams scored three goals apiece until the battered hedgehog perished. After the boisterous fiasco/contest had finally terminated, one of the ruthless buffoons carried the deceased hedgehog into the club's game room and on cue, forcefully stuffed the motionless furry creature inside a pool table's side hole.

Half a dozen homesteading planters had just arrived from the south, and I recollect Fleete actively protesting to my ears that we all were guaranteed to be growing nasty planters' warts in our soles, heels, scrotum balls, and in the balls of our callused feet too.

Liquor and wine abounded throughout the building's shelves. The fellowship had commenced *our* totally British party by singing a dissonant version of "Auld Lang Syne" in Arabic, with the second verse being inadequately harmonized in Hindu. Then the assembled revelers were drinking screwdrivers from the Polo Trophy Cup and next methodically dissecting and disgustingly eating the deceased hedgehog raw. Everyone in attendance swore that we were excellent eternal friends, even though in reality I wasn't acquainted with half the obnoxious assholes who' were also chronically farting and discourteously burping and belching every five or so seconds.

Several military blokes bragged about heading to Burma for more challenging adventure, a rather hostile territory which was soon to be annexed from the Mother Empire. Those brave devil-may-care assholes desired erecting and opening-up a shaving cream factory in Burma to service the "who gives a shit?" local hut dwellers.

Others in our un-illustrious company promised to migrate to the Sudan, where the implausible idiots believed that the social environment would be a vast improvement over that of despicable Northern India. And then finally, according to *their* wholly distorted logic, the "Fuzzies," rug-headed black Africans, would indubitably patronize the illegal marijuana and cocaine drugs the British itinerants planned on illicitly manufacturing and selling there.

For appetizers, Fleete began his outrageous night of misery swallowing-down large amounts of sherry and merlot, alternating gulps of each wine from two separate glasses. For his entree, the already-disoriented fanatic imbibed shots of rye and scotch intermittently, and for dessert, the bizarre jerk-off drank a full bottle of cheap champagne, later switching to diluted 'cabernet' sauvignon, telling everyone able to still listen to his dumb-ass drivel that he was once in a Paris *cabaret* that had been commonly frequented by hemorrhoid-troubled Dr. Damien Dumoise.

"Bartender, give me a glass of Old Turkey before I go cold turkey," Fleete demanded in an uncontrived inebriated stupor. "I need alcohol in my system to protect my frail ass from radical Indian insurrectionists, those pathetic pussies who are inspired by Islamic fundamentalist preachers and by cock-sucking Marxist ideology. Long live exploitive British capitalism, that's what the fuck I proudly say and believe! Long live British prostitution too! Fuck! I think I'm changing into a sleazy Indian lowlife. Already I'm feeling Sikh in my stomach, ha, ha, ha!"

"You're as plastered as the fuckin' pink wall over there," declared Strickland, standing right next to Fleete. "A drunken sailor in port after spending twelve months at sea has nothing on you! Is that a fresh bottle of Amaretto in your hand?"

"Speaking of walls," Fleete awkwardly slurred, "one of my best friends is Harvey Wallbanger, who unfortunately was a stud who got his erect dick stuck in a solid wall stud and now his pecker is bein' tested for termites. And that's not to mention my other close pals too: Tom Collins, Jim Beam, Jack Daniels, Johnny Walker and finally my favorite relative on my loser father's side, Old Grand Dad! Ha, ha, ha!"

"Well, at least you haven't gulped-down any Russian hard vodka yet!" Strickland commented and chastised. "Then you'd be tellin' me all about your Ma's cow!"

"No, but soon I"ll be *rushin'* to ask for some of that' nasty potent shit to drink too, ha, ha, ha!" Fleete clumsily answered and guffawed. "Before the night's over, you're gonna' have to give me a serious enema treatment Strickland! My freakin' aching bowels are in an uproar already! Ha, ha, ha!"

"You're speaking in a heightened intoxicated condition Fleete!" I diplomatically cautioned the idiot, not wanting the very big man to beat the living shit out of me. "You better lay off of my rum!"

"I'll do what the fuck I want if I feel *rum*bunctious enough!" Fleete hollered and punned. "Here's to another old comrade of mine, Captain Morgan!"

By the time it was 3 a.m. on the vintage wall clock, Fleete had downed five whiskey sodas and had chewed and ingested the remainder of the foul-smelling hedgehog, which incidentally looked like rancid greasy offal with lots of fur. The frosty outside temperature was then a frigid fourteen degrees, certainly not a lot of diplomas at any respectable high school or university.

But upon reaching the rear police station stable, Fleete became excessively upset that his horse was having a severe coughing bout. Standing atop the animal's wooden stall, our half-berserk companion un-majestically leaped upon the saddle, but *his* ordinarily docile steed violently flung the dumb shithead onto the manure-laden ground. Strickland and I formed a guard of dishonor around the overindulgent fallen clown, who was then munching on hard straw, and since the gate to the equine's stall was partially open, the anxious animal bolted-out of the huge barn, never to be seen anywhere again.

It was at that precise moment when I nearly earned a hernia. I desperately struggled and lifted Fleete onto Strickland's old gray mare, that is, after the horse's owner had already mounted *his* more-tame mode of transportation. Then I put my left foot into my filly's low stirrup, and upon *his* hand signal, Strickland and I rode-off into the desert, heading toward a God-forsaken place that the uneducated "Who gives a shit?" natives call Hanuman.

* * * * * * * * * * * *

In India there are myriad gods symbolizing numerous things, and also there are many eccentric priests representing those same eclectic gods and oddball things. But one "powerful" god in *our* vicinity, Hanuman, is particularly special to the illiterate natives that pay homage to the cult deity of "the great apes of the hills." But to all-too-prejudiced Fleete, the dark-skinned local inhabitants were all basically of the same ilk, essentially either alien dot heads or moronic foreign towel heads, or perhaps "a blasted combination of both contemptible quasi-religious classifications."

On the unpleasant ride from the police club to the Hanuman Temple, bouncing up and down upon Strickland's obedient horse, Fleete was loudly bullshitting to his remote friend how he once was on a well-disciplined British diet and consequently managed to lose a hundred pounds in a single day while gambling in a popular London "speak-easy casino." My horse was galloping alongside Strickland's and it was very convenient for me to eavesdrop on Fleete's weird remark, and so I softly laughed in a perfunctory manner, simply because I assessed the drunken speaker to be in an exceptionally jolly frame of mind.

When we arrived at Hanuman fifteen minutes later, my eyes perceived that a dull light was being emitted through the temple's windows, and my ears could hear the enthralled worshipers inside chanting hymns, or what the hell sounded to me like hymns way back in the more familiar British Christianity of materialistic Western Civilization. This sort of impromptu religious service is quite characteristic of the region, for the sinister priests apparently have insomnia and commence with their praying at any hour of the day, and their superstitious disciples will show-up at any hour also, habitually entering the temple and unobtrusively joining the very zany congregation in what constitutes "group-therapy pray."

But before *we* could continue enacting our arduous ride, Fleete compulsively leaped from the rear of Strickland's slow-trotting horse, landing hard on the dirt and then rolling over and over, causing an eddy of dust to rise-up from the dry ground. By the time my riding companion and I could dismount our steeds and secure *their* reins to available rail posts, drunken Fleete had already stepped into the sacred building and had begun causing great havoc yelling, "Where's the goddamned tabernacle? Who the hell's being brutally sacrificed on this dump's missing fucked-up altar?"

In the next embarrassing scenario, Fleete lit a fresh cigar, puffed strenuously and then maliciously ground the hot ashes directly into the forehead of the revered monkey god Hanuman. "That's what the fuck I think of your Third Eye, you phony fucked-up chimp statue. Back in England we have monks, but here in India you assholes have fuckin' monkey gods, ha, ha, ha! You hick assholes don't know the damned difference between a gay pansy and a lesbian chimpanzee! Ha, ha, ha! You stupid-fuck wannabe' Simian shits!"

Strickland and I tried to subdue the intoxicated jerk and drag his corpulent ass out of the mysterious service-in-progress. I looked around during *our* extended fracas and I comprehended that the grim-faced local peasants in attendance were both shocked and staggered at Fleete's rather irreverent deportment. Then the insolent ingrate dashed-up five wooden steps and mercilessly punched the head priest on the left side of his thin skull, knocking the already stunned temple official unconscious from the heavy unexpected brutal blow.

"See that blemish on the gorilla's forehead I had made with my cigar," Fleete vociferously ranted to Strickland and me. "Shee that mother-fucker? Well I'll tell ya' my salubrious Friends; that fucked-up stain I'll now call and refer to as the 'Mark of the Beasht'. I made the fucker all by myself with the aid of my super-fine cigar," Fleete slurred. "Ishn't the new beauty mark super-fine? All these fucked-up towel heads and dot heads here can *mark* my words, ha, ha ha! Holy crap! I've wasted my good cigar on *that* fuckin' fake toy idol!"

The irritated natives assembled inside the poorly constructed stone shrine began yelling a variety of threatening insults and protests, and Strickland, who had been casually known to the now-unconscious priest, was worried that massive trouble had been initiated by our alcoholic pugnacious colleague. But unexpectedly, recalcitrant Fleete soon collapsed upon the rudimentary stone floor, breaking our sturdy grips upon his two arms during his unanticipated plummet.

"Now I want to climb atop *that* monkey's shoulders, pull my pants down and shit on the fucked-up primate's head!" the whiskey indulger wildly shouted. "I want to see all of these faggot worshipers go stark-raving ape, ha, ha, ha! Is this fucked-up archeological museum a fuckin' gay and lesbian brothel, or what?" Fleete illogically shrieked. "Ha, ha, ha! I'll make that monkey god into a real shit-head! All that matters is fecal matter! Hey Guys! Just look at all of the transgender transvestites! Ha, ha, ha!"

Then, without any imminent sign or warning, a totally devious butt-naked "Silver Man" emerged from a shadowy corner, and the creep's hideous leprosy shone like wintry frost inside the extremely old temple. At that moment my brain remembered that the Holy Bible describes such a ghastly, horrible, pathetic wretch as "a leper white as snow."

But this most peculiar Silver Man exhibited no distinct facial features, and the devastating disease was obviously flourishing in a very advanced stage of development. As Strickland and I attempted raising Fleete up from the cold floor, *our* out-of-control madman associate screamed out, "Hey you flat-faced ugly mother-fucker! You need some lousy skin conditioning cream real bad! You've got pathetic gray wrinkles growing out of your fuckin' hideous gray wrinkles, ha, ha, ha!"

"You shouldn't have knocked the main priest out!" Strickland futilely scolded Fleete. "To these dumbfounded worshipers, you've just committed a major sacrilege, a vulgar profanity of the highest degree, an act that would be aptly defined as a despicable mortal sin in the Christian faith!"

"I clobbered the wimpy prick in the temple right here in this fucked-up temple," bellowed and boasted Fleete, "and if the jerk-off was a rabbi, I would've clobbered him in the G.D. synagogue, ha, ha, ha; and if the mother-fucker was a perverted screwball Muslim, he would've felt my wrath with a right cross to the mosque, ha, ha, ha; and if the sanctimonious shit-head was a bastard Buddha enthusiast, the fuck-head would've been given a healthy palooka punch right in the old pagoda, sending the Buddha pest all the way to Budapest, ha, ha, ha!"

As the insulted worshipers became more boisterous and even more antagonistic, the grotesque-looking Silver Man, mewing like an otter in great distress, suddenly sprinted over to our location and impulsively, tightly grabbed Fleete around his massive chest. Before the enraged leper could be wrenched away from applying his strong bear-hug, the unstable assailant stooped-down and deliberately dropped his head onto Fleete's noggin, their brows instantly making contact.

Then the diseased crazed participant rambunctiously scurried to the other side of the chamber and kept on mewing like a distraught sick otter. Meanwhile the angry mob members blocked the front and rear exit doors. The three of us were suddenly dangerously trapped, and the Hanuman Temple was then our frightening jail cage.

"I'm gonna' shit on that circus freak's head too, after I first crap on the monkey god's scalp and cure all of his fuckin' dandruff," Fleete defiantly boomed, his mocking nomenclature surely referring to the devil-possessed Silver Man. "You aboriginal assholes here don't know it, but my shit doesn't stink, and it also makes for a super-fine shampoo, yes it does! Ha, ha, ha!"

"Fleete, please calm down!" Strickland intelligently advised. "You need anger management classes bad!"

"I've incensed all these dark-skinned shit-heads without even using any fuckin' incense, ha, ha, ha!" Fleete hollered-out for all to hear, whether the appalled audience of bystanders understood English or not. "Tell me Guys, how do you say 'fucked-up' in the inferior tongue of these inferior jerk-off assholes?"

"They just know that you're ridiculing them and their god," Strickland perceptively commented. "Pretend you're a Trappist priest and keep your trap quiet until we get the hell out of here! Stop your disrespectful discriminating!"

I had noticed from *their* body language that the other two still-conscious priests had been very infuriated right up to the point where the foul leper had touched Fleete. The weird head nuzzling episode appeared to have soothed *their* mounting angst.

Much to my astonishment and mental relief, one of the two standing Indian priests (wearing British oxfords) then spoke perfect grammatical English as if the fellow had been an erudite honor graduate from Cambridge.

"I firmly suggest that you take your foolish comrade away from this sacred sanctuary immediately," the new-found prophet emphasized. "Your uncouth friend is done with Hanuman, but Hanuman is not finished with your prevaricating crony, as you and he will soon discover!"

And to *our* satisfaction, the previously riled-up crowd dispersed away from the doorways, allowing us three Englishmen access to the escape portals. Strickland cautioned me that we might still be knifed or attacked, and totally soused Fleete kept jabbering that he was seeing so many stars swirling around inside his thick cranium that his entire dense head was turning into a "fucked-up erratic galaxy."

"What slaughterhouse are we near?" Fleete frantically exclaimed, his immense lungs gasping for more oxygen. "Could we be in Cow-cutta! Ha, ha, ha! Ya' gotta' admit, this fuckin' place stinks to low heaven! Ha, ha, ha! Take me home to bed please! I want to sleep under a blanket of snow and on a sheet of ice! Ha, ha, ha! Is Roosevelt still President over there in America? Listen shit-heads! I need my fuckin' Teddy Bear! Ha, ha, ha!"

As we hastily departed the alien premises, Fleete indiscreetly blurted-out, "What the fuck was *that* idiotic mumbo-jumbo those frivolous assholes were chanting? What was that stupid-assed jargon those cretins were reciting?" the loud-mouthed lush reiterated. "They couldn't be Cretans because we're nowhere near Greece! Ha, ha, ha! Oh, now I fuckin' get it!" our ungracious acquaintance speculated and naughtily stated. "I'm a big tall husky three hundred pound Englishman. That's the fuckin' 'jumbo' part of the puzzle! Now what the hell does the insane 'mumbo' part mean? Ha, ha, ha!"

"Stop your incendiary cursing Fleete! You've exacerbated your situation and put the three of us in serious jeopardy!" Strickland imperatively reprimanded in an exasperated tone of voice. "Haven't you done enough damage? Don't you know that you're accursed already without you doing any more random cursing?"

"That fuckin' faceless naked ghoul in there' needs moisturizing cream bad, all over his hideous deformed body!" Fleete crazily insisted. "I don't think that gray-skinned freak has any fuckin' skin pores whatsoever. Now tell me Gents, how does that un-human bastard' even begin to sweat! Someone tell that freak-show *ashhole* not to sweat it! Ha ha, ha!" Fleete persisted in his wild tirade. "That miserable son-of-a-bitch must be a goddamned reincarnated pallid-faced zombie ready to be resurrected and shipped back to hell again! That skinny gray monster might even be a fucked-up bloodsucking vampire disguised as a leper! Ha, ha, ha! I think the putrid son-of-a-bitch looks like he needs ten simultaneous blood transfusions just to get a recognizable tiny hard-on again! Ha, ha, ha!"

* * * * * * * * * * * *

Strickland and I gently tucked Fleete into the gigantic bed situated inside the spare room of the police investigator's apartment that had been built above the aforementioned lucrative "all sex brothel." After our mutual acquaintance had dozed-off, the brilliant government official and I reminisced about how Fleete used to be a somewhat tranquil, placid individual, but conversely, his recent quantity intake of hard liquor mixed with vintage wine appeared to transform the normally docile homesteader into a veritable volatile vindictive villain.

But before I retired to rest on my assigned bed, I checked-in on the toxic nincompoop and alertly observed him lying on his right side, and while being restive in his deep sleep, Fleete was fiercely scratching his left breast precisely where the "Sign of the Beast" had been established by the mewing Silver Man.

My vacillating thought processes were in a turbulent quandary, and it wasn't until seven in the morning that I finally went to sleep, but at ten a.m. I was awakened by severe shouting. Downstairs Fleete was vigorously yelling at Strickland's cook, griping that his breakfast pork chops weren't rare enough.

"I want my meat served pure red!" the crazed rancher screamed in a dictatorial tone of voice. "What do you usually serve? Tennis balls? I repeat Asshole! I want my meat to look like a shaven cunt that's having a heavy menstrual period! My appetite is quite ravenous, so throw those well-done chops out the friggin' window and cook me some delicious raw carne immediately."

I nervously entered the kitchen area where Strickland and his mercurial guest were uncomfortably sitting around the small circular table. I noticed that our sobered-up visitor was fanatically scratching his chest, and then I humorously asked Fleete if he was "itching to get back home to the serene Himalayas."

"This shitty part of the Indian hell-hole breeds an odd species of bothersome mosquitoes," the religiously condemned man replied. "I've been mortally bitten many times, but surprisingly, only in one fuckin' place here, right on my left breast. You two goofballs probably think I'm a sight for sore-eye-a-sis! Ha, ha, ha! Christ," Fleete arrogantly pontificated, "I wish one of you fuck-heads were a

G.D. dermatologist who could prescribe the proper medication to alleviate this terrible itchy blotch of mine!"

Strickland thoroughly examined the alluded-to mark and then divulged, "It was merely pink in coloration just this morning, but now the strange growth is jet black and actually four times its original size."

"Holy shit!" Fleete loudly exclaimed, carefully scrutinizing the ominous mark, his beady eyes peering into a hand-held mirror. "I must be turning into one of those repulsive African rug-heads we always read about in *National Geographic!* In another week my fucked-up pigmentation might be totally black! I mean Fellas', I think I'm beginning the initial stage of some type of horrible mutation; you know, just like a tadpole evolving into a frog or a freakin' caterpillar changing into a butterfly."

"You mean a metamorphosis?" Strickland offered and smiled. "But I suspect that now you're experiencing some sort of accursed religious metamorphosis!"

Fleete then quickly stuck his right hand down into his pants to his crotch and answered, "Good news Friends. I still have human male testicles and not fuckin' moth balls! Ha, ha, ha! But I gotta' do something about this third black nipple I'm growing. Am I becoming a weak woman against my will? Am I becoming involved in some sort of fucked-up trans-gender bullshit?"

The abused cook fearfully delivered the fresh pork chops from the adjacent "stove room," and the liquid-like meat looked just like bloody animal flesh: red, slimy and juicy. Fleete avariciously gobbled-down the ordered nauseous-looking food, indeed rather voraciously. The preoccupied brute was scarcely chewing the largest fragments with his gigantic pearly white teeth.

Strickland and I both stared at each other and shrugged our shoulders in unison, each of us endeavoring to fathom why Fleete was only eating his sloppy meal with the right side of his mouth.

Also, we noticed a certain neurotic twitch or tic that was evident in the rowdy man's involuntary movements, inadvertently done as if St. Vitus disease (or some other rare neurological malady) had been aggressively debilitating him. But we both watched with heightened curiosity as the mountain pioneer persisted in his neurotic mania, and despite his deleterious palsy, the obsessive-compulsive journeyman easily completed eating six red-raw pork chops in three short minutes.

"I've never been so famished in all my freakin' life," Fleete remarked almost apologetically. "I felt totally carnivorous and had no desire for either fruits or vegetables. In fact," the beleaguered homesteader declared, "I haven't been this *hungry* since I left Budapest twenty years ago! Ha, ha, ha!"

Being very concerned about his psychotic guest's physical welfare, Strickland pulled me into the nearby water closet and asked me if I could stay at his residence for at least a day to help him attend to Fleete's unusual physical and psychological needs. I reluctantly consented to honoring my host's request, but then our ears heard "the accursed one" again shouting uncultured commands from the kitchen area.

"I want more red meat!" Fleete deliriously demanded. "Not scarlet in color, mind you! Red I say! And this time don't cook it so long on the friggin' stove! I want to feel like I'm home on the range back at my rural Himalayan ranch! Ha, ha, ha!"

After the offensive greedy eater swallowed-down a half dozen more almost-raw pork chops (which the intimidated native cook never dared to place in the oven), we three Englishmen marched-out to the rear stables, even though Fleete remained existing in an unstable mental condition. The instantly-disturbed creatures started neighing and then all together snorting wildly, the steeds obviously experiencing a paranoia-type of heightened group anxiety.

"Quit horsing around!" Fleete admonished his special animal named Outrage. "Why can't you be more benign and act like that mannerly talking horse over there in Spain, Signor Eduardo!"

We three left the smelly paddock and climbed the rickety stairs leading-up to Strickland's more-than-sufficient apartment. After gingerly tucking Fleete into his inviting bed and then reading the afflicted mountain hillbilly two nursery rhymes and next singing the lyrics to the lullaby "Rock-a-Bye Baby," which was sung for a full hour to the curse-smitten hellion, benevolent Mr. Sandman finally admitted the brawny Limey into Slumberland.

Late that afternoon Strickland and I had an important parley in his parlor. Immediately I was fascinated with my gregarious host's knowledge of Indian culture, particularly the practices and rituals of the various religious sects, most of the cults absolutely abhorring sex, either conventional, oral, bisexual or gay.

"That Silver Man leper was not one of the regular temple priests," the renowned police investigator confidentially disclosed. "If the delusional asshole was not contaminated, I think I would've eagerly put my hands around his bony throat and energetically strangled the fanatic. I believe that if this diabolical leper would become dead, then Fleete's evil curse might be miraculously lifted."

A minute later our' dual auditory perceptions detected a distinct rustle coming from directly below, just outside, somewhere in the rear garden. Strickland and I promptly scurried down the rickety planks and swiftly paced outside the rectangular building. There near the scrawny shrubs we observed an uninhibited Fleete groveling and crawling around on his hands and knees as if he were a common predatory hound dog stalking its targeted prey in a local farmer's corn field.

"What the hell is this half-ass shit all about Fleete?" questioned *our* surprised host. "I'm the only certified sleuth around here! I'd show you my badge but I lost the damned thing last night amidst all of the bizarre temple confusion!"

"Nothing!" answered Fleete, rapidly rising to his feet. "And when I say 'nothing', I really mean 'no thing'! I was just performing some fundamental botany experiment, you know, engaging in a little impromptu gardening. So now, my garrulous Host, do you have any extra golf clubs! I'd like to putter around some more in the garden!"

"Are you hungry again Fleete?" Strickland coyly asked. "I hope you weren't about to eat some garden ants or spiders. Come inside for more dinner and I'll have the servant light the supper lamps."

"No thanks," the infected human-turned-animal gruffly insisted. "I feel illuminated enough roaming around under the light of the full moon. Don't you like full moons Strickland? They're much better than your half-assed ideas! Ha, ha, ha!"

"And what's on your personal menu for tonight?" I innocently asked Fleete. "Ravioli, spaghetti, pizza, lasagna, fried rhino' balls?"

"I want to chomp on two dozen uncooked pork chops taken directly from freshly slaughtered pigs!" Fleete wishfully announced. "I fuckin' intend to go hog wild this evening!"

* * * * * * * * * * * *

Strickland eloquently convinced Fleete that we should enjoy our splendid dinner inside the upstairs apartment, or else instead, *our* famished guest would have to eat three pounds of spinach and six pounds of broccoli before ever downing two dozen completely raw neatly-butchered pork chops. Reluctantly, a fully-disappointed Fleete begrudgingly complied with *our* strategic persuasion, for in truth, the daft traveler had eventually realized that it would be far easier for him to devour already-prepared red flesh on a safe dinner table than to awkwardly venture-out into the dangerous desert wilderness to hunt and kill a vicious swine or an angry sharp-tusked boar all on his own.

When our afflicted Himalayan companion was hypnotically transfixed looking at tempting pictures of chickens, hoglets, lambs, ducks and steers, himself being perched upon the bathroom hopper, Strickland revealed to me a fine and clever plan which his savvy cerebrum had keenly devised, a rather cunning scheme that might indeed cure the "affected fellow" taking a prolonged dump in the apartment's minuscule W.C. Strickland and I then exchanged myriad relevant ideas and eventually determined that Fleete's dual emotional and physical dilemmas had to be soon resolved, or else the mentally disturbed Englishman was certain to die from being possessed by invisible hostile evil spirits.

"And remember, Fleete was skittering around on his hands and knees in the back garden ridiculously maintaining all the while that he had been performing some necessary experiment in botany," I commented, "so therefore, the confused nutcase probably thinks that your silly potato patch is an exotic botanical garden!"

"Yes, exactly," Strickland agreed, affirmatively nodding his head. "But plants growing in any garden solely produce vegetables and not meat. I think that our sick guest was childishly covering-up his urgent lust for freshly obtained red animal flesh! The botany reference was merely a flaccid excuse! It's now my personal opinion that the doomed frontiersman requires the expert services of a skilled exorcist."

Our fairly interesting academic conversation was soon interrupted with the eminent Dr. Damien Dumoise showing-up at the police investigator's tidy upstairs living quarters. As soon as the dubious medical man made his nonchalant entrance, a queer baying noise akin to the moaning of a rabid wolf or dog was heard coming from a spot located near the downstairs bordello's back door.

"Possibly some whore getting banged by a big-dicked sailor," Dumoise stupidly joked. "I know about such sounds because I used to do plenty of business with the now-defunct law firm: Fox, Wolfe and Howell! Ha, ha, ha."

Not paying any attention to Dr. Dumoise's counterproductive skepticism, Strickland and I sped like marathon runners down the hall and soon hastily dashed into Fleete's room. The addled imbecile was caught climbing out of the second story window with no ladder existing between him and the solid ground. The London loon was making peculiar animal grunts along with loathsome howls sourcing from his raspy throat, and the Hanuman priest's new apprentice refused to verbally respond when Strickland and I assiduously questioned his obscure motivations.

Then to free the mammoth victim from his insidious trance-like state, Strickland leaned over and grabbed a bootjack that was ten times the size of a regular shoehorn, and next the accomplished police inspector severely conked the heavy object onto Fleete's head, bending the formerly straight metal bootjack into an almost perfect oval shape. Instantly the poor dazed Goliath fell to the floor and had been effectively immobilized from receiving the terribly harsh strike.

"I believe he's turning into a werewolf," I surmised and related. "You yourself heard the awful howling."

"It's all been dramatically happening in the present tense," Strickland suavely countered in a contrarian fashion, "so therefore I theorize that Mr. Fleete is not in the process of becoming a werewolf. Instead, the lunatic is fantastically becoming an 'is-wolf."

"Stop uttering all of this preposterous fantasy-fiction nonsense," Dr. Damien Dumoise cynically communicated. "This rather unfortunate bastard lying before us is obviously suffering from hydrophobia, at least that's my gut diagnosis based on my clinical knowledge of commonplace Indian health disorders. Strickland," the noted area physician continued his flawed analysis, "what do you recommend we do with this formidable wretch before he wakes-up and militantly attacks and maims all three of us?"

"I have the appropriate hostage-taking materials stashed in the corridor closet," my police friend pertinently answered. "First we'll bind the hands of this rabid beast with rope imported from Hempstead, New York," Strickland austerely instructed. "Then secondly, we'll adroitly tether together his thumbs and his big ties so that the poor devil cannot escape our guarded custody. And thirdly, we'll use *his* colossal size-eighteen shoehorn as a makeshift mouth gag and also as an indispensable tongue depressor."

"Great gonorrhea!" Dumoise hollered. "The patient is spitting-out the king-size shoehorn. He's foaming at the mouth and please notice Gentlemen, he's beginning to howl like a horny coyote in heat. I'm certain the bloke has hydrophobia," the zany doctor evaluated and declared. "No doubt he's been bitten by a rabid dog, or maybe the bewitched mountain dweller had once traveled across the Atlantic to America, and over there his microscopic dick had been penetrated by a hungry raccoon while the poor fellow was taking a long piss in the deep woods. Maybe Strickland, you should consider sticking the curved end of your crowbar down his gargantuan throat?"

"Can't you do anything for him doctor?" I anxiously asked. "Surely medical science must have some kind of unique treatment to soothe his horrendous un*bear*able infirmity, even though this mate Fleete's acting and sounding exactly like a wolf and not like a grisly grizzly."

"I'll return to my office and swiftly prepare the Death Certificate," Dumoise volunteered. "This hysterical guest of yours belongs in the grave more than Biblical Lazarus ever did. I'll check and see if I have an ample amount of embalming fluid to fill this asshole's enormous tank up! I'm also the overworked village undertaker," the fatigued doctor complained. "You never have enough of *that* wonderful embalming shit around, ya' know!"

After the cut-and-dry medical man exited the apartment, my bland host was inspired to make a pertinent revelation. "I have my own methods to deal with this rather frightening crisis," Strickland confided. "All we need is a functional shotgun that's been heated in a fireplace flame, a length of utilitarian fishing line, some durable cord, and most importantly, the heavy frame pole of *his* extra-strength bed. Now listen closely," my good friend whispered. "That sound outside is the unearthly intonations of the leprous Silver Man I had heard before. The asshole was earlier scurrying about outside the building exchanging un-harmonious mew calls with Fleete's reciprocating, very haunting wolf howls."

Strickland soon went right to work and artfully manufactured a large loop. The genius had imaginatively created a snare by tying the length of cord together into a tight double knot, the purpose of which was to first isolate the raunchy leper, to next secure the loop (attached to the sturdy sawed-off bed pole) around the Silver Man's neck, and then using the invented noose in a like manner as a circus animal trainer would control a ferocious leopard or tiger, the policeman-turned-inventor intended for us to drag the captured curse-giver upstairs into the apartment in order to compel (by torture) the nude Indian to reverse Fleete's black magic curse.

"Damien 'Diogenes' Dumoise had made a major discrepancy when he had explained away this sensational 'werewolf event' as being a mere nondescript case of 'advanced hydrophobia'," I weakly uttered and stuttered. "Sometimes that guy doesn't know shit about shit! Yesterday the fool invited me over to his pool for lunch and a beer and the freakin' thing turned-out to be a goddamned cesspool!"

Incredibly, amidst the dark bushes, together *we* managed to leap onto the foul-smelling creature and then capture the noxious man/animal, effectively harnessing the atrocious scumbag with the stout noose, all occurring at the bottom of the rickety outside stairs. Strickland and I had figured that if we could singe and burn the nefarious demons out of the repugnant leper while using the heated rifle barrel, we reckoned that there was a remote chance that Fleete's life could be salvaged; yes, spared without having to give the visiting rancher a monotonous battery of painful enemas.

"Don't you dare touch the S.O.B.'s filthy skin!" Strickland imperatively directed. "You'd have a much happier, more peaceful death by imitating Socrates and ambitiously imbibing a pint of hemlock, or by committing suicide swallowing-down some lethal arsenic!"

After we tightly tethered-down the leper upon the wood-planked floor (in a similar manner to which we had incapacitated Fleete), the clever policeman and I sadistically tortured the reprehensible leper all over his exposed skin using the heated shotgun barrel, but instead of crying aloud or screaming like a banshee, the enigmatic Silver Man remained relatively passive, and the outlandish freak only mewed softly, no matter how much we frenetically scorched and scourged his rancid-looking epidermis and maliciously cauterized his scrawny grotesque-looking asshole.

"Thank goodness we wrapped the white sheet around him," the police prosecutor orally conveyed during our less-than-routine persecution session. "This current Indian leprosy epidemic is highly contagious, and I don't want my dick and scrotum sac rotting off my lower abdomen any time soon. Such an abdominal horror would be absolutely abominable!"

Our victim not once surrendered to *our* explicit repetitious ordering that Fleete's detestable curse be reversed; it was then quite evident that our punishment methods were not achieving efficacious results. As our last resort, we lifted the stench-laden leper up to Fleete's face until their foreheads finally touched, just like they had done inside the madhouse Hanuman Temple.

Without wasting any precious time, and with our intended mission fully enacted, Strickland and I mightily hurled the flimsy leper out of the open window where luckily, the foul being landed squarely upon a howling wolf, instantly killing the mangy beast from the terrific impact.

Realizing that the repulsive-looking lowlife had received a prized souvenir from our "experimental life-saving project," we noticed the diseased Silver Man gathering-up the deceased wolf and next, the mystical shaman sprinted off the property like a two-legged cheetah, zooming away and heading in the direction of the foreboding Hanuman Temple.

The ancient tower clock in the city center gonged, registering exactly seven o'clock, precisely twenty-four hours since the visiting Londoner had gone under the leper's evil influence.

Within six hours Fleete had advantageously recovered from his "diabolical werewolf possession." But instead of contracting rabies or leprosy, the awesome giant of a man began scratching his ass and his itchy testicles rather intensively, the sufferer utilizing all ten of his super-long fingernails.

"Holy shit in Shetland!" Strickland prodigiously marveled and thunderously yelped with a broad smile beaming upon his florid face. "Gentlemen, I must confess this very simple fact. Lord Byron was positively right. Truth is often much stranger than fiction. My dear Fleete," the erudite policeman finished his rhetoric, "somehow you've just obtained a bad case of hemorrhoids that's ironically been mystically transferred to you from the infected rectum of our own dear colleague, the very distinguished Dr. Damien Dumoise."

Rudyard Kipling (1865-1936)

Rudyard Kipling wrote stories about India that appealed to lovers of quality literature all over the world. Kipling lived in India in the days when the mysterious land was part of the British Empire. Between the ages of six and seventeen Rudyard attended school in England, but after receiving a solid basic education, the aspiring writer returned to India and worked as an avid newspaper journalist. Many of Rudyard Kipling's most celebrated works, including the classic animal tale "Rikki-Tikki-Tavi," appeared in a masterful work, *The Jungle Book.*

In 1889 Kipling ventured into London with a stack of stories to hawk to publishers. After successfully selling eighty short stories and poems to receptive editors, the enterprising author remarkably became an "overnight sensation." During that same year Kipling also visited the United States and was able to meet with Samuel Langhorne Clemens, better known as Mark Twain. The famous American writer is quoted as saying, "Between us we covered all knowledge. Rudyard Kipling knows all that can be known, and I know the rest!"

"King Midas"

Midas was King of Phyrgia in Asia Minor and most people living inside and outside Phyrgria didn't give a fast fart about the egotistical ruler or about any of his irrelevant imperial bullshit. Despite the public's apathy about their royal guardian, Midas was extremely wealthy and very powerful because he taxed his subjects to death and used their labor and their money to break almost everyone's balls or puncture their tits. The emperor never took any crap from anyone, preferring to pursue his own foolish inclinations, making hasty and irrational judgments without the consent of his distinguished transvestite advisers, whom *he* thought were simply charlatans and assholes instead of harmless deviant transvestites.

One day Dionysus, the always drunk Greek god of wine and frivolity was traveling through Phyrgia with his entourage of naked nymphs and retarded satyrs (creatures half man, half goat, and fully fucked-up). One member of the troupe was Salenus, an old, fat bald-headed prick who was barely sober while nodding his noggin on his donkey', which all of a sudden smelled some asses' asses a mile away in King Midas's royal stables.

The donkey surreptitiously lagged behind and then strayed from the caravan of merrymakers, who continued to party without even realizing that the old fart and his mount were missing from their elite company. The independent ass took Salenus's ass west, and an hour later, arrived at the king's incomparable rose garden where Salenus's ass fell off *his* ass and tumbled into an *asinine'* clump of thorny asshole rose bushes.

The King's alert gardeners discovered Salenus bleeding and laughing on the ground and helped the comical idiot stagger to his feet and think of words to say. Meanwhile the gardeners searched in vain for Salenus's eight other asses.

"Where the fuck am I?" the fat bald-headed old codger inquired. "Who wants to fuckin' tickle my armpits and scratch my balls with both ends of an ostrich feather?"

The notorious revels of Dionysus had become common knowledge throughout Phyrgia, and the alert gardeners perceptively recognized that Salenus was one of the wine-god's intimate colleagues. They wrapped a wreath around *his* neck consisting of assorted flowers and discarded marijuana butts, dragged his corpulent carcass up the palace steps, and gracefully dumped the intoxicated Salenus on the floor. Greedy King Midas was then summoned to entertain his new eminent guest.

The King introduced himself to Salenus', who was still so inebriated that he believed *he* was speaking with a male prostitute in a city ghetto. Midas was thrilled that one of Dionysus's close acquaintances had visited *his* palace, and he insisted that Salenus stay for a feast that would rival any that Dionysus had ever attended or provided.

"You must stay and enjoy my hospitality! I say hospitality because after you get done days of partying, drinking, eating and screwing you'll fuckin' wind-up in my royal hospital," Midas told the still dysfunctional Salenus. "In this country there is always feast and never famine! And when we run out of food, we suck on each other's genitals."

"That's wonderful!" Salenus exclaimed while groggily staggering around and hiccupping. "My throat, my stomach and my loins are all famished! Bring on the strippers, the switch-hitting lesbians and the goddamned male couch dancers you stingy parsimonious bastard!"

Much preparation and attention to detail at the palace was done, with servants flitting around setting tables, carrying wine jugs and baskets of food and placing sweet-smelling ancient aphrodisiac elixir at strategic places.

A fantastic orgy followed that lasted for ten whole days and nights until all the men ran out of sperm fluid and all the women's hairy pink wells went dry. Lyres and pipes were played by female minstrels having their menstruals, and the musicians were exempted from participation in the orgy and when not tooting away, had to sit all by themselves at a designated "periodic table" where they had some "good chemistry and lousy biology" to share while periodically taking their daily physics.

Midas next conducted Salenus through the festooned halls to the King's favorite palace bath, where the two frolicked and toyed with each other like a pair of horny homosexual chimpanzees. These flirtatious activities went on for another two whole days until Midas collapsed on the mosaic tile floor from sheer exhaustion and Salenus had drunk all of the dirty scummy water from the hot tub, thinking and believing that it was sweet-tasting wine mingled with aphrodisiac elixir.

Dionysus heard about Midas's wild celebration and arrived at the King's palace to retrieve his wayward friend Salenus. When the god of wine learned of the wonderful hospitality Midas had extended to *his* "salubrious comrade," Dionysus promised to grant the emperor any gift *he* so desired, either reasonable or extravagant.

The King's heart possessed many non-virtuous negative qualities such as lust, greed, pride, hedonism and vanity. So naturally, *his* exploration of pleasure was predicated on satisfying one or more of those particular vices. Midas's mind was still fatigued from all of the ten-day biological indulgence and the two-day private orgy with Salenus, so his selfish mind was now in total disarray, a facsimile of his fat bald-headed guest's erratic thought patterns.

Midas's cerebrum envisioned the golden cups his revelers had dented and hurled upon the palace marble floors and he thought about *his* golden honeycomb that the famous Greek architect Daedalus had engineered for the king's honor. 'Those drunken shit-faced imbeciles have ransacked my entire palace, have vandalized my cherished golden honeycomb and have smashed or ruptured all of my treasured golden possessions,' the emperor imagined and concluded.

"Dionysus," Midas answered the quasi-deity that preferred reveling with scumbag mortals down on earth rather than associating with *his* condescending almighty pompous peers on *Mt. Olympus*, "I wish to have golden statues of you and Salenus to commemorate your fine visit to Phyrgia and to pay tribute to your amusing friend's memorable stay ay my palace." The King then realized a once in a lifetime very *golden opportunity*. "Therefore," Midas continued as he finally announced the true reason for his veiled plan, "give *me* the power to transform everything I touch into solid gold. This gift will protect me from gold diggers, goldbrickers and from *Golden Fleecers*. It will be like my own personal golden parachute sheltering me from potential poverty, even though I don't know what the fuck a parachute is, let alone a goddamned golden one!"

"I suggest you give the matter some more thought," Dionysus advised while cautioning to his new acquaintance serious deliberation and sober discretion. "Don't do anything 'rash' for I have no ointment or lotion that can cure major skin irritations!"

Kings of Asia Minor tended to be obstinate and stubborn after committing to and announcing their intentions, so Midas was adamant about his innermost desire. "Dionysus, that is my wish," he selfishly maintained. "I would like to be conferred with the *Golden Touch*. Now I insist that you keep your promise and afford me that luxury!"

"Okay Your Motley Majesty, you win!" Dionysus replied, shaking his head left and right to demonstrate his obvious skepticism and objection. "When Salenus and I exit your magnificent gardens, the *Golden Touch* will go into effect. But always remember dear Midas," the god of wine lectured, "the only things' that should be golden' are silence, sunrises, sensational sunsets and your later years."

Ten minutes later Midas was so exhilarated from the official implementation of *his* new magical power that the emperor couldn't decide what object he should touch first to convert into solid gold. He chose a branch of a tall oak tree in the garden not far from the palace wall, and after he touched the tree's limb, its leaves slowly made a spectrum transformation from green, to yellow and then to pure solid gold.

"These stellar leaves are better than the ones Daedalus and his son Icarus had manufactured in the royal workshop!" Midas marveled and uttered. "They are worth a small fortune, and I have only begun to proliferate my' wealth," the King laughed. "I can't wait to fuckin' touch the royal falcon and make it into a golden eagle! Ha, ha, ha!"

Midas was now the greatest and most demented king in the ancient world. He stooped down and touched his garden's lawn and the blades of grass instantly converted into strands of gold. He grabbed a stone and it astonishingly transformed into a lump of pure solid gold. He next touched a familiar root crop vegetable growing in his private garden and the object immediately turned into *twenty-four 'carrot' gold.*

The joyful King was delirious upon contemplating his new ability. Midas playfully held his hand out and sprinted past a row of six white marble pillars and after he touched each one they' all magically changed into solid gold. The ecstatic ruler hypothesized that he would make his entire palace into a beautiful gold edifice, but then he considered that the six golden pillars were a nice contrast to the majestic white marble structure that rivaled any god's temple in Greece, Egypt, Philadelphia or anywhere else in Asia Minor.

Then Midas had an inspiration. He grabbed a golden delicious apple from a fruit bowl and held it up to his lips. 'This apple is already *golden*,' he mused. 'I wonder what will happen if I attempt biting into it!'

The anxious King bit the apple and much to his dismay chipped two of his formerly perfectly shaped front teeth. 'How stupid I was!' Midas acknowledged. "I should have asked Dionysus to grant me the *Golden Touch* in just my left hand so that I could use my right hand to eat, to write edicts and to fuckin' jerk off. I must experiment more to evaluate the extent of this remarkable gift. Then I should be able to ascertain whether it is or is not an evil wretched curse in disguise!'

The regal King ordered his royal servants to set their master's table and Midas amusingly entertained himself by converting the dishes, saucers, cups and tablecloth into pure gold. He accidentally touched the table but then realized that it had been pure gold *before* he had acquired the phenomenal *Golden Touch*.

When Midas's chatty gossipy servants had finally exited his personal dining room, the king tampered some more with his newly acquired special talent. He gingerly grabbed a slice of bread and inserted one end into his mouth. The emperor nearly lost several incisors from *their* crunching down on the flat solid metal surface. The King suddenly became extremely terrified by his "new damned power."

'I will attempt biting, chewing and swallowing a morsel without using my hands!' he theorized. 'If I just use my lips, I ought to be able to eat that second ordinary slice of bread on the table. Thank *Olympus* my lips don't fuckin' have fingers!"

The King bent over and used his nose to move the slab of bread closer to his mouth. Then he bit into the slice, but it too had become solid gold. Midas's emotions quickly shifted from disappointment, to frustration, to shock and then to exasperation. "What the fuck's goin' on here!" he finally yelled out to his servants, who perceived their master's anger and hid behind the six golden pillars in the botanical garden. "If only I had waited and thought the situation through," the King regretted. "Then I would have wisely wished for the *Golden Touch* to only exist on the index finger of my left hand! Shit! Now I can't even finger Mrs. Midas's love canal! On second thought that's not such a bad fuckin' idea!"

Midas reached for a 'goblet' of wine, but soon became aware that he could not drink from nor *gobble it*. The substance solidified inside his mouth and throat, nearly choking the incensed imbiber to death. The distraught King violently spit the golden chunk out, finally fully fathoming the futility of his extraordinary gift of touch.

"This is fuckin' insane!" Midas exclaimed. "If I hold my dick while I'm taking a piss," he orally considered to a wall mirror, "then my bird will turn into a goldfinch and my balls will transform into golden nuggets. Holy shit!" the emperor cried out as he experienced *social insecurity.* "And I'm still two decades away from my goddamned Golden Years! And if I feel or scratch my ass with the

Golden Touch, my ass will become a *golden tush* and I'll be shitting out gold bricks that will scrape the feces right out of my colon and clear out of my semi-colon!"

Out of sheer desperation and extreme anxiety, the now penitent ruler lifted his cursed hands up in the air and earnestly prayed, "Oh great and wise Dionysus. Forgive my greed and my lustful need for ostentation. Please show me mercy by removing the *Golden Touch* that *you* have so generously conferred upon your humble suppliant!"

A familiar voice descended from the sky and instructed, "Midas, you would have been better off if you had discreetly requested a dozen additional assholes to complement the big one you already carry around with you. Go to the mountain of Tmolus', who as you know was a minor god that had been punished by being transformed into a solid precipice. Bathe in the nearby stream," Dionysus's voice loudly directed, "and then the *Golden Touch* will be washed away. And the next time a powerful asshole like me offers you a favor, make sure you have assessed all of the *goddamned* consequences. Show more prudence and less impudence, you stupid ingrate fucked-up jerk off!"

Midas was very grateful to Dionysus for providing him with the solution to *his* terrible dilemma, but in his haste, the king heeded the wine god's instruction but unfortunately ignored *his* sage advice. He journeyed to the mountain of Tmolus, cleansed his entire naked body in the gentle shallow stream, and noticed that the sand at the bottom of the narrow river reflected a bright gold color that has been that particular hue ever since.

The Phyrgian King was absolutely delighted to have been returned to normal. However Midas still retained much of his arrogance, vanity and greediness. The stubborn fellow soon resented and then despised gold as well as all of the other trappings associated with massive limitless decadent wealth.

Midas soon became a quasi-environmentalist, appreciating the sounds of babbling brooks and singing meadows and whispering pines. The ruler distanced himself from his splendid palace, his gossipy staff, his marvelous festivals, his fancy embroidered clothing and tunics and his fantastic harem of fifty horny harlots sporting eager beavers. While partaking in *his* "communion with nature," Midas coincidentally neglected the important political and economic affairs presently going haywire inside his burgeoning empire.

Now the satyr mini-god Pan had made himself' a pipe to play, and it just so happened that the minor deity of amusement was cavorting around in the woods near Mt. Tmolus. Pan delighted in playing his new flute when he wasn't exercising, thrusting or having his own impressive skin flute sucked on by some blind forest nymph that always craved oral gratification while providing sexual satisfaction in return. Hence the well-endowed satyr had the appropriate nickname "Peter Pan."

As a result of Pan giving his new flute a major blow job because he had just received one from the aforementioned blind forest nymph, the beasts and the creatures of the woods became very active and happy, making exotic sounds and enchanting dissonance and loudly farting all over the "Fuckin' Forest." Midas encountered Pan in the deep woods and requested that the goat-god continue playing *his* alluring melodies for hours and hours until the chirping birds and the buzzing bees and the squealing squirrels all developed chronic laryngitis and genital atrophy.

"Apollo, god of music and the lyre will be proud of my new musical instrument," Pan told Midas. "I will be glad to serenade you and the forest animals until my lips grow weary or until the end of the world arrives, or until my dick falls off, whatever happens first!"

But if Midas possessed one major fault in addition to greed, vanity and arrogance, it was the fact that he never learned when to keep his big mouth shut. "Great!" the idiotic emperor turned idiotic naturalist answered the forest satyr. "I will ask *Olympus* in a prayer that Apollo and *you* compete in a musical contest and that the honorable Tmolus will judge who' is the more skilled musician. The pleasure of the music will be much more satisfying than possessing the *Golden Touch* or having a dozen additional assholes to crap out of!"

Now naturally, Tmolus himself' was a woodland deity and would be biased toward selecting Pan while discriminating against Apollo. The god of music's harmonies had a classical rhythm that edified the *Olympians*, extolled Greek heroes and praised dignified rational virtues such as justice, truth, honesty and generosity.

But Pan's revolutionary music suggested emotional expression and freedom of thought, loose social and immoral behavior and the pursuit of physical pleasure. It was a competition between "mind and conscience versus heart and body," and Pan had the definite advantage as far as Tmolus was concerned, because Tmolus used to enjoy getting laid, getting blown, working his stick and wiping his ugly asshole a thousand times a day. Hedonism appealed much more to Tmolus than intellectual activity ever had, so Pan was destined to emerge victorious in his not-so-amicable rivalry with Apollo.

But Tmolus soon discarded his favoritism for Pan and his prejudice against Apollo. He awarded the coveted laurel-wreath prize to the god of music, being fully aware that Apollo was an *Olympian* and had far greater clout among the immortal "Powers That Be" than the less influential Pan had. "I don't want to be a friggin' immobile mountain for all eternity," Tmolus said to a neighboring ridge named Cliff. "I don't even have hands or a throbbing dick to jerk off with!"

Midas however was not quite as prudent and as diplomatic as Tmolus had been. He too was biased in favor of Pan and had completely shut and covered *his* ears when Apollo had been singing and playing his splendid lyre. The king was spoiled because in the past when *he* yelled "Leap," his courtiers and servants would always request "How high?" And then the subordinates would always jump to the exact height the emperor had arbitrarily stipulated.

"No one has dominion over the way I think!" Midas muttered to his reflection in a crystal-clear forest stream. "It's now time for me' to speak-up for the forest god's legitimate triumph over that pompous *Olympian* loser Apollo!"

The King of Phyrgia came out of his self-induced stupor and vehemently protested to the heavens that Pan had decisively won the musical competition and not Apollo. Tmolus peered down at Midas indignantly, wishing that 'the asshole should incinerate himself' in a nearby active volcano's crater.' Perceiving Tmolus's rejection of *his* boisterous verbal appeal, Midas beckoned to Apollo, furiously criticizing the "unfair judgment rendered by Tmolus."

"Go suck a wet one you dumb fuck!" Apollo nastily retorted. "Oh fucked-up King, you must most certainly have defective ears," the god continued. "I now feel compelled to give *them* their true shape." The falsely victorious god' of music, medicine, literature and the lyre swiftly whirled around and then proceeded northwest toward *Mt. Olympus*, thoroughly convinced that *his* final judgment pertaining to "that asshole Midas" was far too lenient.

Midas raised his hands up to his long furry ears and screamed out to the sky, "Great Zeus in heaven! I've been given an ass's ears. At least Apollo could have granted me a long donkey's dick to go along with these exaggerated animal ears!"

Upon returning to his palace after his bizarre Mt. Tmolus and woods' escapades, Midas felt ashamed of his animalistic appearance and wore a large purple turban to camouflage his abnormally large asses' ears. The Ruler attempted to explain to his advisers and counselors that wearing the purple turban was a privilege that only the King could exercise, and the chief consultants were happy to hear *that* proclamation because no one desired to look so horribly unstylish and unfashionable as the "fucked-up eccentric Monarch" did.

After the King's hair grew so long that his tresses and braidy bunches had to be sheared and trimmed, Midas summoned the services of the royal barber', who was also a royal gossiper and a royal pain in the asses' ears.

"Cut and groom my straggly shaggy locks," King Midas commanded, "and if *you* dare tell anyone of my secret, you will have to sleep with the royal zoo's 'twelve dozen' female gorillas when they are all in heat. Can you think of any punishment more fuckin' *gross* than that?"

The royal barber was tempted to relay the King's personal problem to almost everyone he saw or met but *he* intensely feared he would be mauled and mangled by a hundred forty-four aggressive, sexually' aroused affectionate female gorillas. Consequently, the intimidated fellow quietly bit his tongue so often that it was now two inches shorter than it normally would be. 'I don't know what's worse,' the barber painfully thought and anguished. 'Being emulsified by twelve dozen horny female gorillas or sleeping with my corpulent five hundred-pound wife; that choice is really a very tough decision. I'll have to seriously think about this lousy option. The ugly gorillas are looking better and better in my mind every damned minute!' the neurotic barber concluded. 'And besides that, crazy King Midas also might get pissed off at me and send my' tender ass all the way to America to fuckin' become a Yankee clipper!'

In bed the troubled barber tossed and turned, and his obese wife rolled over on top of him thinking that the poor fellow desired sex when actually all that *he* wanted was more oxygen. The paranoid barber even made mysterious noises and nebulous utterances in his sleep, and when *his* subconscious was about to reveal the King's awful secret, in desperation the diminutive barber would beg for more sex, and his steamrolling wife would accommodate his irregular request at least five times every single night until he was steamrolled flat as a pancake.

Feeling as flat as a table, one afternoon the bedraggled barber strolled down to a distant meadow to take a leak in a waterlogged pond. When he noticed that no one was in the vicinity to observe his *private* behavior, the barber then stuck his head inside a groundhog hole to relieve his extreme tension by then shouting into the cavity. A belligerent woodchuck surfaced, bit a chunk of flesh out of the bad-luck barber's scalp and then burrowed back down to its dark den.

"I'll have to dig my own hole to get the necessary relief that I seek," the aggrieved hair trimmer said. "I will not despair despite my great apprehension! I fuckin' never want to be a goddamned Yankee clipper!"

It required six minutes of assiduous excavation, but then the resolute barber finally accomplished his prime objective. Without hesitating, he pressed his head inside the newly created hole and bellowed, "King Midas has asses' ears! King Midas has asses' ears!"

The hole eventually filled up with scummy stagnant pond water, and several weeks later, a colony of wild reeds began growing all around the cavity's circumference. When the thin reeds sprouted even higher, they rustled as the wind briskly blew between them. A court messenger happened to stop at the distant "pissing pond" to take a leak, and then *his* ears sensed a rather peculiar refrain. The young courier dashed to the King's majestic palace and alerted everyone he knew of the strange articulations originating from "an enchanted hole" down near the isolated palace swamp.

A hundred or so curious imperial employees darted down to the secluded pond area to observe and listen to "the most fascinating phenomenon ever." As the crowd gathered nearer to the hole that had been dug by the neurotic barber, the naughty reeds were melodically whispering and repeating, "King Midas has asses' ears, and King Midas's ass has asses ears too! King Midas has asses' ears, and King Midas's ass has asses' ears too!"

"Dr. Tarr and Professor Fether"

Someone might think my tale is humorous but to me, it was all quite disconcerting. During the mild autumn of 1840, I was touring France's southern provinces trying to locate a certain *Maison de Sante*, or a notorious local nuthouse that specialized in advanced psychology methods and techniques. Since I had never had the pleasure of visiting an eminent "experimental asylum" of that kind, I proposed to my French traveling companion that we should set aside an afternoon so that I could avail myself of the opportunity to gather some pertinent research for a short story on mental health I had wished to write.

"This place to which you allude is a lunatic magnet and I wish not to visit it," my Parisian friend replied. "If I were you, I'd fuckin' seek asylum from that wacky asylum and avoid the goddamned place as quickly as you can. But if you insist, I'll tell you how to get there but I intend to ride on to Marseilles and rest my weary bones. I'll meet you at the designated waterfront inn that is expecting us later tonight. Then we could enjoy an excellent supper together."

"Do you know the superintendent of *Maison de Sante*, a distinguished fellow named Monsieur Maillard?" I asked my friend Gaston. "I had heard his renowned name mentioned while I had been speaking with some notable published men in the medical profession back in Paris."

"Unless you have some meritorious letter of recommendation or an official state certificate of admission from the national government," Gaston said in a regretting tone of voice, "then I doubt whether this Monsieur Maillard will allow you to enter and tour his avant-garde facility. Quite frankly, I've heard that Maillard is a trifle fucked-up in his organization skills and that he's quite suspicious about unexpected or uninvited visitors," Gaston confided. "But Edgar, since I'm a medical doctor and had known this Maillard five years ago back in Lyons, I'll accompany you to his clinic and introduce you to him. The rest will be entirely up to you."

"I see," I answered Gaston, my ordinarily rational mind being somewhat confused. "You *are* a doctor of the body and just like your Parisian colleagues, you' condescend those that study the activities of the human mind, thinking that they're all a monstrous gaggle of fucked-up incompetent quacks!"

We rode our fatigued horses on a dirt trail that meandered through a dank and dismal forest and at the base of a mediocre-sized mountain we finally arrived at *my* destination, the *Maison de Sante*. At first glance the edifice was a fantastic-looking chateau, but upon closer scrutiny, its appearance was a bit dilapidated from neglect and from lack of maintenance. My initial inclination was to turn around and head towards Marseilles with Gaston but then my heart gathered the courage to stay and satisfy my original curiosity about the rather intriguing place.

Monsieur Maillard was quite a vigilante administrator who immediately detected our presence while peering out of an iron-barred window. The short portly superintendent anxiously exited his clinic and upon recognizing Gaston, courteously invited him and me inside. Maillard at first impression struck me as a man of genteel and polished manners whose general demeanor reflected dignity and authority. 'Always trust your first perception,' I thought as I keenly evaluated the strange-looking fellow.

"My friend Mr. Poe would like to stay the afternoon and tour your nationally famous *Maison de Sante*," Gaston blandly disclosed. "Unfortunately I have important business to attend to in Marseilles and will have to take a rain check on your offer to stay. Would you mind accommodating my dear friend Mr. Poe in my absence?"

"No, not at all," Superintendent Maillard graciously indicated. "Why don't you alight from your horse Mr. Poe and I'll gladly give you a guided tour of the premises."

After I thanked Gaston for his invaluable assistance, and after he rode off in a fury towards Marseilles, Monsieur Maillard politely ushered me into his "experimental facility." A cheerful fire blazed upon the hearth and a very beautiful and talented young woman was preoccupied playing an aria from Bellini on the piano. She paused upon realizing my intrusion into the room, casually greeted me with a graceful smile and then continued with her rehearsal of the complicated composition.

I had instantly detected an element of sorrow and melancholy in the young woman's disposition but being a refined gentleman of good breeding, I never explored pursuing *that* possibly embarrassing aspect of conversation. I had heard at the recent academic conference in Paris that the acclaimed *Maison de Sante* (under the direction of Monsieur Maillard) had been managed (by the vulgarly used term) "system of permissive soothing" so I asked the now-garrulous superintendent about his innovative method of mental care.

"Well you see Mr. Poe, according to my revolutionary creative method, all types of punishments have been disposed with and the novel concept of 'rewards' is implemented whenever possible," the superintendent enthusiastically explained. "Although the patients are secretly watched, they do have liberty of the house, that is to say, they have and enjoy complete freedom of mobility. And instead of wearing uniforms like inmates in prisons do, my pampered patients are allowed to cavort around at will in civilian apparel and mingle and bond with their peers whenever they so desire," the esteemed executive of the asylum informed. "Such a tolerant atmosphere could only engender the development of independence and self-sufficiency among my 'guests' as I like to call them."

"I see Sir, you run your remarkable institution as if it were a high society hotel," I commented. "Very interesting indeed Mr. Maillard. Very fascinating too if I may add."

At that time I had resolved in my always-skeptical mind to confine my remarks to general topics so as not to offend either Monsieur Maillard or his sensitive-minded patients. A footman then brought a tray of fresh fruit into the room along with wine and other refreshments and I made myself comfortable taking a glass of merlot along with a red ripe apple.

"Was that young lady in the other room playing the piano one of your patients?" I diplomatically asked my host. "She seemed very normal to me."

"No Mr. Poe, that pretty young lady is pretty young and she happens to be my beloved niece Florence, just visiting here for the week," Monsieur Maillard laughed and then loudly burped, nearly regurgitating a large chuck of cheese he had just swallowed. "Flossie as I call her is a most accomplished musician and plans to do some major theater concerts in the near future. All she needs right now is a booking agent and a manager!"

"Are you feeling all right?" I asked Maillard as he began burping and farting loudly. "I do have adequate knowledge about gastro-intestinal remedies, you know!"

"You must excuse my chronic belching," Maillard said while exhibiting a degree of mortification. "For you see, under the previous system that was in place here, a harsh system that enforced martinet discipline and punishment, the inhibited patients were often abused. So that's why with the utilization my new 'permissive soothing method' I had to exclude visitors from the outside interfering with its administration. My patients must learn to trust the friendly staff in the building and not be subject to the prejudices and discriminations of those encroaching outsiders that can't relate to *their* often complex mental health issues."

"How long has your permissive soothing system been in operation?" I innocently asked as I began to think that Maillard was an idealistic impractical dumb fuck university academic doing irrelevant quack research on his own. "I would like to analyze and document the entire intricate process if I may?"

"Why that would be impossible Mr. Poe!" Monsieur Maillard surprisingly exclaimed. "Just last week I found it necessary to return to the formerly obsolete martinet discipline approach. I'm sorry Mr. Poe that you had not visited us last month when the controversial permissive soothing method was being employed."

'This dumb fuck is really a fickle doltish asshole,' I concluded. 'No doubt he farts and shits out of his mouth and probably eats out of his asshole. What a fucked-up hypocritical omnivore' this pathetic jerk-off Maillard is!'

"You see Mr. Poe, while I was utilizing the 'permissive soothing method' of mental treatment," Maillard defensively stated and equivocated, "some of the men actually thought that they were chickens, more specifically roosters, and the fellows would run around the house trying to screw any female whether the ladies said or screamed cock-a-doodle-doo or not! And then we had several gay roosters in the pack that were trying to have sexual intercourse with other male patients! And then a few of the more serious hens spent their entire day attempting to lay eggs! The entire psychological experiment proved to be an abominable abysmal failure where all semblances of civility had been abandoned with the ineffective ultra-liberal permissive soothing philosophy going completely amuck!"

"Did you still have dancing, music, sports, card playing and reading books as alternative amusement activities?" I inquired.

"Well Mr. Poe, for a while we did try those standard therapeutic things and we also relied on the patients admonishing each other for alleged misbehaviors and indiscretions," Maillard lectured without a lectern, "but the really bad maniacs we had to discharge to a local regular hospital for rehabilitation. We wanted to find a perfect medium, somewhere between those punitive methodologies of the ruthless Marquis de Sade and those Christian charity-oriented methods of Jesus Christ. But Mr. Poe," Maillard warned, "I strongly advise you to believe nothing that you hear and only half of what you see in regard to you assessing the *Maison de Sante*. Whatever you do," the rather strange superintendent cautioned me, "don't be misled by the false teachings of those medical ignoramuses over in Paris! Now then, I'll show you the gardens and the conservatories and then we'll have a delicious dinner after six."

"Mr. Maillard, where the hell are your' patients?" I inquired. "I haven't seen one of them since I've been here."

"Oh, they're around here somewhere," the chief administrator obtusely answered. "I'm sure they're hiding from us somewhere in the dense foliage or perhaps playing Hide and Seek behind sofas and chairs just to break our balls!"

And before I could explore the next uncultivated garden and weed area, I heard around twenty zany voices all' zestfully yelling in unison, "Cock-a-doodle-doo!" in a queer dissonant cacophony, sounding much like some sort of out-of-control lunatic chicken coop.

* * * * * * * * * * *

At six o'clock dinner was announced and the superintendent and the footman conducted me from the chateau's comfortable-but-sterile living room through in-need-of-repair French doors into a large dining area containing a huge eight-leafed solid oak table with what I assumed to be thirty dignified people seated around it. Twenty-five of the chatty diners were well dressed women, all of whom were wearing expensive-looking evening gowns, necklaces, wrist and arm bracelets, gold medallions and finally, jeweled diamond rings. The ostentatious women all seemed gregarious and also appeared to be dominating the myriad conversations that were occurring.

I next noticed that the warped floor was rug-less, that the dirty windows were indeed barred (both horizontally and vertically) and that the oak table had been set with an abundance of food with veal and ham as the principal meats and with rice, salad, potatoes, yellow squash and corn being the main vegetables. A great many anecdotes were being exchanged among the guests and my mind tried to absorb all that was being discussed around the gigantic oval table.

"We had a gentleman here about a year ago," prefaced a man two seats down from my right, "and the old geezer fancied himself' being a goddamned teapot, always whistling, not like a human mind you but like a goddamned common ordinary kitchen stove teapot. And do you know what?" the self-serving speaker continued his monologue. "The dumb shit jerk, I think he was from Cannes, would polish himself every night to stay shiny and silvery."

"It's a good thing he didn't think there was a hurricane inside of him or else he would've been a wicked tempest in a teapot!" I mused and then foolishly declared.

Next a tall gentleman seated three down from Monsieur Maillard piped-up, "About eight months ago we had a stubborn asshole staying here who thought he was a hungry donkey and he would eat pine cones, hay and thistle all day long," the fellow with the good memory stated. "Well then, when I kindly asked to see his pecker I saw that the lying son-of-a-bitch didn't have any goddamned donkey-dick after all, ha, ha, ha!"

Immediately Superintendent Maillard felt obligated to reprimand and chastise the loose-tongued fellow. "Mr. DeKock," the flustered administrator said, "stop acting so naughtily. You're beginning to make an ass out of yourself just as our former guest Mr. Muleskin had done when he was hee-hawing his damned tonsils out every single morning, noon and night."

Everyone at the table was merrily drinking wine as if it was fresh cold water. Bottles of chardonnay sauvignon, of cabernet merlot and of white zinfandel were randomly scattered (or distributed) all over the immense table. I was busily feasting on ham and veal and was so engrossed in my consumption of food that I paid little heed to the nonsensical hubbub happening all around me. But in retrospect, the scenario was even worse in magnitude than any chaotic nonsensical episode out of *Dante's Inferno*.

And then a cadaverous-looking lady sitting six chairs down to my right testified, "We had a screwed-up patient living here at the chateau a while back that thought she was a slice of Cordova cheese and every time she picked up a knife at breakfast," the raunchy old bag emphasized, "at lunch or at dinner, a naked Lady Cordova would attempt to slice off a sliver of herself, honestly thinking that she was the goddamned Big Cheese around here!"

"I'm Mr. Chardonnay and I'm a chilled bottle of red wine," the transsexual cross-dressing woman four chairs down to my left announced as she put her finger inside her mouth and made the popping sound of a cork flying off a champagne bottle. "Now which of you' asshole men wants to corkscrew me so that I can pop your weasel too!"

"These weird stories are not only amusing, but they're quite visceral and graphic too," I leaned over and confidentially related to Monsieur Maillard. "Are these people fucked-up, or are *we* fucked-up just sitting here and listening to their incredible bullshit?"

Before Maillard could reply to my keen observation, the asshole woman sitting thirty-feet down at the far end of the table boisterously yelled out to Maillard and me, "Hey you two shit-heads down there! Don't you know I'm a frog? Yesterday I was a horned toad, but now I've changed into a horny frog that doesn't want to croak until I get laid at least twenty times tonight." And next the dumb shit toothless woman noticed a huge disgusting insect crawling on the wood-planked floor, got down on her hands and knees and then extending her long tongue, captured the very large black bug in her mouth and began chomping away."

My mind was in a quandary but I was again subjected to listening to additional bizarre bullshit. "And what about that fuck head Petit Gaillard who thought himself to be a box of snuff and wanted everyone in the house to sniff his smelly asshole that he thought was his box's opening?" a woman in the center right of the expansive oak table hollered-out for all to hear. "And don't forget that dumb shit Jules Descartes who believed he was a pumpkin and who would beat up the cook before every meal because Jules suspected that the always bruised-up chef was going to change him into a pumpkin pie to be eaten by all at dinner."

"What the hell is this stupid shit all about?" I demanded to know from Maillard. "Either these pea-brained fuck-heads are all raving imbeciles or they're an insolent pack of retarded morons? Which is it Monsieur?"

Before the beleaguered superintendent could ever garner and utter a response to my imperative/interrogative statement, a really ugly lady who was now half naked shouted out, "What about good old Bouffon Le Grand who thought he had two heads, the first one being Cicero and the second one being Demosthenes. And then good old debonair Bouffon would leap-up upon this same dinner table and render to us in a an extemporaneous speech saying, "That asshole Greek Demosthenes might have pebbles in his mouth but that fuckin' roamin' Roman Cicero always had rocks in his head! Ha, ha, ha!" the female zoo candidate shrieked. "And then good old bonny Bouffon finally graduated into being a top and would spin around all night long until he finally shit and pissed his pants!"

'My riding companion Gaston was indubitably right,' I finally realized and concluded. 'I too need asylum from this fucked-up asylum! These son-of-a-bitches sitting here have to be the fucked-up patients and I now think that they certainly aren't goddamned sophisticated aristocratic guests at all!' I determined.

But before I could grab Maillard by the collars and start strangling a feasible explanation out of his throat, an elderly gray-haired promiscuous bitch (with her hideous flabby tits hanging out of her dress) stood up and began redundantly bellowing, "Cock-a-doodle-doo, any cock'll do! Cock-a-doodle-doo! Any cock'll do!"

"Monsieur, she's trying to start a sex orgy at the dinner table! Do something Maillard! I say fuckin' do something before I violently squeeze your neck until your goddamned windpipe disintegrates!" I boomed as I took out my frustration by pounding my right hand against the asshole superintendent's chest, but to no avail or personal satisfaction.

"Mr. Poe, I must tell you that Madame Honeywell is in heat," Maillard explained to me with a very pallid face. "She thinks she's a female poodle in estrous. There's little I can do to salvage Madame Honeywell, or 'the Bitch' as she wants to be called! And incidentally Mr. Poe, Madame Honeywell sometimes thinks she's a modest young lady who when she meticulously dresses herself, she always gets outside rather than inside her clothes."

"Just like the goofy Cicero/Demosthenes jerk-off that was just discussed, your Mrs. Honeywell is what the modern psychologists call a person suffering from a split personality, yes, I believe that the mental condition is now referred to as schizophrenia! But truthfully Monsieur Maillard," I screamed above the ever-ascending dining room din, "I now truly feel like I'm the goddamned chief cashew inside the nuthouse!"

And before basic order could be intelligently restored, Mrs. Honeywell again stood up and once more cockily yelled out, "Cock-a-doodle-do! Any cock'll do! Cock-a-doodle-do! Any cock'll do!" while ripping off her ornate dress and accompanying undergarments and then the crazy old bag "Bitch" began wildly masturbating her vulva and her clitoris in public.

"Maillard, exactly who has devised this retroactive treatment of a compromised medium that exists between your' former liberal permissive soothing method and the more Draconian Marquis de Sade martinet punishment method?" I hoarsely gasped.

"Why it was none other than that famous dynamic duo Dr. Tarr and Professor Fether," Maillard recollected and loudly replied. "Don't tell me you've never heard of those two very prominent contributors to the psychology field?"

"I must admit that I'm forced to acknowledge my uneducated ignorance," I confessed in a raspy hardly audible voice. "If I recall, those two gentlemen were not in attendance at the recent Paris medical conference."

Suddenly a massive food fight originated at the other end of the colossal oval table with apples, oranges, bananas, ham, veal, and hot potatoes flying all over the damned place and soon the airborne objects were accompanied by torrents of wine from recently opened bottles of chardonnay sauvignon, cabernet merlot and white zinfandel. I stood up and weakly screamed, "You're all going berserk! Stop this bullshit buffoonery right this second!" at the top of my faltering lungs and vocal cords but regrettably, the voice of a minnow swimming under faraway Niagara Falls could have been heard much better at that crazy fiasco scene located not far from the Riviera in Southern France. "Maillard, if you can't immediately put these thirty insane lunatics in straightjackets, then I suggest that you get out the fuckin' crooked jackets instead!"

"Certainly Mr. Poe," the short obese baldheaded superintendent loudly articulated into my ear, "these thirty patients need one-on-one individual attention, which because of economic reasons, cannot be supplied. I have only two reliable employees assisting me and we're pretty damned overwhelmed, wouldn't you agree?"

"Well then," I yelled in a puzzled frame of mind, "where the hell are Dr. Tarr and Professor Fether? Can't they help you re-tool and reorganize this fucked-up place?"

"I'll tell you a little secret Mr. Poe. They're both locked-up in the chateau's cellar," Maillard confessed without remorse. "They had taken over this institution from me but then I became an activist patient here myself, shrewdly coordinated a counter-revolution just like Napoleon Bonaparte had done, and I coyly got together these thirty uncouth rebels and convinced them to recapture the asylum from the control of those two quack shrinks Tarr and Fether."

"Holy shit!" I exclaimed amidst the tumult of the ever-escalating dining room food fight. "Then really and truly Maillard, the patients have taken over the goddamned asylum! That's fuckin' even worse than the goddamned chicken hawks and foxes being given the keys to the chicken coop!"

Three nude men then clumsily hopped onto the table and started kicking plates and serving bowls and eating utensils off the already abused oak surface while the deranged triumvirate simultaneously and non-harmoniously was singing "Yankee Doodle."

And while all of the unbearable noise and frenzy was in progress and reaching a crescendo, a formidable army of experimental baboons and chimpanzees (that had been caged-up in the asylum's cellar) savagely invaded the dining room and the vicious animals were led by the demented Dr. Tarr and the equally demented Professor Fether, who both had broken free of their shackles and had gotten the Simian troops to support *their* battle assault.

Needless to say, during the hectic and ferocious combat that ensued, I had received a tremendous brutal thrashing and was maliciously scratched all over my face, hands, chest, testicles and arms. I instinctively feigned mortal injury by falling to my hands and knees and then accelerating my ass by swiftly crawling out of the terrible madhouse *Maison de Sante*. I staggered and hobbled outside to the chateau's outbuildings, and I next struggled to saddle and then mount my refreshed horse, which had been moved to the nearby stone barn. Five minutes later my rested steed was ambitiously galloping in the direction of Marseilles.

After my hasty departure from the crazy asylum, I traveled extensively throughout France and researched inside each and every Paris, Marseilles and Lyons library for the collective thesis works of Dr. Tarr and Professor Fether, but alas, in the end my well-intentioned efforts all proved to be abject failures.

Edgar Allan Poe (1809-1849)

Even though Poe had died at a very young age, he still managed to remarkably write over nine hundred pages of imaginative short stories and poems.

In addition to being a superb writer, Poe was also an excellent editor and literary critic and is widely regarded as one of the most important authors in American literature. The now-esteemed writer is often referred to as "the father of the American short story" and as "the inventor of the detective story."

Edgar Allan Poe was born the son of traveling professional actors and was orphaned at age three to the wealthy Allan family of Richmond, Virginia, and that is how Edgar acquired his middle name. Mr. Allan never adopted Edgar because he disapproved of Poe's literary ambitions, the two often quarreling about authors seldom being able to make a decent and respectable living.

Poe was expelled from the University of Virginia on suspicion of gambling and other misdemeanor behavior. He enrolled as a cadet at West Point but was dismissed from that military academy as a result of poor grades. Realizing that reconciliation with Mr. Allan was impossible as long as he wished to become an author, Poe became disenchanted and depressed and intentionally dropped out of the prestigious school on the Hudson. But today there is a commemorative statue at the academy dedicated to Poe claiming that the famous writer had once attended college there.

Edgar married his thirteen-year-old cousin Virginia Clemm and made a very modest living as a writer and as a newspaper journalist. Poe had a nasty temper, took drugs as painkillers and because of his volatile disposition, couldn't keep a job for any length of time. In 1847 Virginia died of tuberculosis and Poe, underfed, pale and gaunt-looking, passed away two years later.

Poe's detective stories "The Murders in the Rue Morgue" and "The Purloined Letter" made him famous in addition to his classic horror tales "The Pit and the Pendulum" and the genius' eerie epic "The Tell-Tale Heart."

"The Rocking Horse Winner"

Hortense Cresswell had always been a beautiful woman who after marriage had given birth to two obnoxious children, Joan, now age twelve, and Paul, now age eight. Hortense was wedded to quiet and reticent Seymour, who unfortunately had then become blind, developing the permanent condition when his gorgeous wife had involuntarily regurgitated in his face while standing in line at a fast food restaurant, the potent stomach bile from her acid reflux immediately and egregiously obliterating her husband's retinas.

Seymour's optometrist Dr. Lidell Hindcite told the bad-luck man, "Eyeglasses and operations can't help you now Mr. Cresswell. I wholeheartedly recommend that you stay away from dangerous vomiting women who love fish and chips, and whatever you do between now and your next office visit, don't make a damned spectacle out of yourself!"

Hortense was very stern-but-doting when raising her two raunchy delinquent children, both of whom shared immense disdain for their' bad-luck parents, the prodigies both wishing that they were other parents' progenies. Joan's mind would often enter a pretend fantasy world and the sister would play with her transvestite dolls and lesbian dollhouse for hours-on-end each and every day, but her toxic brother Paul would incessantly ride his hobby horse Winston six hours at a time. Today was always a carbon-copy of yesterday and also a stark harbinger of the next twenty-four hours to come.

'I married for love and look where the hell love's gotten me,' Hortense lamented and thought, wallowing in massive self-pity. 'My children are fucked-up, my blind husband is fucked-up, and I'm fucked-up too! Thank goodness for my dear brother-in-law that my lamebrain kids affectionately call 'Uncle Oscar'. Yes, Seymour's brother is always lavishing Joan and Paul with wonderful expensive gifts. That's how the hell Joan got her marvelous dollhouse and how Paul received his terrific hobby horse last Christmas,' Hortense recollected. 'The little pecker-head rides the damned plastic thing relentlessly for hours until a worn-out spring finally breaks. That friggin' toy horse is more than a hobby to my asshole obsessive-compulsive son! It's an addictive preoccupation that's friggin' become his sole occupation! Winston will never make it to Churchill Downs!'

The Cresswell family had little money or property. Not even the local post office would give the ridiculous suburban London fools food stamps. The lowly Cresswell's often had to borrow sums of cash from their parsimonious gardener/butler/chauffeur named Bassett, whose animal face was sad and dour in appearance, making Bassett's head and countenance look something like a "melon-collie hound dog."

"Where does Bassett get all of his money?" Hortense asked Seymour at the rickety supper table. "Does he travel to Italy and import and sell Venetian blinds to sightless people? If that's the case Seymour, we need to borrow twenty pounds from either Bassett or from Oscar and purchase some shades for the living room."

"I've overheard gossip that Bassett gambles quite heavily at the race course on his weekend days off," Seymour reported. "The fellow has a one track mind, going to Ascot all the time and wearing that absurd polka dot scarf of his, trying to impress his whoring prostitute girlfriend who works dayshift at the Palladium Picayune Porn Palace over on Piccadilly."

"I guess that if our servant hit the Daily Double," Hortense speculated and stated while the bratty children were busy with their toys in the cluttered play room, "but then I've heard other juicy gossip at the grocery store that Bassett goes straight to the Palladium Picayune Porn Palace on Piccadilly and has a circus robustly screwing two gaudy, grotesque-looking nymphos in the room right above the counter where his whoring prostitute girlfriend is stationed!"

But the egocentric children who were vociferously arguing in the adjacent play-room were fully aware that despite the sensational toys they had always obtained from dear Uncle Oscar, the mischievous brats' sensed that their penniless parents were basically indolent, destitute loser-type paupers.

Hortense worked part time as an art designer but the attractive lady *drew* a pittance for a weekly salary at the shoddy studio situated atop the Cockney Contemporary Cultural Center. On the other hand, Seymour never could *see more* money coming into the domestic household either, being partially dependent on government welfare after losing his job driving the town garbage truck up until the time an aberrant tractor trailer/dump-truck had violently blindsided his "indestructible vehicle" at a major traffic intersection. Seymour had been blamed by the police officers investigating the accident, and the poor fellow instantly lost his *"j*ust-*o*ver-*b*roke" job two months before going blind.

And no one assembling two-piece pen sets at the corner Trafalgar Blind Center truly personally knows their fellow worker

Seymour, and the three chatty legally blind female employees nevertheless absolutely despise ill-starred Cresswell because the working trio could never see eye-to-eye with their colleague on any popular subject or irrelevant controversial issue.

'I'm treated like I'm a Cancer,' Seymour grieved to himself, 'but astrologically speaking, my horoscope is really more of a horrid horror-scope. Those three cunt assholes bullshitting over there don't know it,' Cresswell further evaluated his lackluster situation in life. 'Those gossiping shit-heads have never realized it, but I'm actually a diamond in the rough,' the distraught fellow sulked. 'I'm not a fuckin' Cancer. I'm a fabulous Gemini despite what the hell Hortense, Oscar, Bassett, Paul, Joan and those three worthless almost-blind scumbag bean-counters think!'

But opportunity had never politely knocked on the Cresswell family door, and both Hortense and Seymour believed that opportunity never ever had grown any knuckles with which to loudly rap. The pathetically paranoid couple never purchased any church or mosque raffle tickets simply because they were always too timid and too intimidated to take any chances. But both adolescent Joan and diminutive Paul perceived the Cresswell family mantra quite well, although it had never been spoken or even communicated by hint: 'There must be more money! There must be more money!'

"Where did Joan's dollhouse and my prized Winston come from?" Paul asked his disconsolate mother one late spring afternoon. "Did you extort those things from Santa Claus, the Tooth Fairy or the totally fake Easter Bunny?"

"Your rich Uncle Oscar gave you two hellions those special presents," the mother replied. "Isn't he a fantastic Uncle?"

'That stupid asshole prick bores the hell out of me,' Paul negatively thought. 'That greedy bastard is so selfish that he probably made all his money selling fish on Fridays to gullible knuckleheaded Roman Catholics!' Then the irascible lad all-too-shrewdly switched his devious mind back to the mediocre conversation at hand.

"Yes Mother," Paul coyly answered. "Uncle Oscar is such a swell guy that if he were a hot air balloon, the dumb-ass clown would burst his fat gut before ever floating-up into the lower atmosphere."

"Be more discreet when speaking about your generous Uncle Oscar," the mother admonished, as was her characteristic bad habit, addressing Paul as if he were an obedient educated adult. "He's done a lot for you and Joan."

'I have a real bitch and a half for a mother,' Paul sarcastically concluded, giving his mom the royal middle finger underneath the kitchen table. 'I wonder if she's really my' biological parent? I heard her once telling Uncle Oscar that he had a tiny dick and that Pappy Seymour had a huge dork in comparison. I suppose,' the naughty child pondered as his mother conscientiously prepared some tomato soup on the kitchen stove-top, 'poor men have really hard and long colossal-size dicks and wise-ass rich men have small limp peckers.'

"Paul, when you ride Winston after your hot lunch, be sure to wear your jockey shorts," Hortense jested as she continued swirling the soup around with her large wooden spoon. "Remember Paul, your boxer shorts are to be worn only when you're in the play room fighting with your sister!"

'My mother's really a royal super-bitch to the third power!' academically precocious Paul regretted, frowning wickedly in her direction, the unaware woman's back to him as Hortense meticulously stirred the pot of tomato soup upon the less-than-ordinary kitchen range.

* * * * * * * * * * * *

After the rather bland tomato soup lunch had been served, Paul deliberately-but-candidly asked his troubled mother, "Mom, why are we so darned poverty-stricken? Pretty soon we'll be living in some shabby crack house in a ghetto slum or barrio. Why aren't we rich like Uncle Oscar?"

"You ask too many impertinent adult questions for an eight year old boy," the peeved mother chastised. "Why don't you go into the play room and ride Winston all the way to Inner Mongolia or perhaps to the Sudan for several joyous hours. You need to relax Young Man and learn to appreciate where you are at this callow stage of your carefree life. In all honesty Paul," Mrs. Cresswell cavalierly resumed her sanctimonious lecture, "you seem to have too many frustrations for a normal boy your age."

'My mother's such an old nag that not even Winston would wink or whinny at her if she was a Dover Downs Derby filly,' Paul imagined before swallowing the last tablespoon of his tasteless tomato soup. 'Grandmom must've had a hunch about Mother's lousy domineering personality, naming the now-haughty hussy Hortense, since obviously,' the lad reasoned, 'the bossy witch has probably morphed into a tense whore who makes under-the-table money to help pay the friggin' bills and keep the family going! And Dad's a total dud, a complete parasite, even worse than the Seine River I studied at school!'

But soon self-centered Paul snapped out of his miniature fantasy world and again started conversing as if he were an intelligent adult. "Mother, I need to tell you something important. Actually, it's really something pretty paramount. You and Pop might be unlucky losers out there in the real shilling and pound world, but I have some good news for you. Your one and only son is a sure winner!"

"What makes you say *that* sort of immature stupid crap?" Hortense abruptly challenged. "If you can't act your size-five shoe fit, then try acting your silly-assed age, you wily little scamp, you!"

"God told me that I am to be lucky," Paul strangely revealed without ever invoking the *Book of Revelations*. "He told me stuff while I was riding Winston to the finish line, somewhere between Moscow and Helsinki."

"Stop busting my sensitive tits that have been hurting me ever since I had idiotically breast-fed you!" Hortense simultaneously protested and laughed in a rare demonstration of motherly humor. "And what the hell did Jesus, Mary, Joseph and the Holy Ghost have to say after Almighty God, having nothing better to do, needed to communicate with big-shot you?"

Being pissed-off with his mother's disapproval and with her sharp-tongued acerbity, disenchanted Paul swiftly abandoned his mom in the kitchen and propelled his little ass straight into the playroom to secretly ride Winston from London non-stop to distant Winston-Salem, North Carolina. 'God will send me luck and I shall use it again to make money,' the crazed kid contemplated, his vernal mind almost fully immersed in a self-induced trance.

Then the indignant little ingrate conjectured some more. 'I'm pretty smart for my age and am mentally more advanced than many teenagers are right now. Everyone with half a brain knows that most girls want to get laid by big-dicked barrio guys but then eventually settle-down later living in huge mansions with little-cocked wealthy shitheads like Uncle Oscar.' Feeling great anxiety, Paul then began rocking back and forth upon Winston very aggressively.

"Paul, Uncle Oscar's here to see you!" Hortense Cresswell shouted from the adjoining parlor room. But the stubborn boy ignored his mother's news' announcement and proceeded to rock Winston back and forth even more wildly.

'I need a good luck skein to help my deflated ego survive this hell-hole bungalow, and these freak geeks called parents are very hard for me to tolerate. Let's see now; what in formal society rhymes with the weird-sounding word 'luck'? Hey, what about 'suck' and 'fuck'? They sound cool enough!'

"Paul, Uncle Oscar's coming into the play-room to talk to you right now!" Hortense hollered from the parlor, but to no avail.

And then the warp-minded little maniac increased his effort upon his faithful hobby horse, and in the awesome frightful frenzy, began riding Winston toward Bristol near the English Channel so that the steed could then deftly gallop across the vast Atlantic southwest toward North Carolina.

No one in the family (and counting Bassett too) had ever before dared enter *his* play-room "paddock" when the defiant imp was frenetically rocking back and forth on Winston's prefabricated brown plastic saddle. 'Take me where luck can be found!' the enraptured equestrian wished. 'Someday I'll be able to pop my first glorious sperm load, once I learn how to get a hard-on! I'll just imagine I'm screwing a hot harlot with big tits and nice nipples bouncing around on her chest! That first big orgasm will be a real bonus added to my next good luck message I'm able to receive from Heaven, delivered right into my nifty head. I'll ride all the way to America until I finally fall off of good old Winston from sheer exhaustion!'

The alarmed mother, still casually chit-chatting with Uncle Oscar, was annoyed at hearing the tremendous next-room racket. She quickly opened the 'paddock's door', angrily sped into the play-room and yelled, "Paul! You'll break poor Winston in half riding so wildly like that! You'll also break your tiny little testicles bouncing up and down like a lunatic basketball gone berserk. Are you being pursued by tribes of hostile Apache and Comanche warriors? This might actually be your Seminole (semenal) moment! Ha, ha, ha!"

After verbally administering her humiliating rhetoric, Hortense left the play-room in disgust and then more docile Uncle Oscar suavely stepped inside. The aggravated boy had lost his concentration and now appeared to be rather insulted from being matronly reprimanded. The spoiled tad ceased his dynamic rocking and rolling, and then remembering his treasured hobby horse Christmas gift, the cunning young fellow reluctantly greeted his sometimes-generous relative.

"Well Paul, last week you won the Kentucky Derby," Oscar Cresswell satirically joked. "Are you now getting Winston ready for the annual Preakness and for the super-lucrative Belmont Stakes?

Honestly now Paulie Boy, you'll be better-off than Queen Elizabeth II. You'll have a triple crown to her one!"

"It's my only pleasure in life and you're making fun of it," Paul acknowledged and balked. "Someday I'll have more mature adult pleasures like you do, Uncle Oscar."

"Aren't you growing a little too old for that silly worn-out rocking horse?" the amused half-sympathetic uncle suggested. "You'll be approaching puberty soon, getting hair under your armpits and all that other biological human growth and development shit too. Pretty soon Paulie, you'll be wanting to get your' dingle wet inside a hot pink vagina, if you know what the hell I mean? Have you learned to work your utility stick yet?"

"Well Uncle," Paul responded with an instant blush flashing onto his face, the little schemer specifically desiring to change the awkward sex subject to something else. "I finally got there. Yes sir, I finally got to where I wanted to go again!"

"You're going back to Kentucky?" Oscar Cresswell mocked and laughed. "The next Derby isn't until the first Saturday in May, almost a year from now, ha, ha, ha. I just have to admire your ambition, riding that dumb-ass hobby horse to nowhere eight-to-ten hours every single day. When you get older Paulie," the scrupulous uncle stipulated, "and you're feverishly competing in the very real adult business world, you'll need a legitimate profession, or perhaps a profitable career to pay the rent or the mortgage, and not some asshole hobby or hobby-horse to foolishly occupy your valuable time. Do you understand my sage advice Young Man?"

"You just mentioned the corny word 'legitimate' Uncle, but I had a wonderful horse last week," Paul confidentially divulged to a now-rather fascinated Oscar Cresswell. "Its name was 'Illegitimate'."

"You gotta' be kidding me Young Fella'!" the amazed dapper man exclaimed. "Illegitimate handily won the prestigious Ascot last week by five lengths. In fact, the long-shot pony went off at ten to one odds! A few bettors won big bundles on their low-chance-of-winning wagers! Who told you about Illegitimate?"

"Our goofball servant Bassett," Paul replied in a low voice so that his over-curious mother would not be eavesdropping. "He and I are always discussing the races. Bassett and I both have one track minds, ya' know. His limited thinking is usually at Ascot, and mine is riding Winston all over creation."

"Oh yes, your gardener, butler and chauffeur, Bertram Barnabas Bassett!" Uncle Oscar recalled and stated. "He had his testicles along with half his bloomin' ass blown-off in the war. Now he's a sperm-less half-assed jerk-off that looks like a depressed hound dog. I felt sorry for the miserable bloke so I got him this low-paying job at your parents' dump here. The only reason he's stayed so long in this nightmare disaster is not because of his paltry salary. It's because of the squalor-like lodging in the back garage that he loves and it's because of the meager meals Bassett eats there for free!"

"He's really and truly my only good friend," retorted and defended Paul. "Mr. Bassett lives for the races, and don't argue with him when he's on his own turf, reading newspapers all the time to study the changing odds! Mr. Bassett's very knowing when it comes to horse-racing," the boy attested. "He's the one who convinced Mom and Pop not to put a padlock on my paddock."

"Your paddock, you say?"

"Yes Uncle," the boy answered with a tight expression shown around his small mouth. "A lock on the door of this room; it's 'off-limits to adults', my kiddy play-room."

Being intrigued with young Paul's totally zany testimony, Uncle Oscar hastened outside to the weedy garden to interrogate Bassett on the essential matter just discussed. The searcher found the half-assed fellow busy digging a hole to bury a stray cat that had just died from old age in the cottage's unkempt jungle-like back yard.

"Master Paul occasionally asks me about the Ascot races, so since I like the little over-abused chap a bit," the wounded war veteran-turned-gardener explained, "I tell him what the hell I know about the exciting sport." Bassett's florid face was by now quite solemn, as if the race course addict were seriously talking about Bible religion as well as expounding on the Immaculate Conception, the Crucifixion along with the Glorious Resurrection.

"Did Master Paul ever give you a shilling or two to bet on a race?" Oscar Cresswell inquired. "I'll bet the punk kid wagers what little he can afford to gamble."

"I don't want to get into any major trouble with his folks," Bassett diplomatically remarked with sweat now appearing on his brow. "But the boy is definitely interested in horse racing, that's for damned sure. Now Sir, if *you* were to ask *him* about his activity involving me betting small amounts of dough for the lad, I'll bet he'd show enthusiasm on the subject and be very cooperative with you, Mr. Cresswell. But in truth Sir," the neurotic gardener orally stressed, "I don't want the eccentric hooligan to feel like I had given his little race-track secret away. I want to keep the tyke's trust, ya' know. I'm basically his only true friend that he ever confides in."

* * * * * * * * * * *

If curiosity killed the notorious ill-fated cat, it also inspired Uncle Oscar to escort his only nephew for a long ride in the remote countryside inside his new plush luxury automobile. The odd pair's initial dialogue was rather jocular.

"What do you think of my new expensive car?" Uncle Oscar asked. "Isn't it a beauty? There're only fifty of these cherished babies in all of London just like it."

"It looks and rides like one of those silly-looking weinermobiles that are big deals over in America," Paul absurdly equated. "On second thought, this silver tin pig is shaped like that famous Hollywood statue, you know, the asinine award given for Best Picture, Best Actor and Best Actress."

"Are you making fun of my Rolls Royce and my name too?" the suddenly upset uncle asked. "This terrific thing cost the average factory bloke around five years' wages."

"Get bent!" the provocative ornery kid replied.

"What did you say!" the quickly offended driver yelled across the capacious front seat. "I hope it isn't what I think I heard! Repeat what the hell you said!"

"Get a Bentley!" Paul smartly re-configured his former exclamatory sentence. "It's a nice car you have here, but I prefer Bentleys! They're much more acceptable to the middle class."

"Say Paulie, I was wondering," the Rolls Royce operator interrupted. "Did you ever bet on any horses?"

"Once I almost bet on the Indianapolis Colts, and another time I almost put a few shillings down on the Denver Broncos," the disingenuous twerp prevaricated. "But then I chickened-out and bet on the Delaware Blue Hens!"

"Stop irritating me with a ludicrous litany of dumb-ass evasive answers!" Uncle Oscar vehemently protested, almost losing his tonsils on the winding way to Cresswell's rural lodge out in Hampshire. "You ninny! Please show some culture and be sincere and honest for a damned change. I had been referring to wagering on British horse races, not on stupid-shit American football games. I thought you would give me a tip minus the dumb frivolous bullshit. Now what's a fair-to-Midland hot scoop on the upcoming Lincoln Park agenda?"

"I like LBTG in the fourth," the addicted kid predicted. "Yeah, LBTG is definitely gonna' triumph in the fourth. What do those letters stand for anyway? Is it some sort of idiotic code for Lesbian, Gay, Bisexual and Trans-gender?"

"Who the hell ever told you *that* nonsensical rubbish?" Oscar Cresswell hollered, nearly avoiding a box truck speeding in the opposite direction while also nearly bursting a major blood vessel in his throat. "Everybody knows that LBTG stands for 'Let' us Gobble Bacon and Tomato', you know, a very cute allusion to tasty BLT sandwiches!"

"Well, how about it meaning Let God Banish Transvestites?" the argumentative boy offered. "That little ditty sounds much more logical, doesn't it Uncle Oscar?"

"I strenuously doubt if LBTG has an icicle's chance in hell of winning its next race," the snobbish driver snottily driveled. "I'm considering putting a few stock dividend pounds from my brokerage account on more experienced Mizra, it behooves me to say. Yes, I like Mizra's chances."

"I only know the Winner and not the names of the unimportant Place and Show horses Uncle Oscar, and besides," the wise-ass kid resumed his extended monologue, "the damned Winner is going to be LBTG. But please don't repeat this vital info' to anyone else. I promised my partner Bassett I would keep *that* can't miss tip a secret. The guy had lent me the first five shillings I needed to start building my gambling empire. It was sort of like my seed money."

"Well, how much do you plan on betting on this old gray mare LBTG?" the Rolls Royce owner asked.

"I have three hundred and twenty pounds saved-up, and I'm betting all but twenty just in case I lose and have to start building my financial empire from scratch again. But Bassett's not half as brave as I am," Paul related. "The coward's gonna' plunk-down only a hundred and fifty smackers over at Sam's Bookie Parlor."

"You got to be joking!" the dumbfounded driver choked and coughed, almost swerving off the two-lane asphalt road and careening into a deep drainage ditch. "Look Paulie. I'm gonna' give you a royal treat you'll never forget. Instead of you doing business with that Jew swindler Sam 'the Scam' Schultz, I'm gonna' take you to Lincoln Park where I'll gladly place your bet for you right then and there. You'll wager on this LBTG nag, and I'll personally put my five winning pounds on Mizra."

The following Saturday afternoon Uncle Oscar picked-up Paul in his shiny silver Rolls Royce and then motored-out to the always crowded race track. The trembling Uncle was positively astonished when LBTG came in first, Lancelot second and Mizra finished a respectable-but-miserable-distant third.

"Holy shit Paulie! You won a staggering fifteen hundred pounds!" the shocked uncle whooped. "I couldn't believe that you had three hundred pounds to plunk down, but somehow you did. Frankly, I was happy to bet the enormous sum for you. Are you sure that you and Bassett didn't rob a bank or a thriving brothel?"

"Look Uncle, if you want to be Bassett's and my silent partner, ya' gotta' pledge to remain silent, and secondly, ya' gotta' talk to him in the privacy of the dumpy family garage," Paul adamantly insisted, brazenly establishing the general inflexible terms of the impending oral contract.

"I'll speak with that half-ass sperm-less shit-head when I return you back home to your loser parents," Seymour Cresswell's very successful brother informed. "I always thought that Bassett was full of shit, but now I'm beginning to wonder otherwise!"

Inside the grimy garage Bassett was readily amenable to the new three-member betting covenant, so the following Saturday the now-enamored rich uncle drove Bassett and Paul out to Richmond Park to attend the scheduled "big stake races."

"I want to play the Super Trifecta today?" Uncle Oscar audaciously mentioned on the scenic drive out to the bustling horse race stadium. "What stallion do you' like in the first?"

"Well Uncle, Mr. Bassett and I have thoroughly reviewed the thoroughbreds in the entire field," the sagacious nephew indicated, "and we both like Connie Lingus to Win, Phil Lay-Chio to Place and Feed-the-Cat to Show."

"What the hell are you saying?" Uncle Oscar shouted across the new car's front seat. "I've never heard of those obscure hapless equines. You two fucked-up amateurs must be wholly mistaken."

"Master Paul is never wrong Sir," Bassett confirmed. "I think the lad's a descendant of either Ezekiel or Isaiah!"

Two hours later the thrilling main race outcome was phenomenal with all three chosen horses speeding across the Richmond Park Finish Line in the exact same order as the incredible "pipsqueak prophet" Master Paul Cresswell had correctly prognosticated. The "oracle kid" and Bassett had together won a spectacular five thousand pounds, and conversely, avaricious Uncle Oscar a mere one hundred upon his much less daring wager.

"A bird in the hand is worth two in the bush!" Bassett jubilantly enunciated on the very smooth luxury ride back home. "Life is a lark at Richmond Park!"

"That insane gibberish you're uttering Bassett sounds like you're saying that jerking-off once is better than getting laid twice," Uncle

Oscar obstinately bitched as his immaculate polished Rolls Royce pulled-off the paved lane and was recklessly maneuvered into the Cresswell family's narrow gravel driveway.

"Before you leave Paulie, who do you and Bassett like in next Saturday's highly publicized British Derby? I'm throwing my standard conservatism out the proverbial window, so I plan to get a trifle bolder in my wagering on the next Big Trifecta."

"We like Adultery to Win, Master Bates to Place and Little Dick to Show!" forecast the grammar school Moses. "Golly Uncle Oscar! I can't believe you're taking Bassett and me to the fabulous British Derby! Bassett promised to buy me some condoms from the wall dispenser in the upper level Men's Room."

"Good then!" Uncle Oscar concurred, not hearing one syllable about the mass-market condom machine. "I'll drive you two avid racing buffs out to the track grandstand next Saturday. But before the gates open Paulie, I'm gonna' procure triple fancy lower level box seats for the three of us!"

Sure enough, a week later Adultery, Master Bates and Little Dick finished Win, Place and Show, just like young inimitable Paul Cresswell had amazingly predicted. After the outstanding supernatural event, Uncle Oscar drove himself' and his two passengers home to rustic Hampshire, drank a pint of Beefeaters pure gin, and then the gambler fell into an inebriated deep sleep.

* * * * * * * * * * * *

Uncle Oscar again hurriedly visited the inferior Seymour Cresswell bungalow, the rejuvenated racing fanatic requiring some fresh predictions from the accomplished child-prodigy turned soothsayer, who was again perched upon his beloved hobby horse, violently rocking back and forth as if the juvenile's very life depended on his energetic enterprise. Hortense and Oscar worriedly watched the seemingly possessed lad perform his arduous daily mania, the dedicated boy sweating profusely in almost a hypnotic state of mind, fully oblivious to any adult spectators scrutinizing his laborious activity.

"Seymour's busy doing his menial monotonous job at the corner blind person's workplace," Hortense reported to her only brother-in-law, just when Paul was gradually ceasing his prolonged exercise session upon overused Winston. "I suppose you've come here to find-out some hot tips on the upcoming races. I've recently learned at the beauty salon that Paul and Bassett have accumulated a small fortune betting on the races, and rumor has it that you've profited quite well too."

"Oh, hello Uncle Oscar," the perspiring petite augur' lethargically greeted as the weakened kid slowly dismounted from his toy riding horse. "I suppose you're here to find-out who's going to win the Grand National and the Lincolnshire. I've just found-out the results while riding Winston. Either Heaven or God has told me the exact winners, maybe both have."

"This horrible gambling chicanery isn't moral or healthy," Hortense assessed and nastily criticized. "I think it's not God's work but instead, it's the Devil's doing! It's more demonic than blessed, that's my humble opinion, despite all of the easy money that's being made by you imbeciles! It's all evil, quite plain and simple!"

"Okay then Master Paul," Oscar Cresswell nonchalantly stated, adroitly avoiding direct conflict with his sister-in-law's expressed objections, "what's the Grand National and the Lincolnshire look like? I can't wait to find out!"

"Well Uncle Oscar, Cox-Stucker is gonna' come in first in the big Grand National, and my favorite horse Adultery is gonna' win the Lincolnshire by an easy seven lengths. God told me these certain facts. You can bet your mansion and your Rolls Royce on either of them! You can bet your fat ass too!"

"This wicked information isn't originating from Heaven," the skeptical mother declared. "It's all coming straight from Hell!"

"Never mind your nervous mother's ranting," Oscar commanded Paul. "Give me some more pertinent race details, like the Lincolnshire Daily Double for instance."

"Forget the Daily Double! Here's a swell Trifecta for you, Uncle Oscar!" the now-spiteful boy exclaimed with heightened animosity showing in his intense brown eyes. "I've been studying the dictionary and now I have the whole ugly thing all figured-out."

"Figured what out Paulie?" the surprised uncle asked. "You're talking in riddles!"

"I hate Joan, and Bassett's really the only one I trust around here," the irate boy stated. "And Uncle Oscar, you're a lousy no-good mother-fucker!"

"What foul thing did you just say?" the normally sophisticated aristocrat loudly answered. "Did your mother and I hear you correctly? We're gonna' wash and rinse your dirty mouth-out with strong detergent!"

"Yes, the winning horses in all the races have spelled it all out for me," youthful Paul insolently and pompously related. "You and

Mom have committed Adultery. Pop is not my biological father Uncle Oscar. You are! That fact obviously makes me Illegitimate!"

"Stop the vulgar innuendo! Your mother and I resent these false accusations, these unfounded allegations, these gross insinuations!" Oscar Cresswell objected, completely losing his temper. "I think I'm about to give you the thrashing you've deserved these past eight years! You need your tender fanny tanned good!"

After Hortense burst-out in tears, Master Paul continued with his all-too-honest indictment. "Yes Uncle Oscar, you did it all with your Little Dick. Mom began the sinful affair with Master Bates being done to you. That extra-curricular bull-shit was followed by Connie Lingus and then by Phil Lay-Chio. And LBTG is the new rich people's secret sex club over in Hampshire that you and Mom recently joined, you disgusting sneaky Feed-the-Cat jerk, you mentally sick pussy stuffer!"

Mrs. Seymour Cresswell suddenly felt lightheaded, and her thin pale body soon crashed upon the nondescript parlor's faded brown carpet. Uncle Oscar bent-down and immediately tried reviving the fainted woman by rapidly slapping her face.

"And there's one more thing I have to tell you," vengeful Paul Cresswell austerely voiced to his mother's secret paramour. "Greedy Uncle is gonna' win the coveted Oxford Stakes three weeks from today!"

D.H. Lawrence (1885-1930)

David Herbert Lawrence was a famous British novelist, poet and short story writer. A childhood friend of Lawrence named Jessie Chambers secretly had copied the fledgling author's poems and sent them to *The English Review,* and the superb works were published in November of 1909. D. H. Lawrence became an overnight sensation in London literary communities.

The author's first novel *The Rainbow,* published in 1915, was immediately banned, being judged in a court of law as being obscene, but most probably disallowed from public consumption because the author's characters questioned England's involvement in World War I. A later famous novel, *Lady Chatterley's Lover,* was banned in many countries because the important work was also believed to be indecent and contrary to strict Victorian morality.

"To Build a Fire"

Dawn had broken under a cloudy sky and the self-confident man deviated from the Yukon trail and climbed up the steep earth bank to a higher but less used pathway that led eastward through the spruce timberland. After ascending the incline and walking along for several hours with his wolf dog behind him, the man inspected his watch and observed that it was already nine o'clock. The absence of the sun made the entire physical environment seem drab and gloomy. But still, the man was determined to persevere.

'In a few more days the sun will be visible on the southern horizon,' the cocky man believed from past experience witnessing similar atmospheric phenomena. 'My fuckin' wolf dog has no concept of the sun, of its function or of its necessity! The stupid beast is probably much better off having its ignorance of nature and its cruel laws! Basically, it's all the old reason-versus-instinct bullshit and I possess the goddamned knowledge and my low-intelligence dog does not!'

Surveying the distance beyond from his lofty vantage point, the man saw the mile-wide Yukon River frozen solid with ice three-feet-thick with several foot deep snow drifted upon the hard surface. The river wound its way around several spruce-laden islands in the same direction as to where the man would meet up with friends later that afternoon and then continue their trek southward. The newcomer to the North stubbornly believed that the icy fifty-degree temperature was fairly tolerable and not potentially dangerous to anyone with any element of courage in his character and who possessed a spark of self-reliant determination in his spirit.

'Mittens, ear muffs, warm moccasins, fur hat and coat, flannel shirts, thick socks and woolen underwear will insulate me from these abnormal elements,' the man rationally thought. 'But how the freakin' Eskimos ever have wintertime sex up here is far beyond my comprehension!'

The man spit some mucus from his mouth and was amazed that a sharp explosive crackle occurred when the liquid solidified in the cold air temperature before ever hitting the snow. 'The boys will be meeting me at Henderson Creek at six o'clock as has been planned,' the man recollected. 'In an hour or two I'll take out a biscuit and have it for lunch. But I'll have to eat that son-of-a-bitch in a hurry before it hardens like the spit did in the air and then breaks my teeth. There aren't too many fuckin' dentists up here on the trail so

I'd better be careful how I use my damned choppers!' the adamant man concluded.

And each biscuit was rich in fatty grease and wrapped in a nourishing slice of bacon. 'Not exactly a meal fit for a king but up here in Northern Canada, it sure beats fuckin' starvation! Although I'd rather eat pussy, the bacon-covered biscuits are definitely more nutritious! I'll just pretend I'm eating Sir Francis and then the delicious bacon will taste all that much better! Too bad I couldn't be devouring the fucked-up Earl of Sandwich too!'

He and his wolf dog ambled along the deep snow trail as the man occasionally rubbed his nose and cheekbones with his mittened right hand. 'It's a little uncomfortable out here but I'll endure,' the traveler haughtily convinced himself.

But the wolf dog knew that it had been too cold to be traveling anywhere even though the animal lacked the arithmetical knowledge that the temperature was actually seventy-five degrees below zero and not fifty-degrees below as his master had erroneously believed. A hundred and seven degrees below the Fahrenheit "frost-point" is an unbearable condition that is hostile to the survival and sustenance of human life. The animal knew from past experiences with humans that its master should either seek shelter or enter a camp to get warm and wondered why the man persisted in struggling his way through the fierce harsh cold winds.

Every time the man attempted to expel juice from his chewing tobacco, the fluid would freeze and attach itself to his red beard because the brown liquid would not shoot out over his chin onto the ground. In fact, an amber icicle was forming between the man's mouth and chin from the extremely cold Arctic weather. 'This is not the time to give my boots a spit shine, or even a fuckin' brown spit shine!' the audacious man thought in an effort to amuse himself. 'Christ! If I was born in Belgium I'd be even more fuckin' 'phlegm-ish' than I am right now! And this phlegm I'm discharging from my mouth can't remind me of my old girlfriend back in Fairbanks because she was a real spitfire!'

Several miles ahead the trekker stumbled down a slippery snow embankment and reached the foot of Yukon Creek, a mere ten miles from the forks. 'Let's see now,' the anxious fellow considered. 'If I average four miles an hour, I'll arrive at the forks by around two in the afternoon. I'll hold off my stomach pangs until then and enjoy swallowing down my bacon-flavored biscuits. Then between six and seven o'clock I'll rendezvous with the boys at the camp and I'll finally be able to examine some of their wonderful porno' magazines. Shit, I hope they've gotten some new nude centerfolds! Oh well. I'll just keep my current pace and extend the length of my amber icicle beard. Shit, the thing's already twice as long as my dick!'

But then the man noticed that his nose and his cheeks were numb and that his facial skin no longer felt the sensations of warmth, touch or pain. 'I'll put up with these frosty numb cheeks and numb nose for six more hours. A little discomfort never killed anyone! Fuck!' the sufferer realized. 'How will I ever know if I piss myself if my dick becomes numb too! Oh well, I'll just think about those porno' periodicals at the camp. They'll keep me movin' on. It's amazing how the power of pussy can motivate a guy to ignore terrible things like fifty-to-sixty degree below zero temperatures out here in the bitter wilderness.'

* * * * * * * * * * * *

The man's locomotion was not impeded despite the frigid cold and the high snow accumulation in his path. His awareness knew that although no deep-water creek could avert being frozen over, still, pockets of springs bubbled out from the hillsides and the reality existed where the trekker could accidentally fall into a pool of water. Such a horrifying misfortune would mean immediately building a fire to dry out and then promptly changing his socks to prevent getting frostbitten toes. The covered pools might be three inches deep or three feet deep, the latter scenario representing a life-threatening situation to be certainly avoided.

'I must be careful, because if I fall into a pool of water,' the man thoughtfully evaluated, 'I might as well be authoring my own self-destruction. And I don't need the delay of building a fire if I could instead use my intelligence and my savvy to evade having to do it. And besides, I strongly desire to continue living so that I could go back to Fairbanks down in Alaska and hump and pump my old spitfire girlfriend. Now that I've eluded the soft snow water pool traps, I can resume my four-mile an hour gait. I'm not going to allow nature's obstacles to fuckin' stymie my progress, so sir!'

Two hours later the man encountered another patch of soft snow that he recognized and suspected might be hiding unexposed water pools, so honoring an inspiration, the wanderer decided to make his wolf dog go first, but the beast refused to take an unaccustomed leadership role in the expedition. The man forcefully pushed the dog forward and its weight suddenly broke through the thin ice, instantly wetting its front paws.

Immediately the canine licked its paws and instinctively bit out the ice between its pads, a natural reaction to its need for self-preservation. Fearing a loss of time the man ripped-off his' mitten and helped the animal scrape-off and removed the remaining embedded ice chunks. Realizing that his right hand had become numb is less than a minute of exposure, the man quickly put his mitten back onto his hand and then pounded his chest thirty consecutive times to get vital circulation flowing again back into his wrist and fingers.

At one-thirty in the afternoon the man arrived at the designated 'forks' to stop and consume his bacon-flavored biscuits that had been strapped inside a pouch concealed underneath his warm fur coat. Again his exposed fingers became numb at locating and removing his lunch food. He then struck his hand two dozen times against his right knee to get the circulation and his feeling sensation going again. Now the beleaguered traveler realized that his feet were wet, his nose, cheeks and fingers numb and that perhaps starting a fire would be not only advantageous but also fully necessary.

'That son-of-a-bitch old geezer back at the lodge at Sulfur Creek knew what the hell he was bullshittin' about when he said that it gets unbearably could out here in the country,' James Philip Monahan recollected as he continuously stomped his feet and thrashed his arms about as if performing gym class calisthenics.

Using twigs and small branches from nearby spruce trees, the man built a fire to sit beside and then commence swallowing down his three biscuits while the obedient wolf dog sprawled out just far enough from the roaring flames to not get its fur singed. After warming his hands and briefly smoking his pipe, Jim Monahan speedily pulled on his sealskin mittens, adjusted the flaps of his fur cap over his tender ears and then proceeded up the left fork trail that paralleled the newly found Henderson Creek. But as the trekker and his dog advanced onward, the canine knew that it was far better to dig a hole in the snow and curl its body into a semicircle to keep warm rather than to be walking along a creek in such severe weather conditions.

'Ah, no signs of underwater springs on this left fork!' Monahan gratefully assessed. 'I should be able to maintain my schedule and meet the guys before seven. I hope the fuck those zany assholes don't wanna' play strip poker! Oh shit! I've just broken through down to my goddamned knees! That's what the fuck I get for losing my concentration for a second and then letting my fucked-up imagination run amuck! It's imperative that I lose another damned hour to build another fire or else risk freezing my fingers, toes and dick off!'

At the top of a rocky hill the man industriously gathered grasses, twigs, sticks and branches, for time was of the essence. Monahan removed a piece of treasured birch bark from an inner pocket, scraped a match and managed to ignite a fire. He very methodically fed the flames with dry twigs and grass and much to his elation, the sparks and flames became greater and soon began to roar.

'When it's more than fifty-degrees-below-zero, there's no margin for error,' Jim plausibly concluded. 'If my feet are dry, I can run in the snow for a half a mile and get my blood flowing in my extremities again. But if my feet are wet, I gotta' build a fire and expose them to heat otherwise I'll be even worse off than that Venus de Milo statue, having no legs in addition to no fuckin' arms! I must complete my route without any further complications! I can't get cold feet! Ha, ha, ha,' the man mentally laughed at his moronic cliché. 'No way!'

* * * * * * * * * * * *

The encumbered wanderer was not used to such terrible adversity and realized that he should have adhered more diligently to the old-timer's advice back at Sulfur Creek. 'I gotta' act fast and not fuck-up again!' he frantically conjectured. 'It's early March and I can't be as slow as molasses in January because damn it, it's even colder now than it fuckin' was two months ago!'

To build his second fire to an appropriate level of heat and power, the pathetic man had to remove his mittens and his overtaxed brain comprehended that his hands in addition to his fingers were numb, and also, his feet were now objects simply attached to his body. The full force of the swirling wind added even more harsh reality to his treacherous dilemma.

'It's so fuckin' cold that I won't know if or when I shit my pants!' the perplexed victim comprehended while shivering. 'My blood is staying in the center of my body and my arms, legs and head are feeling the hellish consequences. My skin can feel the loss of blood and diminished sensation but let's hope this fire flourishes because I don't know if I have the wherewithal to fuckin' start another one!' Monahan lamented and regretted. 'Now I know. The next time the temperature drops under fifty degrees below, I should stay the fuck under the covers in my bunk bed. Hell, my uncooperative hands can't even feel the twigs that I'm feeding into the fire. Forget screwing my kinky spitfire girl down in Fairbanks! Oh, if I could only be alone in my bunk and be jerking-off one final time!'

The man attempted untying his ice-coated footgear however the strings seemed like rods of straight steel, but upon acknowledging the folly of his actions, the desperate trekker drew his sheath knife to sever the laces. But then an unanticipated fate occurred that would send shock waves from his brain down his spine. Jim had made the crucial mistake of building his fire under a large spruce tree so that twigs and wood would be readily available.

The tree had a tremendous weight of snow upon its boughs. While yanking the fifth twig from the tree, that minute agitation precipitated disaster as a load of snow descended from the top branches until virtually all of the accumulated ice had descended into a mini-avalanche and had in five seconds extinguished the fire that the determined man had labored so assiduously to ignite. A foot-deep mantle of snow now occupied the space where the benevolent fire had existed just thirty seconds before.

'The old fuck at Sulfur Creek was right. I should've been travelin' with another prospector. It's as if my death sentence has just been cruelly announced,' Jim Monahan hypothesized with disgust. 'I'm never gonna' read those porno' magazines at the camp or ever get laid again by my spitfire bitch back in Fairbanks or by any other horny whore anywhere else! I gotta' try one more time to build this fuckin' fire, but even if I succeed, I'm certain to lose a few fingers and toes to frostbite!'

The perplexed man gathered some twigs using his two hands like a primitive machine, but his next endeavor was performed out in the open away from any snow-laden overhead tree branches. Jim could not separate the twigs from the worthless green moss around them because of the lack of dexterity in his fingers. All the while the confused wolf dog sat in wonder staring at the incompetence of the desperate man who was ordinarily the skilled fire provider. Monahan then fumbled in his pocket for his second and last piece of birch bark to start the flames but presently he lacked the motor skills to effectively clutch it. Realizing that his feet were also frozen, the man's mind entered a panic-state frenzy.

'I gotta' beat my hands against my sides to get some feeling back into my fingers,' Jim anxiously thought. 'Just look at that dog peacefully lying there all fuckin' curled up in a ball, still warm and vibrant! Believe it or not, I would trade places with that dumb animal in a Seattle minute. I think that all-too-comfortable beast has more of a future than I fuckin' do! I can't believe it. I actually envy that furry complacent son-of-a-bitch who was basically really a son-of-a-bitch when he was born!'

For an ephemeral minute the overwhelmed man enjoyed with satisfaction an excruciating ache in his left hand as marvelous sensation again existed there. Jim was able to remove his pack of matches, which unfortunately then fell into the snow. Unable to pick the matches up with his numb fingers, he devoted all of his energies on how he could ignite a fire.

Monahan again used his two hands as an improvised 'scoop shovel' to grab the elusive pack. Wearing his mittens, he was able to again manipulate his palms like two hand-spades. The beleaguered distraught man managed to get the entire match-pack between his knuckles and then he awkwardly raised his mittens up to his mouth, which had difficulty in opening because his lips had been ensconced in ice. Then the *overmatched* man succeeded in lighting one flare, which then set the entire pack on fire, and burning brimstone soon ascended up into his nostrils and down into his lungs, causing the accursed victim to excessively cough. The burning pack of matches plunged into the snow and then its accompanying flames quickly faded out.

* * * * * * * * * * * *

Jim stared avariciously at Czar, his curious-but-defensive minded wolf dog. 'You must think that I'm a total asshole if you have any fucked-up concept of what the hell a total asshole is!' Monahan thought during a moment of self-serving black humor. 'Once you realize that I'm dying and am no longer your personal fire provider,' the master visualized and considered, 'you'll sure as taxes and death abandon me as if I was a hard turd that had just dropped out of your furry ass.'

The battered man peered again at his bewildered dog and the master's faltering mind successfully manufactured a fleeting idea. 'That's it!' Jim imagined as he again briefly glanced at Czar shifting his weight back and forth with curious wistfulness as he lay in the snow. 'The old-timer back at Sulfur Creek had once told me about a man caught in a blizzard who had miraculously killed a caribou and then crawled inside its partially gutted-out carcass to stay alive until someone accidentally discovered him. That's exactly what I have to fuckin' do in order for me' to stay alive! I'll try to kill Czar and then stick my hands into its warm body to get the sensation of feeling back into them. It's my only chance of survival in this goddamned surreal supernatural life-or-death raffle that my unlucky name has been entered into! That's my only hope. I must fuckin' live at Czar's fuckin' expense!'

Monahan beckoned to Czar to come to him but the skeptical animal was used to listening to stern commands and detected fear in Jim's weak voice. The dog's suspicious nature also sensed that things were out of kilter and that his normal relationship with his master had somehow drastically transformed from dominant man' and subordinate beast to something else.

Czar's ears flattened as the dubious animal ignored the man's feeble solicitations. Jim then got down on his hands and knees and bizarrely crawled towards his furry companion but again becoming wary and apprehensive, Czar slowly sidled away. The thwarted master then became cognizant of one important fact: he must rise to his feet and tower over the wolf dog if he expected Czar to obey his commands in any way, thus again rendering his allegiance to his master. 'If I don't watch myself, I might somehow weirdly become a serf to Czar in a power-structure reversal of roles!'

After achieving the arduous act of standing erect, Jim had to wait a moment to verify that he was indeed in a vertical position perpendicular to the ground, for his energy reserve was rapidly sapping and he had no distinct feeling in his legs, feet or toes. The doomed man attempted clutching the dog's neck but instead, he collapsed upon the animal, endeavoring to strangle or smother Czar beneath the weight of his body. All the while the surprised dog snarled, whined and struggled.

'If only I had the coordination and the needed strength to stab Czar with my sheath knife,' Jim thought during his mental and physical mania. With virtually all of his stamina expired, the exhausted man released the wolf dog from his greedy grasp. The creature wildly plunged away with its tail curved between its hind legs, panting heavily between snarls.

Then Czar, with his ears pricked forward, halted a distance of forty safe feet away from Jim to survey the man and his miserable plight. The dog's keen instincts detected weakness and craziness and Czar did not value either alien entity.

Jim looked down at his gloved hands in order to locate them and was surprised to see them still attached to his dangling arms. 'I've never before had to use my fuckin' eyes to find out where my goddamned hands are,' the grieving man's mind fancifully thought. 'I'm just as destined to die as the last asshole standing at the Alamo had been destined to die!'

For five whole minutes Jim violently pounded his hands against his knees and his heart was able to eventually pump enough blood to temporarily make his persistent shivering cease. But still, his extremities remained frozen and numb. 'Even my hard head is feeling no damned sensation. I'm truly the epitome of a human *numb*skull!' Jim mused as hysteria began settling inside his brain. 'I'm no longer afraid of having my damned fingers and toes amputated! I'm now dreading the thought of losing my friggin' life! I swear there is no paradise but I fuckin' pray there isn't any goddamned hell!'

Out of sheer desperation, Jim Monahan attempted to jog toward the distant logging camp, still situated several miles away and the now-cautious Czar reluctantly and subserviently followed his trail. As the disoriented man floundered and staggered forward, his eyes perceived certain familiar objects that gave him renewed strength: the banks of the creek, the timber jams, the leafless aspens, the spruce trees and finally, the dull gray sky.

'Fuck. If I'm not careful, I might soon be stiff and dead, just like I want my useless pecker *not* to be!' the emotionally defeated Monahan poignantly assessed. 'I must make it to the camp before some carnivorous nocturnal animal finds me. Even if I lose part of my face, hands, feet and ass,' the vanquished man decided, 'I don't give a diarrhea shit! I gotta' somehow survive this awful mess and write a goddamned novel about it!'

Jim was both astonished and confused that he could run at all on feet that were so terribly abused and so horribly frozen. The weight of his body was now indiscernible to his mind's perception. His feet had no relationship to the solid earth and ice as he clumsily advanced, skimmed and skated ahead.

'I must not fall!' his stressed-out brain kept registering and reviewing. 'I wonder if that winged-helmeted Greek god Mercury could move as fuckin' swiftly as I'm moving now! And as for that fucked-up son-of-a-bitch bastard Prometheus, where the fuck is *he* when I really fuckin' need his fire-lighting services the most!' Jim illogically hallucinated. 'Why the fuck couldn't I be lost in the steaming hot Amazon jungle! At least I wouldn't be fuckin' freezing to death up here in nature's icebox! Shit!' Monahan realized during a moment of elevated frustration. 'I gotta' make sure I don't lose my balance tripping over a goddamned crocodile or giant anaconda! Jesus Christ! I'd rather be nailed to a cross than to mentally and physically suffer like this! I don't have the endurance to survive!' the man sobbed. 'My only fuckin' hope is to be miraculously found by the boys! But they're all egotistical self-indulgent assholes! I'll bet they're all reading their fucked-up porno' magazines in their warm bunks and looking at pictures of nude crocodile and anaconda centerfolds! Am I becoming fucked-up or what?'

Then the negative pessimistic thought of his frozen arms and legs extending their numbness and advancing to his chest and abdomen horrified Jim as he valiantly staggered onward. 'I'm more fuckin' afraid of panicking than of fuckin' dying!' the brave man concluded. 'I want to walk but actually I need to run! Shit! When I used to play baseball in my youth back in Portland, Oregon I used to walk all the fuckin' time!'

Jim abruptly fell to the ground and Czar parked his gray and white furry body ten feet in front of the frenetic victim as if deliberately taunting him and his futility. The warmth and security of the animal angered the jealous man, now wishing that Czar' was a ferocious crocodile or a ravenous anaconda seeking to devour a near-frozen human being.

'I'm gradually losing my battle with the frost!' Jim academically reckoned. 'Why the fuck couldn't I have been a soldier at Gettysburg, or a frontiersman at the Alamo and had died battling other humans rather than being defeated by a goddamned relentless mean-spirited woman named Mother Nature?'

Then a certain peculiar simile entered the disenchanted man's distorted disarrayed mind. 'I must sit-up and meet death with some degree of dignity. No sense in running around like a chicken without a head' because I'm not a goddamned chicken even though I can't feel or even touch my goddamned head!'

Monahan stoically decided that he must encounter death decently and peacefully by going off to sleep and then subconsciously surrendering his will to live. That imagined quiet scenario appeared to be the best solution: to use sleep as an appropriate anesthetic since the sensation of pain had been reduced to a mere conceptual fantasy, totally devoid of reality. Jim's last random thought was his ghost accompanying his concerned friends and together the quartet had discovered his frozen body lying upon the tundra. The man's spirit had finally been persuaded by his diminished will to abandon its imprisonment and exit his body in pursuit of its predestined place in the invisible Universe.

In his final thought, Jim's erratic mind conjured-up an image of the old-timer at Sulfur Creek being the immortal God-the-Father sitting on his Olympian-like golden throne inside His marble palace in the center of Heaven. The dead man's initial words to his omnipotent Deity would be, "You were right Old Boss! I should've had a strong fellow along with me on the trail. You're always right, and quite truthfully God, Your damned ubiquitous eternal irrational wisdom makes me want to puke!'

Then Jim drowsed-off into the most comfortable and satisfying sleep' that is humanly possibly on even the softest and most desirable bed mattress. The puzzled wolf dog sat restlessly waiting for his master to awaken and to eventually remember to ignite a warm fire. But the man's soul, half-Mercury and half-Prometheus, had peacefully journeyed into the afterlife.

As the twilight drew closer and dusk was imminent, Jim did not stir from his sitting position with his head bowed between his knees. The eerie silence was quite extraordinary and particularly foreign to the canine's experiences.

A half hour later Czar whined loudly and then aggressively yawned. The furry creature crept closer to its former master and smelled the scent of death. The baffled animal instantly bristled its fur, recoiled and then backed away in confusion. A short interval of time elapsed and then Czar howled under the canopy of night stars that had appeared overhead, the baffled creature inadvertently growling-up at the constellation Canis Major.

And finally, out of despair and disappointment, Czar turned and trotted up the trail in the direction of the camp that his limited brain had memorized in a sort of biological map. From its knowledge of the local terrain, the wolf dog knew exactly where the other fire providers could be easily located.

Jack London (1876-1916)

Jack London died at the early age of forty but the author left behind a rich collection of literature still read and admired today. London was a master at the literary writing technique known as *Realism* where he skillfully describes struggles and life-or-death situations pitting man against man, man against hostile environments and often man against himself.

Jack London was born in San Francisco and helped to support his family at age fourteen, dropping out of school to do so. Spending plenty of time in city libraries, London was a voracious reader who studied hard and eventually passed the entrance examination into the University of California. He stayed as a student for one semester but then went to work as a sailor and a laborer. During the Gold Rush of 1897 London spent a year in the Klondike and Yukon territories where he gathered material and information about interesting characters that later would appear in his novels and short stories.

Very fascinated by the Darwinian theory of "survival of the fittest," many of Jack London's works focused on the endurance of strong men driven by atavistic instincts and primitive emotions. His two famous novels are actually direct reversals of each other. In the *Call of the Wild,* Buck, a very large dog, is stolen from a wealthy family's Santa Clara, California home and is transported to the Alaska/Canadian Yukon to eventually become the lead canine in a dogsled team. In the classic novel *White Fang,* a wolf dog is taken from the tundra wilderness and then becomes domesticated.

The settings of most Jack London stories are in California, the Klondike/Yukon regions of Canada and the South Sea Pacific islands in and around Tahiti. London graphically described the great San Francisco Earthquake of April 18th, 1906 in his newspaper account "The Story of An Eyewitness."

"The Notorious Sleeping Beauty"

Once upon a millennium an old King and Queen loved each other but complete happiness had always eluded them because their marriage never produced any children. The King had a dreadfully low sperm count and the Queen's ovaries produced but one egg in her entire lifetime and that one egg had a shell so thick that not even a hundred million sperms with a catapult could puncture through the damned thing. And besides that phenomenon the Queen was a terrible bitch since every day of every month from age thirteen right through age fifty she was having one continuous bloody period the whole bloody time. Not even the King's most well manufactured band' aids could stop the stenchy prolonged bleeding.

"Oh well, I guess we have to go with the flow," the Queen confided to her depressed husband.

"Okay Florence, from now on I'll call you Flo'," the King imaginatively volleyed.

One bleak *April Fool's Day* a slender moonbeam had penetrated the King's stained glass bedroom window and also the Queen's vagina, so miraculously the next morning (forget about this nine month crap) her Highness gave birth to a beautiful daughter. The King and the Queen were so joyful that they screwed each other all night long for the first time in four decadent decades.

Alas (at last) the King and Queen sent out invitations to Fairy Women all over their kingdom because the royals didn't want to be condemned for being biased against lesbians or dykes, or clan dykes or Klondikes.

"Hey, we sent the Christening invitations out without any messengers to deliver them," the Queen informed her forgetful husband.

"Maybe I should make a decree for the establishment of a bona fide postal service," the King affirmatively stated. "But for now we'll have to send the invitations out by means of courier."

Dark valleys and rolling hills abounded in that map-less remote kingdom and it required several weeks of intensive preparation for all of the festivities to finally commence. But a few of the clueless couriers deliberately got lost and never came back to the castle to report their' missions (or their intermissions) being completed.

Soon the clopping of horses' hoofs could be heard all day and all night long over the drawbridge crossing the alligator-filled moat and then into the colossal 'white castle,' which often doubled as a hamburger stand for hungry knights and jesters from *jesteryear*. The

Fairy Women journeyed from afar to participate in the gala occasion because basically the old bitches had nothing better to do. Each faggot lady brought a special rare gift to present to the newborn Princess, who was destined by fate to own luxurious hotels and fantastic ocean liners in many tropical lands, especially in the Caribbean.

A full week later the last of the Fairy Women (who was a hoary lesbian whore) rode across the lowered drawbridge and into the castle on a white ass that had numerous bells jangling so loudly that they jangled everybody's nerves. The old Fairy Woman however possessed incredible potent witch's abilities in the arcane black arts, which of course she kept secret all to herself.

The very Potent Bitchy Witch entered the castle's main hall, dismounted from her white ass and discovered the infant Princess fast asleep and being attended to by the royal family's 'head nurse,' who frequently serviced the King's erection when the constipated Queen was out in the garden taking a long crap in the tall grass. Much to the King and Queen's shock the old Fairy Witch gazed down at the innocent sleeping infant and instantly gave an ominous pronouncement:

"Plan as you may, but the day will come,
When spinning with spindle, she'll prick her thumb.
Then in dreamless sleep she shall slumber on
Until a hundred years have come and gone.
Be glad that I have given this curse,
For I originally planned for the spell to be worse,
So forget all your worries, your pain and your cares,
Your precious Princess will sleep a hundred years!"

Then the formidable old bitch Witch wrapped her mantle tightly around her shoulders, hopped her exposed pale butt onto her white ass, yanked the reins and rode the obedient animal out of the colossal hall. The jangling of the bells on the ass's reins, saddle and bridle jangled everyone's nerves even greater than before as the old Fairy Woman crossed the rickety drawbridge and soon disappeared into the night's gloom.

"Why didn't you invite the old Fairy Woman to the Christening feast?" the King chastised his wife. "If you had remembered to do so then she would not have pronounced this horrible curse on our royal daughter. How could you have been so damned negligent?"

"If our daughter lives for a hundred years in suspended animation," the Queen pessimistically stated, "then she'll wake up being an old wretched spinster even without ever again having the pleasure of using a spinning wheel and a spindle."

"And the old Fairy Woman didn't even tell us if our daughter would awake as an old woman or as a young girl after her century-long slumber," the King realized and added. "May the old Hag's smelly asshole shrivel up and then experience immediate atrophy."

The King and the Queen were really pissed off as a result of the old Fairy Women's disconcerting hex. "Can't we get the court magician to say some elaborate words like 'curse be gone' or 'hex-a-gone'?" the Queen (who was also known as Mrs. King) asked her bewildered spouse.

"This is really fucked up!" the Monarch moaned and sulked. "Now we gotta' watch our bratty kid day and night when we could be out carousing around the gay and lesbian community looking for some carnal pleasure. I could be gratifying my ego by committing sodomy while making a royal pain in the ass out of myself. What an absolute bummer this friggin' hex is!"

"We should have had the foresight to invite the old Fairy Woman to the Christening party," the Queen returned. "Now we must pay the price for our grievous omission. I'm so damned angry I can't even shit!"

"Who'd want to invite that grotesque-looking ancient Bitch anywhere!" her regal husband yelled and maintained. "She's uglier than all of history's mortal sins put together times ten!"

The King sent his loyal royal messengers throughout his troubled land instructing the public that every spindle should be destroyed or brought to the castle to be demolished. Some spindles were burned to ash', others were splintered by axes while still others were infested by termite colonies at the King's imperial command. But most of the couriers sent out got lost or escaped to lands that were more citizen-friendly than the King's deplorable domain, while still the remainder of more ambitious messengers simply became priests, monks, pedophiles or entrepreneurial male prostitutes.

"After all of the spindles have been confiscated and incinerated," the merciless King proclaimed, "anyone caught hiding a wooden wheel will have their penis severed or their tits slashed off and then suffer being decapitated before eventually bleeding to death!"

"Say Husband," the Queen unconstructively interrupted, "we could now make a fortune selling spinning wheels out of some unknown artificial material that would take the place of wood."

"Please keep the remainder of your brilliant ideas to yourself!" the King loudly opined and criticized. "A poisonous mushroom has a higher damned *IQ* than you've got!"

Several decades passed and one evening the royal couple conversed about what had transpired after their hexed daughter's Christening. The Princess had now grown into a beautiful maiden, who had to wear seven heavy iron chastity belts with rusty locks so that no yeoman or pauper could pork or masturbate her. But the young heiress was never told why she was being overprotected or why her pubic area was being "chastised." And furthermore, the gorgeous curvaceous naïve Princess knew nothing about the nasty old Fairy Woman and her "very abominable spindle curse."

"What goes up, must come down," mentioned the Queen to her peeved husband, "spinning wheel turnin' around!"

"Shut the fuck up!" the King balked. "It's bad enough I have to give my blood, sweat and tears grieving over something as dumb as a catastrophe resulting from a cheap spinning wheel! I've neglected my kingdom for twenty-one years now over that shitty-assed fear I possess!"

"And believe it or not," interrupted the very alert Queen," the people are much better off without your insane edicts screwing up their overtaxed poverty-stricken lives even more than they already are! The serfs see this spinning wheel bullshit as a definite blessing from *their* perspective. Some of the serfs living near the sea have even accumulated enough savings to buy surfboards."

The Princess had the privilege of wandering all over the huge white castle and eating as many greasy hamburgers as she wanted. Despite her propensity for acute indigestion, the future queen was allowed to peep through the castle's wet wall cracks but always had to keep her hands off of her own juicy slit and clit. But one particular castle tower was off limits for the Princess. She often wondered if the keys to her seven chastity belts had been cunningly concealed inside "the secret room."

One *April Fools* evening the Princess furtively looked behind a draped wall tapestry and discovered the portal to a passageway she had never before observed. Looking around to make sure that no nosy castle voyeurs were scrutinizing her stealthy activity, the Princess slowly turned the key in the squeaky lock. She opened the ancient door and then bounded up the steps as fast as she could hoping that another seven keys (or one master skeleton one) could be found in the remote turret chamber to unfasten her cumbersome chastity belts. Right before arriving at her destination, the fair maiden looked through a wall slit and perceived a thin moonbeam and a few early evening stars twinkling in the dark night sky.

'Shit! I'll bet this remote tower will be a wonderful place for me to secretly masturbate!' the Princess thought. "Now all I gotta' do is find the magic key or keys that will remove these seven burdensome chastity belts. My crotch really itches badly and I can only have my servants remove the heavy belts with their entrusted keys every morning and evening when I take showers, dumps and leaks. That's the only damned times I can piss or take a crap!' the melancholy Princess meditated. 'Even when I have to go badly or have the damned diarrhea, I still have to hold it until early morning or early evening arrives! Damn it! Why couldn't I have been born a friggin' horny peasant girl with a hundred big-dick boyfriends?'

At the top of the winding staircase another door prevented the curious visitor from entering into the lone mysterious room. Near the shaded gloomy portal the Princess peeked through a slight crack in the poorly constructed castle wall and beheld an elderly Hag dressed in lamb's wool symbolizing that the nefarious Fairy Bitch was there to ingeniously trick her junior majesty by pulling the wool over *her* innocent eyes.

Upon closer inspection, the royal young trespasser noticed that the persistent old Hag was not taking a shit into an "in-house" hopper as the observer originally had suspected. Instead the wicked Witch was using her slender fingers to rotate a spinning wheel while "changing the *composition of flax*," which was never a haunting melody written by Mozart or Beethoven. The old Hag beckoned the Fair Maiden in a sinister but enticing voice:

"If ya' wanna' witness an old bag spin,
Then lift the latch, and enter in!
But if ya' wanna' leave this weird atmosphere,
Then get the fuck outa' here!"

Naturally the courageous and daring Princess yielded to temptation and lifted the latch, which she had learned to do when she had been enrolled as a kindergartner in the King's "early childhood latchkey program." The chamber's interior was dank and cold and as the Young Lady cautiously approached the Old Hag *she* heard other peculiar utterances being articulated:

> "With finger and thumb I whirl my twine,
> Making it weave so smooth and fine,
> But if ya' wanna' give it a try,
> You'll see how time will fly."

The Old Hag spun her flax (before ordinary people had flax machines) with such agility that the Princess envied the elderly wretch's wonderful dexterity despite the old Bitch's quite apparent advanced arthritis and rheumatism. Then the Old Bag stopped spinning and soon pressed her bony cold index finger against the stunned Princess's chest, which incidentally was not covered by any chastity belt or bra filled with falsies.

"Your cold hand feels like a dying bird's claw!" the Princess gasped. "Please touch me again. No one has ever touched my tits before whether the person might have been straight or gay or tri-sexual! Please continue doing it!"

"Take this spinning wheel away and secretly practice with it!" the old Witch suggested without exposing her shaded hooded face to her avid listener. "If you don't my Pretty, you'll end up being an old horny spinster just like me. Ha, ha, ha!"

The intrepid young Princess quickly possessed the tempting spindle from the old Hag's hands and tucked it under her gown to camouflage its existence. Then the comely young lady left the off-limits turret room, descended the spiral staircase in a jiffy and thought on the way down to the castle's mezzanine level, 'This entire palace is a goddamned 'no spin zone'!' I better be careful or things could rapidly spin out of control.'

Meanwhile the paranoid King and Queen were searching every nook and cranny of the enormous castle looking for their beloved naughty daughter. When they finally entered her room a second time, both royal pain-in-the-asses sighed with relief upon locating their child but then the cantankerous royal pain-in-the-ass father mildly reprimanded his aberrant offspring for violating the established and clearly defined house rules.

"Where the hell have you been daughter?" the King admonished with an accusative interrogative. "Whatever you do, don't talk to strangers or discuss your sex life with strangers that happen to be pimps!"

"Yes darling, where have you been?" the Queen injected in a more sympathetic tone of voice than the one employed by her sex-starved husband. "You really had us both worried half to death."

"But certainly Mother," the Princess said, "I'm old enough to take care of myself without either you' or Pop spying on my whereabouts all freakin' day long. After all my dear spying parents, I've passed the puberty plateau, I do have hair on my cookie and besides that particular maturation sometimes my responsive silver-coin-size nipples become erect when I get aroused. I'm old enough to take care of myself, aren't I?"

"Yes my dear," the King politely answered with a sinister smile, "but are you wise enough to take care of yourself when temptation beckons? Forget your silver-coin-size nipples. Can you take care of yourself by using wisdom? That's the billion gold coin question."

And then the very astute Queen queried her cherished Daughter. "My dear, what are you hiding with your hand tucked inside your gown's creases? If it's a hand grenade, don't pull the pin whatever you do! If it's a marijuana joint, let me have it to light up and smoke."

The Princess gave a mock laugh and disclosed to her elders that her concealed object was "a personal secret," but under pressure, she nervously promised her parents that the item wasn't a cucumber, a carrot or a dildo.

"Maybe it is a flower," the sneaky Princess continued under duress, "or maybe I'm holding a token as a lucky charm waiting for a handsome prince or knight to come to this God forsaken castle and expertly deflower me. Maybe it's a pin for my hair or one to use to stick into your fat asses," the Princess screamed at her parents like a maniac. "Or maybe it's neither of those objects but a very graphic nudist colony magazine instead. But I guarantee you two adult dolts that later this night I shall show both of you pathetic retards exactly what the mystery device happens to be."

So the King and the Queen were for the moment satisfied with their daughter's unusual honesty, which was principally based on conniving and also founded on a most devious explanation. "Oh precious Daughter," the King emotionally remarked, "you're so happy and so gay. Maybe in a year or so we'll all take a leisurely vacation cruise to the Isle of Lesbos in the royal yacht!"

After the royal parents finally retired to the *mastur*bation *bedroom* their great apprehensions about their daughter's veracity began haunting their psyches.

"Tomorrow morning we'll tell our stellar Daughter about the old Hag's disappointing hex after *her* Christening over two decadent decades ago," the King recommended. "Our child is now old enough to drink hard whiskey, smoke marijuana, experiment with cocaine and reason on her own."

"She wouldn't dare do anything rash, even if her sensitive skin became severely irritated!" the Queen commented. "Once she knows all about the frightening spindle prophecy, or should I say spindle warning, I'm certain that the Princess will never yield to randomly experimenting with a spinning wheel, even if she had a silly name like Vanna Whitehead, Sarah Yeahvo or Vera Beach."

But when the King and the Queen were discussing their strategy concerning spinning wheels in the throne room the Princess surreptitiously uncovered and gazed at the simple spindle that she had swindled from the old Hag. 'Shit! One end is as sharp as a needle!' she immediately determined. "In fact it *is* a prickly needle indeed. Oh how I wish it were a nice firm long thick male prick instead of a sharp short spindle needle!'

And as the Princess awkwardly fumbled with the common small machine, a screech of an owl was discerned at her bedroom window. The sudden distraction caused the Princess's hand to slip on the wheel and then the sharp needle cut deep into her tender right thumb's skin.

The Fairy Woman's diabolical black magic instantly began taking effect as the first drop of blood surfaced and soon appeared at the end of the Maiden's thumb. 'If I was an 'iron maiden' instead of a human one,' the Princess regretfully thought, 'then I wouldn't have to worry about such a stupid thing as my thumb's skin bleeding and my finger throbbing with pain.'

Soon the victimized Princess felt quite lousy and drowsy and she slowly closed her attractive blue eyes. She plopped down on her comfortable mattress and then fell fast asleep while completely enjoying her 'beauty rest.'

An ominous drowsiness rapidly enveloped the entire castle and at that incredible moment kept all of the inhabitants spellbound. The Chief Treasurer ceased counting his gold and silver coins and put his head down on his table, the Royal Astronomer forgot about the heavenly bodies he had been intensely scrutinizing in a girlie magazine, and the Main Butler fell asleep while peeking through a keyhole observing the Queen's six kinky-minded attendants naked in a pile of horny lusting bodies.

Every person and every living creature in the entire castle from the ants in the walls to the bees in the garden entered into a heavy slumber', even the frivolous and dictatorial Royal King who was halfway through taking a royal shit on *his* most important royal throne. Loud and repugnant snoring was going on everywhere throughout the extensive aristocratic dwelling, but none of the participants was able to hear a single sound, especially the palace's Chief Deaf Mute.

Time glided by as if the phantom had ice skates on, and as the calendar years passed one by one still the disgusting snoring (which no one snoring heard) kept occurring. Even when hard snot balls formed in everyone's swollen nostrils, the vulgar snoring droned on and on throughout the very rapidly deteriorating and now in-need-of-repair castle.

The fair Princess remained young and stunning (even though no one could see her) during her extended sleep and everyone in the castle that was also slumbering hadn't aged (almost a century later) and each person looked exactly as he, she or it had when the castle's residents had been affected by the nefarious Witch's diabolical spell.

But every spring and summer the outside weeds grew taller, the briars and brambles in the garden became wilder and larger and the now vulnerable terraces and walls were eventually covered and laden with moss, algae, fungi, slime and rat turds. And then ninety-nine fierce winters later on another momentous *April Fools Day* a lost Prince from a neighboring land viewed the distant castle turrets and ramparts covered in environmental growth and believed that his senses were indeed deceiving him.

'What a fucked up castle in need of maintenance even if the abominable structure originally was a real bastion of royal lunacy!' the Prince rationally reckoned. 'When I was but a gullible little shit head my nurse told me about a Fairy Woman's spell in a distant land while *she* was busy nursing me and I was busy sucking away on *her* hard luscious delicious nipples.'

And so the handsome lost Prince (who had misplaced his compass and his moral compass too) who never studied a map nor knew how to read one rode his white steed down a steep hill with his rascally hound dogs barking close behind. Soon the visitor approached the thick unkempt hedges and thickets that surrounded the dilapidated white castle that looked so bad that it couldn't now even sell hot dogs or raunchy dog food sandwiches. The fatigued Prince was rather valiant and was not discouraged by the disarrayed quagmire and by the immense entanglements his disconsolate-looking bloodshot eyes were witnessing.

'Don't they have any friggin' landscapers, gardeners or lawn maintenance services in this land?' he imagined. 'There isn't one damned access route through this dense growth that is gradually isolating that decrepit castle from the rest of the world. A tree might grow in Brooklyn, but a fuckin' out-of-control jungle is quite prevalent right here.'

Then the depressed Prince estimated that it would require ten thousand lumberjacks, ten billion ants and ten trillion termites to finally clear the excessive vegetation away. So instead of starting a raging inferno to deforest the area, the stupid idiot removed his hunting knife and began hacking away, pretending all the time that each vine was a ruthless monster or a wild ferocious beast attacking his royal testicles.

So the lunatic Prince slashed and he severed and he sliced with his minuscule hunting knife imagining that the small object was a machete and his hands were soon bleeding right though his cheap gloves he had gotten as an incentive bonus for opening a bank savings account in *his* neighboring land. By midnight the obsessed Prince had managed to carve a hole halfway through the dense growth, which was nearly as dense as his thick cerebrum. And so he therefore decided to camp for the night and made a fire out of twigs, leaves, bark, his own pubic hairs and the least interesting pages from a porno' magazine he had kept safely tucked under his saddle.

Then after eating a turnip and taking a long leak, the Prince was too weak to work his stick and sustain a boner so he dozed off to sleep dreaming of his next hard on. And so by accident the night spring wind blew the campfire flames in the direction of the castle, and the raging inferno incinerated and cut through the last fifty feet of vegetation as if an outstanding miracle had actually transpired.

When the Prince finally awoke he realized, 'It's a good thing that this queer land doesn't have any forest rangers or my ass would be in jail by now!' And then another monumental thought arose in his rather diminutive mind. 'This damned enigmatic kingdom doesn't even have any people, straight, gay, bisexual or otherwise. How fucked up can you get? This strange territory isn't even on a map in any *Atlas* or geography book in any library I've ever been in!'

And as the new arrival slouched down and crawled through the portal into what formerly was the palace's main garden, the inquisitive Prince could not detect any signs of insects, birds, gorillas, rhinos' or space aliens. He next gingerly crawled through the dense underbrush and then stood and carefully walked over the decaying drawbridge, which the former residents had scribbled graffiti symbols all over its beams because it naturally was a drawbridge.

And at the castle's sole entrance the Prince came across several of the land's sentinels frozen in time and petrified like stone statues outside *their* paint-faded guardhouse. The uniformed sleeping soldiers were standing above the muddy moat and pissing into the water onto two alligators below, but the men, their whizzes and the open-mouthed alligators had all been immobilized in suspended animation as if time itself' had been paralyzed.

The brave Prince reluctantly entered the dark dismal castle, and after exploring around several passages he came to the Princess's bedroom door, which was *ajar* in addition to being a door. Ivy vines and ferns were now growing inside the bedchamber, making it appear as if it had been built without a floor right in the middle of a tropical jungle.

The Prince instinctively looked down upon the bed and beheld the beautiful royal maiden resting, and his first instinct was to grab her breasts and incessantly fondle them and his second impulse was to tear her clothes off and pump the poop out of her until she finally revived to mutually enjoy tremendous dual orgasms. But then the newcomer observed the spindle still gripped by the girl's ten thin fingers, so he thought, 'If that thing starts spinning around while I'm screwing this pretty chick, it's liable to castrate me and do more than a basic circumcision to my erect pecker. Perhaps another more discreet approach to get my throbbing glory into her panties sometime in the near future would be a more feasible consideration.'

And so the anxious Prince (who really needed to get laid to help clear away his repulsive facial acne) bent over and smooched the sleeping Princess on the lips while reasoning, 'Now why can't these be her other lips, the ones situated between her firm legs!' the royal interloper thought. 'That would be one time I wouldn't mind having a *hair* lip! Ha, ha, ha!'

Then the Prince lifted his hunting horn up to his parched mouth and gave the inanimate object the best blowjob it had ever had. The loud blast awoke the Princess, her parents and everyone else in the enchanted castle. 'Oh fuck! How dumb can I be!' the Prince immediately thought. 'Now I won't have any damned privacy while I'm pumpin' this terrific-looking Babe silly!'

The Princess lost her grip on the accursed spindle and the item dropped to the ground (for there was no more floor in the room because of the dense vegetation that had wormed its way through the cement and stone masonry). The Princess opened her eyes but not her legs and then smiled at her gallant rescuer. And it was plainly evident that the Prince blowing his horn had awakened the Princess from her century-long sleep and not a sloppy messy kiss as is often erroneously believed.

The King and the Queen each awoke from their century-long siestas and instead of worrying about their precious Daughter they frantically tore off each other's clothes and the Monarch hopped upon his mistress and successfully laid several miles of pipe with his very aroused personal equipment.

And then all of the other humans in the castle awoke from their sleeps and latched onto the nearest person and engaged in a wild un-orchestrated orgy with moaning and groaning echoing off of every wall and tree and vine all over the damned castle. Straights were screwing straights and also penetrating gays so it really was indistinguishable what a person's sexual orientation or disorientation was at that particular time, for sodomy was happening all over the freakin' palace and even in the castle's countless trees and also on the trees' numerous branches.

And even the dumb animals forgot about their own species and then indiscriminately began screwing one another. Dogs were hitting on cats', birds were penetrating frogs, horses were humping away on sea gulls, donkeys were porking pigs, and sheep and bulls were crazily screwing chipmunks and porcupines.

After the remarkable seven-day orgy finally ended the appointed wedding date had been set. And when the triumphant virgin Prince in quest (and in need of) his first piece of ass carried the Princess into a well-furnished recently constructed bedchamber, his mouth went agape and his penis shrank to a centimeter when he observed that the beautiful vivacious maiden had somehow transformed into the wretched old Fairy Hag with a face full of moles, cysts and accompanying warts.

'Oh well!' thought the Prince. 'I'll just close my damned eyes and get this show on the road. An ugly bad piece of ass is better than no piece of ass at all!'

And the beautiful Princess became the next ugly Old Fairy Woman Hag that would hang around the kingdom waiting for the next unfortunate Princess to be appropriately Christened' inside the royal castle.

"Excerpt: The Wholly Book of Exodus"

Background

On April 1, 2002 Mohammed Kareem Jihad, a fourteen-year-old April Fool Palestinian revolutionary, was ascending a rocky ledge along rugged cliffs that bordered the western banks of the *Dead Sea*. Exhausted from his climbing enterprise, young Jihad stopped to rest his weary body. The vernal radical lit a *Camel* cigarette and surveyed the landscape below. Much to his frustration everything seemed calm and serene.

When Mohammed Kareem Jihad leaned backwards his gaunt frame slipped through a narrow crevice between two limestone crags. The disoriented youth rose to his knees, inspected his shadowy surroundings and soon realized that he had fallen into a cave (containing a remarkable ancient artifact). In the center of the small hollow was an urn, a well' preserved remnant from Hebrew antiquity.

Instead of sticking his hand into the urn to feel for any contents Mohammed followed his dreadful terroristic instincts by pulling the pin of a hand grenade and tossing the explosive device into what was surely a great archeological discovery. When the bomb exploded prematurely Mohammed Kareem Jihad had not yet fully exited the cave. Besides shrapnel, two leather objects bound with straps (strapnel) blasted out of the ancient urn and collided with the back of the Palestinian lad's skull, knocking him unconscious.

When Mohammed Kareem Jihad finally regained his faculties *(his rich uncle owned two radical Arab universities)*, he perceptively noticed and then grabbed the leather pouches and fled the scene of destruction. After descending the perilous cliffs the young militant thought, 'I'll bet whatever is inside these two leather packages is worth at least a carton of cigarettes,' so the youth mounted his stolen desert "quad" and motored to the city of Jericho, where his economically struggling father owned a popular café.

Inside the café Professor Phillip Collins of the Semitic Semantic Institute was seated at a table with Dr. Allen Qaeda from the Arab Aramaic Academy. Mohammed Kareem Jihad rushed into the dismal café and approached the cozy table where the two distinguished scholars were conversing.

"How much will you give me for these two leather pouches?" the boy anxiously asked Professor Al Qaeda. "I need to buy some weapons right away!"

"Let's unravel them and see what ya' got!" the suddenly curious researcher replied. The good academic doctor gently unwound the dusty cords that bound the leather wrappings. Inside both packages Dr. Allen Qaeda discovered dozens of remarkably well' preserved papyrus sheets with ancient writings carelessly scribbled on the archaic scrolls.

"Why it's the first two books of the Old Testament!" Professor Al Qaeda exclaimed in astonishment. *"The Book of Genesis* and the *Book of Exodus!"*

Professor Phil Collins, who knew plenty about Genesis, rendered his authoritative impressions. "This translation has much more detail than the presently read first two books of the Old Testament!" he enthusiastically observed and shared. "This type of papyrus dates back to at least 900 BC, which makes it a lot older than the Dead Sea Scrolls that had been re-written by the Essenes during an ancient creative writing class."

"If this historical account is accurate," interrupted Professor Al Qaeda, "then this great discovery will present a *wholly* new perspective to religious history, which is presently very controversial to begin with."

Young Mohammed Kareem Jihad was growing very impatient with the scholarly adults' intellectual evaluation and speculation concerning his fabulous find. "How much are they worth?" he insisted on knowing.

"Two cartons of American cigarettes, definitely!" Professor Phil Collins promised.

"And we'll even throw in an AK-47 and two slightly used hand grenades," Dr. Al Qaeda added.

"Sold!" an elated Mohammed Kareem Jihad gleefully shouted. "Now I can blow up my' younger sister's doll collection and her Jewish friends too!"

And so, Dr. Al Qaeda and my uncle Professor Phil Collins (on my mother's side of the family) became the legitimate owners of the only authentic "First Two Books of the Wholly Bible." The remainder of the "unabridged" Old Testament had been thoroughly obliterated inside the urn when Mohammed Kareem Jihad's hand grenade had quite effectively exploded.

Fortunately Uncle Phil Collins had made a computer file in English of his meticulous translation of the great archeological treasure. Uncle Phil very thoughtfully and confidentially had electronically sent "Wholly Genesis" and "Wholly Exodus" to me as e-mail attachments. The careful deciphering represented my relative's fantastic interpretation of the ancient Hebrew writing, which I had electronically received on April 10, 2002. Regrettably, on April11th, Uncle Phil and Dr. Al Qaeda were blown to smithereens by an errant Palestinian rocket while refining their study of the ancient scrolls in Professor Collins' Jerusalem home. The papyrus sheets and the original computer file had also been destroyed in the malicious terrorist attack.

My treasured e-mail translations are the only remaining evidence of *The Wholly Book of Genesis and The Wholly Book of Exodus*. Uncle Phil sincerely believed that the versions presently in my possession are the original and most reliable documentation of the "Word of Moses," who was believed to be the organizer of the popular *Genesis* and *Exodus* interpretations that appear in the standard *Bible*. Uncle Phil Collins and Professor Al Qaeda strongly believed that Moses had fabricated the Biblical Genesis and Exodus stories around 1400 BC. But since writing (and bona fide alphabets) did not appear until the time after Homer and King David, around 1,000 BC, the Biblical stories had been handed-down and distorted because of the practice of oral tradition with storytellers adding and subtracting important details.

Uncle Phil Collins and Dr. Al Qaeda professed that young Mohammed Kareem Jihad's accidental discovery represented the true unabridged stories of *Genesis* and of *Exodus*. They maintained that the new versions are much more valid in scope and content since the accounts had been written hundreds of years earlier than the stories that now appear in the first two books of the *Bible*. Thus, Mohammed's find is closer to Moses' language and intent than later popularly read interpretations of *Genesis* and *Exodus*. "Careless Hebrew historians and ancient priests recklessly modified the *Wholly Genesis* and *Wholly Exodus* versions into more pious, moral and self-righteous texts," Uncle Phil academically stated in his final e-mail letter. "They did it to satisfy their own selfish purposes and agendas."

Uncle Phil' also indicated in his e-mail, "Moses, who lived approximately 1450 BC around the time of Pharaoh Thutmose III of Egypt, didn't know how to write, even though he had put the stories of *Genesis* and *Exodus* together much like Homer had done with the *Iliad* and the *Odyssey*. In fact nobody knew how to write with any rhetorical expression skills until half a millennium later." According to Uncle Phil, "Moses barely knew the numerals one to ten signifying the *Ten Commandments* etched on the twin stone tablets," my mother's older brother attested.

Now that the essential background of *The Wholly Book of Genesis* and *The Wholly Book of Exodus* is fully known, only the astute readers can be the best judges of the merits of Mohammed Kareem Jihad's discovery and Uncle Phil Collins' exceptional claims. I have placed in *italics* the language that ancient scholars had shrewdly edited out of the *Wholly Book of Genesis* and I have plainly and clearly left the standard and generally accepted script in *Times New Roman* type.

Jay Dubya

Chapter One
"Jacob's Descendants in Egypt"

The second book of the Pentateuch is called *The Wholly Book of Exodus, meaning "Let's get the hell out of here before we are savagely butchered to death by these mercurial-tempered mighty pissed-off Egyptians!"*
Exodus describes the rapid departure of the Israelites *(Jacob's people and clan)* from Egypt, continuing the nightmare adventures of the *Lord's* ill' starred' "chosen people" *(cursed and punished Hebrews) and the text begins* where the *Wholly Book of Genesis* leaves off. *Exodus* recounts the oppression by the Egyptians of Jacob's descendants and their miraculous deliverance by God through Moses,' *(how they all filtered through Moses remains a mystery to this day), who then guilefully guided the Israelites out of Egypt without even the aid of a compass, a fortune teller or a crudely-drawn map.*

Moses led the Israelites through the Red Sea *(which was really blue)* to famous Mount Sinai *where nasty sinus infections were often cured by sneezing into a wicked gusty wind with real gusto from atop the desolate mountain's peak.* There', Moses entered into a special covenant with the Lord where God 'laid down the law' for all *the doltish Hebrews* to *faithfully* obey His Ten Commandments *(Demandments). Hence, the saying originated "to lay down the law," which when translated into colloquial English means 'to read the riot act."*

These are the *everyday* names of the sons of Israel *(Jacob)* that were accompanied by their households. *(Their' households weren't really households at all. They were crude tents that held many wives, children, concubines, prostitutes, whores, hookers and harlots).* These were the people that migrated with Jacob into Egypt and later *trekked* back to the "Promised Land *of Unfulfilled Promises the Almighty Lord had made to Abraham and to his sons Isaac and Jacob.*"

The sons of Jacob were the following *devious and unscrupulous* men: Reuben, *the undisputed sandwich king,* Simeon, Judah and *next was* Levi, *who had invented a strong blue denim-material used for work apparel.* Some other sons' of Jacob were Issachar, *who looked like a burned-out ember,* Zebulan, *who formed a bizarre bazaar four piece singing group called Led Zebulan* and then there was *Dandy* Dan, Naphtali, Gad, *Egad* and Asher', *who was in charge of performing Hebrew cremations.* The total number of the direct descendants of Jacob was seventy *individuals*. Joseph *(Jacob's eleventh of twelve sons)* was already *well situated in a position of power* in Egypt, *being smart enough to stay a good distance away from his crazy family and all of his demented relatives. In Joseph's case, absence made his heart grow more forgetful of his warped and shameful heritage.*

Now Joseph and all his *obnoxious and malicious* brothers and that whole generation died, *but not all at the same time, in the same place or on the exact same day.* The Israelites were prolific and fruitful *because they liked to screw-around all the damned time instead of working and producing like loyal slaves should work and produce.* They became so numerous and so strong that the land was filled with them *like a colossal locust invasion or like swarming bees inside an overcrowded hive. The ancient prehistoric New Stone Age Hebrews were notorious avid pumpers and humpers, no doubt about it.*

Then a new king, who knew nothing of Joseph, came to power in Egypt. *The king's name is unimportant because he knew nothing of Jacob and of Joseph, nor did he ever care to know about them. But somehow, this unknown personage managed to become king of the most potent civilization of that era.* He *(the new Egyptian anonymous king)* said to his *inattentive* subjects *and predicates*, "Look how numerous and powerful the Israelite people are growing, more so than we ourselves," the new Pharaoh declared *to his apathetic listeners. "It is all because the Hebrew men have been circumcised and can squirt their prolific seeds further into vaginas than we uncircumcised but lesser endowed Egyptian men can shoot our juices."*

101

"The fact that the Hebrew men can have all these children proves that they all aren't stupid jerk offs like you think they are!" a cynical court adviser retorted while interrupting Pharaoh's lackluster speech. "Your statements do not circumvent circumcision!"

"Come, let us deal shrewdly with them *(the Israelites)* to stop their increase *in population*; otherwise, in times of war they too may 'join' our *myriad* enemies, *who for some reason always become torn apart and disconnected at their bellybuttons during brutal 'naval' battles.* The *not-too-brilliant* Israelites might *defy their history and surprisingly* fight *extensively* against us, and so leave the country *after whipping our asses good,"* the anonymous Pharaoh verbally concluded.

Accordingly, *the Egyptian* taskmasters were set over the *enslaved* Israelites to *vilely* oppress them with forced 'labor', *especially the women that were giving birth.* Thus 'they' *(the Israelites, here comes the recurrent pronoun-antecedent problem again)* had to *obediently* build for Pharaoh the supply cities of Pithom and Raamses *without any blueprints or available usable materials.*

Yet the more they *(the Israelites)* were *mercilessly* oppressed, the more they *(the libido-oriented Israelites)* multiplied and spread *like fertile rabbits since they always screwed around a lot and seldom worked for their industrious Egyptian masters and taskmasters.*

The *dominating* Egyptians then dreaded the *circumcised* Hebrew men and reduced them and their families to cruel slavery, making life, *vinegar and lemons'* even bitterer for them *during those un-enlightening barbarous times.* The Israelites performed hard work in mortar and brick *many millennia before brick and mortar stores and shops became popular.* They *(the Israelites)* had to do all kinds of field work-*and they were cruelly demoted to field representatives that never had field days, even though some were the best in their fields.* Thus is the whole cruel fate of slaves. *The Israelites had been reduced to mere beasts of burden and were even challenged in court by the strong "National Egyptian Donkey Union."*

The anonymous powerful king of Egypt *(who wasn't important enough to have a name even though he had the authority to repeatedly bust the Israelites' balls and to deflate their women's flabby tits)* told something *in the form of a command* to the Hebrew midwives, one of whom was called Shiphrah and the other *named*

Puah. "*Listen to me.* When you act as midwives for the Hebrew women' and see them giving birth, *try pushing the little sucker back into its mother's snatcheroo.* If it is a boy, kill him, but if it is a girl, she may live," *the anonymous* Pharaoh commanded. *"And quite frankly it's seldom that I'm this goddamned sentimental. You're both just lucky you two bitches caught me in one of my better fuckin' moods today."*

The midwives, however, feared God more than *they feared* Pharaoh *because they had heard all about the deluge of Noah's time and all about Sodom and Gomorrah where fire and brimstone had penetrated up people's delicate ass holes. And if a person had a hairy ass hole, then the flames from the fire and brimstone were fiercer than ever and raged completely out of control, cauterizing sensitive ass hole after sensitive ass hole.* The *now three* midwives *(Shiphrah, Shipwreck and Puah)* did not do what the king of Egypt had ordered them, but let the boys live. *Of course, there were tens of thousands of pregnant Israelites (and remarkably all of them women) and only three overworked midwives to accommodate the needs of all of them randomly spread out over the vast desert country's entire length and breadth. The beleaguered midwives really needed shorter hours and better working conditions but the only unions that the horny Hebrew women knew were post-pubescent Israelites continuously having intercourse and then putting up with the whining babies that resulted from their indiscriminate copulations.*

So the *(anonymous) Egyptian* King summoned the *defiant* midwives and *candidly* asked them, "Why have you acted thus *by failing to act?* You have allowed the boys to live. *Don't you know the damned difference between subtraction and addition? Haven't you learned anything from your female ancestor Basemath?"(The mother of arithmetic mentioned extensively in the Wholly Book of Genesis).*

The midwives answered Pharaoh *all together, which was a bad habit all the Israelites had,* "The Hebrew women are not like the Egyptian women," they all chanted in unison, *simultaneously having the exact same thoughts and words.* "They are robust *and busty* and *certainly* give birth *before afterbirth* and *all that happy nonsense happens even* before the *overtaxed and overworked* midwife arrives *from a remote part of the country. It ain't easy for just the three of us to work this whole friggin' land all by ourselves, ya' know anonymous Kingy, and that's no friggin' bull shit either!"*

Therefore God 'dealt' well with the midwives, *even giving each of them a free deck of playing cards*. The people *(the Israelites)* too, increased and grew strong *because most of them finally went through puberty at age five and were adequately breast-fed until age twenty-one*.

And because the *three overwhelmed Hebrew* midwives feared God, He built up more families for them, *making the poor midwives hustle and scurry all over the damned place, arriving too late to deliver any Hebrew babies into poverty and slavery. The overburdened midwives became frustrated, not even having sufficient time to play solitaire with the decks of cards the Lord had generously given them.*

Pharaoh, *feeling rather petulant*, then commanded all his subjects, *predicates, direct objects and predicate nominatives*, "Throw into the river *(the Nile)* every boy that is born to the 'Hebrews', *except for the children of Reuben, for 'he brews' some damned good coffee and beer to go with his succulent sandwiches.* However," *the anonymous king proclaimed and pontificated*, "you may let all the girls live *so that I may increase my harem at my majestic palace. But I want you to 'a-'nile'-alate' all of those fertile little Hebrew pecker heads as soon as possible in order to accommodate my arbitrary and capricious will.*"

"The Green Door"

The vicinity around the intersection of Broadway and 42nd Street, which is also known to the world as Times Square, represents an area of intrigue and adventure whether the walker is a fascinated visitor to the metropolis or a hard-core native casually strolling along the filthy-but-busy New York sidewalks.

Vaudeville review matinees, a chorus of honking horns, sleazy straight, gay and lesbian bars, legitimate stage plays and a variety of circus and carnival-like sideshows all vigorously compete for the abundant foot traffic traversing the congested area.

A plethora of beautiful enticing women, many wearing lustrous diamonds and sable furs, march right alongside scantily-clad business-seeking hookers and on-the-prowl kinky prostitutes, both of the latter female segments perfectly willing to sell their curvaceous bodies for a "cheap trick." Fresh cash is readily obtained for the streetwalkers' vital services from straight men, from homosexual men or from devil-may-care transvestite lesbians in need of cozy feminine companionship.

Yes indeed, all sorts of imaginative scams and flimflams tempt the senses of the busy thoroughfare's daily trekkers; the dissatisfied pedestrian masses' both expecting and relishing having their attention lured, which in reality represents the mobile lady vultures' first step into accessing innocent victims' wallets or pocketbooks.

All along the notorious avenue loud-voiced hawkers incessantly bally available customers and gullible sightseers into small side street businesses, and to make the chaotic environment even more confusing, direct face-to-face solicitations along the horrendously crowded major artery are quite commonplace. The police endeavor to control the bizarre flow of legal and illegal commerce, but many people who saunter along the famous street's pavements in quest of Holy Grails, Golden Fleeces, lady loves, hot disease-free sex and free dildos are frequently disappointed at their lack of success.

Many itinerant trekkers manage to psychologically adjust to their failed "adventure mission" and ultimately return home to their nagging wives and to their bratty and totally-spoiled kids, mentally accepting the delay of their next exciting downtown exploit. Often times a subsequent excursion to Broadway follows another violent domestic argument (involving a wife or a husband), compelling him or her to leave the house in desperation and methodically search for some empathetic personage of the opposite gender to share and to allay his or her heart-wrenching marital dissatisfaction.

In the center of Manhattan the twin spirits of Adventure and Romance often compete to attract the good, the bad and the ugly elements of human nature. A gallery of curious-minded predatory faces often peer-down out of upstairs windows randomly scrutinizing the endless pedestrian traffic, the gapers' perceptive pupils looking below for vulnerable weak innocent prey to either con or distract. Cabdrivers vociferously yell their redundant solicitations to ferret-out prospective clients amidst the stream of impersonal humanity that clutter the sidewalks of the Great White Way between Thirty-fourth and Forty-third streets.

As far as the eye can see, sophisticated ladies and scumbag harlots drop their dainty handkerchiefs wherever and whenever they size-up an eligible gentleman or "mark." Everyone inside Broadway's surreal perpetual motion illusion seems to be aggressively evading one basic truism: that is to say, no one sauntering along majestic-but-gaudy Times Square wishes to be (on some future day) lying on his or her deathbed singularly regretting that he or she had neglected or missed that elusive once-in-a-lifetime opportunity to pursue and experience an extraordinarily enjoyable human activity. No one lying horizontal and about to receive his or her last rites ever wants to remember a pallid and mediocre marriage or a bundle of wrinkled cash idly sitting in a bank safety deposit box, or recollect a piss-poor sex partner with sleep apnea as his or her eight decade tenure's ultimate thrill and greatest accomplishment.

* * * * * * * * * * * *

Rudolph Steinberg was a piano tuner and salesman by trade in addition to being an after work wanderer prowling along the downtown glitz and glitter of magical Broadway. The fickle-but-feckless fellow was always searching for some romantic adventure outside the perimeter of his miserable marriage and the unhappy man was also in quest of certain adult excitement far away from his obnoxious teenage son and daughter. And besides those specific aspects to Rudolph's lackluster existence, the unfulfilled roaming salesman was also an avid sex addict and porn' fanatic.

'I really need to get laid,' Rudolph kept thinking as he quickened his stride along the popular noisy street venue. 'My wife and kids are visiting her folks out on Long Island so this is the perfect opportunity for me to show some audacity and get my noodle wet. My damned wife doesn't like having wild sex and I think the witchy bitch actually hates her own cunt! But right now I need not worry about time being a factor because I have all night long to literally screw around,' Steinberg concluded with a smile. 'I just got paid cash under the table by my tyrannical boss so I have additional bucks to spend on personal luxury, if necessary. I'll have my pick of the crop in terms of happy hookers. As usual, I'll use my guile and my charm. I just have to be shrewd enough to select a Broadway broad that doesn't have a bad case of transmittable V.D.'

Steinberg hurried along, weaving in and out of the two direction streams of people hastening about and adding to the area's general hustle and bustle. A certain contingent of the New York humanity-in-motion consisted of captivated and enthralled foreign visitors to the legendary theatrical district. The second more familiar aggregate, which included the in-need-of-sex piano expert Rudolph Steinberg, represented the daily native Broadway participants either parading home from their places of employment or eagerly seeking a dynamic bar lounge or the comfort of a friendly brothel waiting room.

'I've tried most of the standard whorehouses,' Rudolph decided. 'I know what I'll do. I'll look for a good-looking doll to pork, a pretty honey standing in one of the many doorways. I'll know the right one the instant I see her. If the babe's asking fee is reasonable, I'll be able to do something constructive with my nagging hard-on. Getting my aching rocks off all by myself' is so friggin' juvenile, so goddamned adolescent!' the disgruntled piano tuner imagined, shaking his head as he paced ahead faster. 'I'm tired of being a stupid jerk-off every time my bitch of a wife is out of town visiting on Long Island! I've read in my favorite book *Junie's Love Test* exactly how to pick-up the right broad on Broadway. Say, that's gotta' be precisely how this fucked-up thoroughfare got its name! To my knowledge, piano tuning is definitely not the oldest profession in human history, ha, ha, ha! Even the goddamned prehistoric Neanderthals had whores and hookers! And I've got money to burn!' Rudolph confidently chuckled as he swiftly passed by a prominent New York City fire department station.

That evening during his later-than-usual urban safari Rudolph's attention was distracted by a set of clattering false teeth hopping around inside a glass case that a man with a cane and red and white striped jacket was loudly describing as a "Living dental specimen from Somalia." Glancing upward while surveying his general environment, the enterprising Steinberg observed the electric letters of a dentist's shingle, automatically indicating that the chattering and clattering uppers and lowers were creatively and appropriately advertising the tooth extractor's legitimate place of business.

Standing alongside the amusing jumping teeth phenomenon was a tall-but-muscular Afro-American dressed in an embroidered red fox-hunting coat, imposing yellow trousers with black stripes down the sides, and the huge fellow was also sporting a tilted red fez atop his shaved head. The formidable-looking black giant was assiduously distributing business cards to the passing public, and anyone he chose to tacitly solicit felt intimidated and was too afraid to decline reception of the small rectangular pieces of information.

"Are you a real Zulu?" Rudolph awkwardly asked the suddenly slightly chagrined black Goliath. "Are you a real Zulu?" he admiringly reiterated.

"Did you call me a real Lu-Lu?" the gargantuan card disseminator asked with a disdainful frown evident on his visage. "Say it again and I'll beat the living shit out of you!"

"No Sir, you are mistaken, er, I mean it was *my* mistake," Rudolph stammered and vaguely apologized. "I didn't say Lu-Lu! I had no intention of insulting your honorable character with any idiotic derogatory remark. I was simply making a historical allusion my Kind Sir. I had foolishly mentioned the word 'Zulu,' which is a distinguished South African tribe consisting of many noble and courageous warriors. Many of those barbarians, er, I meant to say 'brave tribesmen,' are rather humungous in size and quite similar to the famous Watusi lion hunting natives."

"Sounds like a lot of fucked-up bullshit to me!" the black Hercules answered. "But your wild theory is right on-the-money about that African shit! My mother used to tell me that the family originated from Ethiopia. Here Sir! Here's a card that you ought not to discard, ha, ha, ha! Have you ever been to Africa my good man? If by chance you have traveled there, you were probably incontinent on the continent, ha, ha, ha!"

Rudolph Steinberg was so thrilled and relieved at not being pulverized by the enormous black dude that he didn't peruse the print on the card until he had nervously traversed half a block down the avenue. One side was blank but on the opposite side was printed "The Green Door" without any address or other pertinent information provided.

And then being rather vigilant and curious, the self-conscious piano tuner and salesman alertly observed a man toss to the pavement a similar card that the massive Ethiopian had deftly handed-out. Rudolph carefully stooped-down and examined the rejected card, which to his surprise did not read "The Green Door" but instead had printed on its surface the name and address of the aforementioned dentist along with the traditional boilerplate caption: "Bridge Work, Crowns and Painless Oral Operations."

'This is some sort of oddball enigma!' Rudolph conjectured. 'The other guy received from the gigantic black fellow a dental card with specific information given on it while I had been handed a card that only reads 'The Green Door.' Hey, I get it!' Steinberg ecstatically hypothesized. 'I'll bet that The Green Door is a new house of prostitution that's just opened its door for business! Glory be' to the Highest! It's all amazingly materializing right before my eyes! This could be the exotic sex adventure I've been waiting for! I could feel intense throbbing in my lower abdomen already!'

Being intrigued by the minor 'Calling Card' puzzle, Rudolph inconspicuously crossed Broadway, walked a block on the opposite side, re-crossed the noisy avenue and again approached the immense but handsomely dressed Ethiopian. Without making eye contact, the piano tuner accepted a second introductory business card, which much to Rudolph's confusion exclusively had inscribed on it the mysterious phrase that lacked vital context definition and description: "The Green Door."

Then a peevish male pedestrian disgustedly tossed a business card to the pavement that had recently been obtained from the awesome-looking black fellow. Steinberg bent down and automatically read the printed language, which clearly described the dentist's practice and the exact location of his professional parlor.

'How could this be?' Rudolph wondered as his hyperactive penis shriveled inside his trousers. 'I'm pretty damned befuddled by this more-than-small riddle. I'm not exactly fully certain that The Green Door is a newly established cathouse! But damn it, I'm gonna' find out soon! I've got millions and millions of sperm that I need to shoot out of my sex pistol, or should I say blast out of my abdominal cannon! Yes, *that* second thought sounds much better!'

Rudolph neurotically made a second U-turn across Broadway, paced a block south, then re-crossed the street and again approached the hulking Negro standing next to the square glass case containing the clattering false teeth. This time the black behemoth failed to hand the befuddled piano tuner a business card but instead randomly and courteously did so to other less interested but cooperative passersby. Gazing back at the towering Ethiopian, Steinberg received the distinct impression that the menacing-looking black gent had been deliberately ignoring him.

'I now get the apparent connection!' Rudolph perceptively realized while looking up to the blinking electric dentist's shingle tacked above an entryway leading to a steep flight of steps. 'The Green Door paradise I'm dreaming about must be somewhere inside the same building as the anonymous dentist's office. No address appears on the brothel's Green Door card because it's obviously an illicitly operating house of ill repute. What a moronic asshole I was for not being able to decipher the essential basics to this ridiculously simple uncomplicated mystery!'

Changing his attention from his visual recognition of the rather ordinary 'on-the-blink' electric dentist shingle, Rudolph's eyes then looked to his left and promptly perceived the presence of a thin attractive brunette elevated in high heels and wearing a short and provocative black dress. The alluring female was casually puffing on a cigarette and impatiently standing with her ankles crossed in the doorway.

'The building's five stories high,' Steinberg astutely counted and comprehended. 'I'll closely follow that tough-looking hooker all the way up to the fifth floor if I have to! I hope I can still get and maintain an erection after having to expend so much energy climbing up to the top floor! Hope there's still enough oxygen to breath up that high! Apparently she's ardently waiting to receive her next horny customer, who incidentally just happens to be me!'

A moment later, after making serious eye contact with Rudolph Steinberg, the voluptuous woman slowly ascended the wooden steps. The aspiring client, in need of much-anticipated sexual relief, ambled up behind.

The building's second floor, consisting of millinery retail shops and mink-coat furriers, had been closed-off to the public after business hours by a sturdy latticed metal gate. The structure's third floor featured an assortment of still-open barbershops', hairdressers, musicians' offices and doctors' practices, and then the more-seedy fourth floor rooms hosted quack fortunetellers, tealeaf interpreters, palm reading rip-off artists and several non-certified, demented, wacky amateur gynecologist/abortionists.

'Oh yes,' Rudolph alertly surmised and determined. 'The higher I go in this un-inspiring and archaic edifice, the more cheesy the caliber of the offices become. No doubt the fifth and final floor will offer me a most excellent green door brothel and then my brief introduction will be followed by a marvelous lewd interlude with that radiant auburn-haired hussy I had seen standing in the doorway that's situated right next to the all-too-reputable ground floor haberdashery emporium that my fucked-up piano company boss Mr. Snodgrass frequents quite regularly. At least that's what the hell he tells me! But I'll bet Snodgrass uses that excuse as a deception to climb these same steps up to the fifth floor!'

Two pale overhead jets (located on opposite sides of the dingy narrow vista) eerily lit the deserted fifth floor hallway. Directly to the interloper's right was the object the impetuous visitor had been seeking. 'Ah, there it is, the infamous green portal! My curiosity's killing me! I just gotta' discover what's behind the Green Door! I'll nonchalantly rap three times and within an hour accomplish tonight's destiny!' Rudolph fantasized. 'I'm sure there won't be any rowdy gamblers playing poker, any rogues surreptitiously plotting crimes or any bloodthirsty mobsters hanging out. This remote haven has got to be a glorious house of sin and pleasure and nothing more!'

A faint rustle was heard originating inside and then the brown-haired chickadee opened the Green Door's latch. She wrapped her arms around her guest, closed the door and immediately dragged Rudolph over to a ratty-looking faded cloth couch. The non-hesitant young woman began relentlessly kissing her newfound man on his neck and face and next began rubbing his thighs and then adroitly gently stroking his soon erect sex instrument. 'This is an absolute dream come true!' Rudolph considered during the height of his ecstatic reverie. 'This horny nymph must be a devoted daughter of Aphrodite! And last but not least, this lusty doll hasn't even mentioned her fee for performing such tremendous erotic service! Holy shit! I'm about to cream my pants!'

Just prior to Rudolph reaching his first climax the apartment's portal entrance flung open and a colossal-sized figure rushed inside, savagely slamming the door shut behind him. The new arrival unceremoniously lifted Rudolph up off the tawdry sofa, flung the disoriented chap against the gray plastered wall and immediately snatched the victim's wallet from his back pants pocket.

"What the hell's going on here?" the surprised dupe yelled. "I'm an honest guy engaged in an honest transaction! I always pay my debts and I'm gonna' pay for this current piece of ass! Say, who the hell are you?"

"I'm Rocco," the big-fisted brute insolently identified himself. "This is my sweetheart Sally. Not only am I the doll's jealous boyfriend but I'm also her protective pimp so ya' better mind your fuckin' mouth otherwise I'll bust your jaw into at least ten different fragments! Got the picture Asshole!"

"Look Rocco, I'm willing to pay for Sally's special talents if ya' just hand me back my goddamned wallet," the roughed-up piano tuner futilely pleaded. "Whatever happened to the practice of fair commerce being practiced here on Broadway?"

"Look Chump," Sally interrupted the melodramatic discourse between Rocco and Rudolph, "I'm having my monthly period so I can't have sex with anybody right now. It's against my personal ethics! And Rocco and I are starving for a bite to eat and we gotta' get dough right away in order to survive, that is, until my hungry pussy gets back to normal and becomes active again. And besides that, our fuckin' rent is overdue!"

"So you devious Weasel, you perverted Deviate, this ain't no run-of-the-mill hooker's trick being done and paid for on your part; it's a goddamned robbery in progress!" Rocco effectively clarified. "Now Punk, I'm gonna' pilfer all of the greenbacks out of your fancy wallet because Sally and me are sailin' in dire straits and need some instant cash flow to complete the friggin' voyage. And if ya' dare run to the cops and squeal," the intimidating bully vehemently threatened, "then my big brother Bruno will find your lily-white ass and quickly turn it into pig's fodder! Ya' fuckin' understand your dangerous predicament?"

"He probably has an ugly Puritanical wife and a couple of raunchy ingrate kids," Sally accurately guessed and said to Rocco. "That's why this never-satisfied jerk-off needs a legitimate job to support that horrible mess he has at home! But other than that, this mark is harmless. Go easy on the dumb shit-head Rocco once you've grabbed all his dough!"

Rocco rapidly removed the sum of two hundred and ten dollars from the unfortunate victim's wallet, handed the empty leather object back to its rightful owner, hoisted Rudolph up off the grimy rose-floral carpet and then viciously punched the idyllic fool twice in the stomach for good measure. Sally skillfully opened the apartment door and then Rocco fiercely hurled Steinberg into the dank and dirty corridor, the airborne fellow eventually colliding with the solid brick hallway wall.

Staggering around the dark and narrow fifth floor corridor, Rudolph noticed that each and every apartment possessed an identical green entry door similar to the one leading to Rocco and Sally's 'temporary residence.' Steinberg considered that his mandible must have been fractured as he slowly descended the rickety five flights of stairs. At last the dazed and injured thrill-seeker stumbled out onto the cement sidewalk. Above the glittering lights of Broadway, a dusky wan sky had majestically domed the area, making its spectacular eye-appealing appearance during the city adventurer's half hour absence.

'That's the last time I'm ever going anywhere near *that* nondescript shabby fifth floor apartment,' the recently violated attack victim concluded. 'And up until today I had always falsely thought that a jawbreaker was a goddamned hard round piece of candy! Say,' the piano tuner observed, "there's that monstrous African freak-of-nature still out there on the pavement devilishly dispensing those evil business cards!'

Instinctively the extremely perplexed assault-and-robbery dupe valiantly confronted the fantastic Ethiopian. Holding the two distinct business cards in front of *him* Rudolph shouted like an asylum patient, "What the hell's this shit all about? How come there's no damned information on *this* card in my right hand? Where the hell is this sinister non-existent Green Door anyway?" the crazed Steinberg screamed in rapid succession.

"Pardon me Sir," the imposing African suavely replied, "but The Green Door is the name of the new play that's having its debut over at the Hippodrome Theatre tomorrow night. Look over your shoulder to your right and you'll see the handyman putting-up the new title on the marquee. I think the printer down the street was in such a hurry that he forgot to put the most vital information on the newly mass produced business cards," the dignified African explained. "The show's agent is a friend of mine and he asked me if I'd be kind enough to distribute his announcement cards along with the dentist's that I was already handing-out."

"What a crock of smelly shit!" hollered back the thoroughly upset and battered piano salesman. "I should hire you to kick the crap out of a big wise-ass palooka named Rocco."

"Nobody around here messes with Rocco; he's a former Los Angeles heavyweight boxing champion! Say Man, you're bleeding pretty profusely from your gums and mouth," the Afro-American noticed and disclosed. "If your jaw's not broken, then certainly your front teeth have been rearranged by either a smashing left hook or a crushing right cross. If I was you," the sensational-looking black human specimen added, "I'd go straight up to the second floor dentist's office spelled-out on *that* card in your left hand. By coincidence, his office also has a green door just like every other friggin' room in that there' goddamned soon-to-be-condemned building that you had just exited!"

O. Henry (1862-1910)

Even though O. Henry had died at a very young age, he still managed to remarkably write over five hundred short stories and anecdotal sketches. William Sydney Porter's fiction often occurs in familiar environments and settings that he had known well during his short tenure upon this Earth. O. Henry was very familiar with New York City and so his famous stories "The Gift of the Magi," "The Last Leaf, " "The Furnished Room," "After Twenty Years," "The Higher Pragmatism," "The Cop and the Anthem," "The Green Door," "The Caliph, Cupid and the Clock" and "Mammon and the Archer" all take place in Manhattan at or around the turn of the twentieth century during the emergence of the exciting Golden Age of science and technology.

Porter was born in the South in Greensboro, North Carolina, and so the prolific author was quite familiar with the culture of the post-Civil War Dixie states and some of his popular stories are set there: "The Whirligig of Life" (Tennessee), "One Dollar's Worth," "A Call Loan," "The Pimienta Pancakes" (in Texas) and "The Emancipation of Billy" also take places in the American South.

Most interestingly, many of O. Henry's terrific short stories were authored while he was in jail. In 1892 Porter moved to Texas and soon became a teller at an Austin bank where the institution's officials accused him of illegally manipulating funds into his own account. Porter fled to Central America but upon returning to the States after his wife became very ill, the on-the-lam author was captured and then convicted. Thus, one of O. Henry's most famous stories "A Retrieved Reformation" involves safecracker Jimmy Valentine getting out of prison and also, the writer's humorous stories "Shoes" and "Shoes and Ships" take place in Coralio, an imaginary seacoast village in Central America.

It is widely believed that the unique writing name "O. Henry" had been conceived in honor of a certain security guard named Orrin Henry, who had been employed at the federal penitentiary where the literary genius William Sidney Porter had been serving his sentence.

"Punch, Brothers, Punch"

No sir, I'm not exaggerating one iota when I'm now reporting that my formerly invincible brain had been hijacked, that my cerebral functions had been temporarily held hostage and that my immortal soul had been sabotaged just by reading a stupid-ass extraneous jingle rhyme a dozen consecutive times in the morning newspaper. Those poetic catchy fucked-up words took advantage of my mental vulnerability and waltzed through my brain for an entire week every time I ate breakfast, lunch, and dinner, or every time I took a stroll or began writing a story, or even took a perfunctory short piss or a long healthy shit.

To be sure, I was a defenseless prisoner and was relentlessly tortured by this diabolical freaky singsong meter and verse. Now I guarantee you that the whole childish business will at first appear fuckin' innocuous and seem absolutely trifling to *your* mature sensibilities too. I caution you to have your guard up before you continue reading this authentic recounting of an amazingly true and bona fide episode of emotional anguish. Here's the fucked-up language that I had read in that morning newspaper edition.

> Conductor, when you receive a fare,
> Punch in the presence of the passenjare!
> A blue trip slip for an eight-cent fare,
> A buff trip slip for a six-cent fare,
> A pink trip slip for a three-cent fare,
> Punch in the presence of the passenjare!
>
> Chorus
> Punch brothers! Punch with care!
> Punch in the presence of the passenjare!

Sitting calmly at my breakfast table (where I always break my overnight fast), I couldn't clearly recollect whether or not I had eaten anything, although there were plenty of random crumbs on my plate and on the tablecloth and also on my lap napkin. I had been assiduously outlining and organizing the chapters to a newly contrived thrilling novel just the night before the distressing incident had occurred so I rose from my kitchen chair and then casually rambled to the den to continue my arduous brain-drain work.

After I lifted my pen to gently apply to my writing paper, all I could get the goddamned authorial utensil to jot down were the dumb-fuck silly-ass words, "Punch brothers, punch' with care! Punch in the presence of the passenjare!"

I grappled with *that* catchy verse bullshit for a full hour but my basic resistance was totally useless. My captivated brain could not refrain from refraining, "A blue trip slip for an eight-cent fare, a buff trip slip for a six-cent fare, a pink trip slip for a three-cent fare, punch in the presence of the passenjare!" My disoriented mind could not achieve any peace or respite from that barbaric and inhospitable rhyming word invasion.

Well, my day's responsibilities and plans were positively ruined and I could see the futility of any effort on my part quite lucidly. I voluntarily surrendered to my 'word poem enemy' and after sauntering downtown I soon realized that my feet and my strolling pace were keeping cadence and measure to *that* same asinine relentless jingle. When I couldn't tolerate that bothersome and irksome bullshit any longer, I altered the rapidity of my steps, but my anxiety was to no avail. Those annoying beat rhymes accommodated themselves to my new stride and the vexing verses harassed both my left and my right foot as I staggered along the pavement looking like a drunken mendicant.

Exhausted from my hour-long ordeal, I trekked home and mentally and emotionally suffered all that afternoon and next, even cried right through dinner and was even passively farting in the bathtub to the jingle's accursed rhyming scheme. In bed I rolled and tossed all night long so I arose at midnight, picked up a non-fiction book to read but there was nothing visible upon the pages except the confounded bullshit words, "Punch brothers, punch with care, punch in the presence of the passenjare!"

And when the rising sun finally appeared in the east, I got out of bed, remembered to dress and put my shoes on, ventured downtown and everyone I encountered marveled at my reiteration of the stupid fucked-up hypnotic phraseology, "Punch brothers, punch with care, punch in the presence of the passenjare!" The strangers that I confronted, besieged and bombarded were even more upset and pissed-off about that moronic verbal shit than I was!

Two days later on Saturday morning I exited my bed to honor a scheduled appointment I had made the week before. After brutally scarring-up my face while shaving, I dressed and as a mobile tottering wreck, met my valued friend right on time in front of the local pharmacy, the dignified and esteemed Reverend Mr. Biggins, whom I had agreed to accompany on a ten mile-long walking excursion to the Talcott Tower over in Simsbury, Connecticut.

After we initiated our physically demanding ramble, the honorable Reverend Mr. Biggins kept talking, talking, and talking as was his predictable wont, but I said and heard nothing since my mind was definitely preoccupied in its fascination with the fucked-up repetitious trolley car rhyme. At the end of the first mile, the garrulous minister commented, "Mark, I know you're a devout atheist and an occasional agnostic but I've never seen you looking so haggard and so fatigued, not to mention you being profoundly absent-minded. I encourage you Mark, please say something salient to break the monotony of my mediocre monologue!"

Drearily and without any evident enthusiasm I unabashedly muttered, "Punch brothers, punch with care, punch' in the presence of the passenjare!"

The Reverend Mr. Biggins stared at me blankly through his thick bifocals, looking both pretty damned perplexed and amused simultaneously. "I can't comprehend your entire drift Mark. There doesn't seem to be any particular relevance or significance to your strange utterances. Certainly, it wasn't anything melancholy you had mentioned and yet, perhaps it was your dull droning intonation that had negatively affected my auditory perception. Truthfully Twain," my heaven-bound friend indicated, "I've never heard anything so alluring yet so pathetic. What is…."

But my ears were deaf to the Reverend's most perceptive statements. My weak and wimpy mind was already being held hostage with, 'A blue trip slip for an eight-cent fare, a buff trip slip for a six-cent fare, a pink trip slip for a three-cent fare, punch in the presence of the passenjare!'

Now I don't recall what had transpired immediately thereafter during the remainder of the lengthy ten-mile hike but then the exasperated Reverend Mr. Biggins placed his right hand upon my left shoulder and shouted into my ear, "Wake up Mark! Don't daydream all day long! Here now my apostate companion, we've finally arrived at the splendid Talcott Tower man! I've talked myself deaf, dumb and blind the last several hours and I never received any legitimate response from your lips except some nonsensical gibberish that you kept repeating over and over again," Reverend Biggins remarked and reminded me. "Just look at this majestic landscape and admire the full panorama! Just reflect for a moment and feast your eyes upon the magnificent foliage and gaze upon the fabulous shrub arrangements! You've traveled all over

Europe and I challenge you Mark to compare what you're witnessing now to what you had seen in Venice and Rome! Come now my dear Mr. Twain', give me your honest evaluation of your sensational surroundings! What parallels and opinions do you have?"

I sighed wearily and then reluctantly and lethargically declared, "A blue trip slip for an eight-cent fare, a buff trip slip for a six-cent fare, a pink trip slip for a three-cent fare, punch in the presence of the passenjare!"

Well now, Reverend Mr. Biggins, who never deliberately cursed a word of profanity in his life, just stood there biting his tongue. His face expressed a very concerned and gravely alarmed configuration. Then the very distinguished man of the cloth said, "Mark, there is something remotely appealing about your ongoing declaration that I cannot fully understand. Those are the identical words you've been reiterating this entire laborious walk over here to Simsbury. There doesn't seem to be any special substance to them; it's all rhyme without reason so to speak! Yes, it's all basic form without content; that's exactly what you're communicating! Those nebulous-sounding words of yours nearly break my heart. How do they go? Punch in the, sorry Mark, but I just can't accurately remember."

I gathered my sanity and slowly articulated the simple lines six consecutive times with perfect enunciation. The Reverend's face lit up and beamed as if it was an illuminated electric sign. "Why Mark, that's an exceptionally captivating and intriguing jingle you've just related! It's almost music; not exactly Mozart or Brahms mind you, but almost music! Its unique pattern has a certain magical flow to it! I've nearly memorized all of the words myself. Say them just one more time for the sake of redundancy so that I'll be able to fully master the entire sequence."

Well, I accommodated the inquisitive Reverend with those fucked-up words and then the victim attempted to say them all by himself but made one minor mistake in his delivery, which I immediately expertly corrected. The second time he got them all perfect in the proper order and at that rapturous moment, a great burden seemed to tumble right off my formerly oppressed shoulders. The torturing jingle miraculously escaped my conscious and subconscious minds as if I had been a lustful vampire supplying a new red-blooded candidate with my dreaded uncouth cell-sucking deportment. Suddenly a graceful sense of tranquility descended upon and enveloped me simultaneous with the transference of the rhyming malady from me to the readily available Reverend Mr. Biggins.

I was so lighthearted and I sang some popular song lyrics on the entire ten-mile-long trek home. Then my emancipated tongue proudly rediscovered the art of speech again and my formerly pent-up thoughts were finally liberated into viable oral sentences. Those joyous buoyant words gushed out gregariously until my mental fountain was dry and empty. I shook the Reverend Mr. Biggins' right hand at our parting and politely related, "Haven't we had a royal jolly time? But Minister, you haven't said a palpable word ever since we stepped away from the Talcott Tower grounds! Say something lively to break your boredom."

The Reverend slowly turned towards me like an automaton with a lackluster pallid face and then drew a very deep breath into his flaccid lungs. And without exhibiting either apparent animation or alert consciousness he uttered, "Punch brothers, punch with care, punch in the presence of the passenjare!"

A disconcerting pang of rare sympathy shot through my being as I assessed, 'Poor fellow! He's got the dreaded symptoms of that same contagious mental disease right now! I hope he fuckin' remembers where the hell he lives before he's picked up on the street for vagrancy, white collar or no white collar, should he violently rip the damned thing off during a hectic moment of frantic madness!'

* * * * * * * * * * * *

I didn't see Reverend Mr. Biggins for an entire week but then on a Tuesday evening the self-righteous sanctimonious usually confident individual staggered into my presence and met me at my residence for an unscheduled social visit. The about-to-be-appointed bishop looked pretty damned haggard, pale and basically, an exhausted wreck. The holier-than-thou fellow opened his bloodshot eyes enough for me to observe that the perplexed son-of-a-bitch appeared to have a double case of pinkeye.

"Ah Mark, it was a terrible ruinous investment I had made in memorizing those horrendous and devastating rhymes you had maliciously taught me," my disgusted friend prefaced. "They've haunted my psyche like a perpetual nightmare both day and night, horrible hour after horrible hour right up to this present rendezvous. In fact, I'm inconsolable about the whole ordeal."

"Well now Reverend, why don't you gather your wits and then tell me what happened after our pleasant journey to and from the

Talcott Tower," I suggested. "Things are never as bad as they often seem at first evaluation!"

"That's what the hell you think!" the soon-to-be-ordained bishop unexpectedly cursed. "Last Saturday evening I had received an urgent telegraph message and had to hop aboard the evening train to Boston as a result of the emergency. An old friend of mine had died and his family had requested that I preside over the funeral and give an extemporaneous account of his marvelous contributions to his family and to American society."

"So what's so extraordinary about that?" I diplomatically asked before popping a chocolate candy into my mouth. "Your actions were quite humanitarian and altruistic. Essentially, you were acting in compliance to your job description."

"Well Mark, I took my damned seat in the first Pullman car and began organizing the text for the sermon," continued Reverend Biggins, who to my knowledge never before had ever uttered a syllable of either obscenity or vulgarity. "But unfortunately, I never got beyond framing the first paragraph, for then the car wheels rubbing against the goddamned rails began their characteristic and distracting clack-clack-clack, clack-clack-clack, clickety-clack, clickety-clack background noise," Biggins sadly expressed. "Right away those odious rhymes you had conveyed to me came into play and the bullshit things dominated my mind as the train wheels and tracks provided my ears with ample musical accompaniment."

"Sounds like a pretty familiar story to me," I assessed and stated as I nonchalantly reached for a second sweet chocolate. "Nothing too serious that could warp your logical thinking," I added, adroitly-but-suavely busting my holy guest's sensitive balls. "It was just an inconsequential annoyance, that's all."

"That's what the fuck you think Mark!" Reverend Mr. Biggins screamed back into my face with his bloodshot eyeballs nearly popping out of their sockets. "After an hour of deep contemplation and progressively nodding my head to the inane rhythm, I was more fagged-out than a goddamned gay fag after twelve hours of continuous immoral and illicit homosexual sodomizing sex. My noggin felt like a freakin' crapola and I truly felt like a goddamned fucked-up shit-head," my religious guest insisted. "My colossal headache was splitting my skull apart as I restively sat there in total anguish like a mother-fuckin' zombie. I stretched my naked ass out in my berth but all my rapidly disintegrating degenerate brain could contemplate were those corny infectious fucked-up rhymes you had evilly mentioned to me last week."

"And exactly what were those rhymes?" I further baited the Reverend Mr. Biggins, deftly feigning ignorance. "I can't recall all of them."

"Well shit Mark," my incensed usually pious friend bellowed, "it occurred to me that I had a one track mind just like the fuckin' train did! 'Clack-clack-clack, a blue trip slip, clack-clack-clack, for an eight-cent fare; clack-clack-clack, a buff trip slip, clack-clack-clack, for a six-cent fare,' and the abominable agony continued, and so on, and so on and so on. 'Punch in the presence of the passenjare'!"

"Could ya' nod off and catch forty winks while you were simultaneously nodding your head to the rhythmic beat?" I politely asked as I cruelly winked at my visitor and directly-but-courteously mocked his pathetic plight.

"Sleep! Did you have the audacity to fuckin' say 'sleep'!" my saintly and usually extremely devout friend vociferated. "I was a total lunatic when the locomotive finally pulled into the goddamned Boston station. The next morning at the funeral I did the best I could with my prepared oration but every bitchin' sentence I uttered was tangled, laced and woven with 'Punch, brothers, punch with care, punch in the presence of the passenjare!' And Mark, my totally fucked-up delivery, which is normally quite eloquent as you well know, well my entire pronunciation dropped into and matched the undulating rhythm of those cock-sucking rhymes you had shared with me, and my tired eyes actually caught the dumb-fuck assholes in attendance sitting there and mechanically nodding their heads to my fucked-up elocution."

"Sounds like some heavy unprecedented bullshit to me," I amiably replied before pouring myself a cup of hot coffee. "It's a good thing you weren't addressing your congregation here in Springfield or else your name might've been swiftly removed for consideration for your upcoming hierarchal promotion."

"Well Mark, much to my utter astonishment, the entire audience, the stone-faced undertaker and the grim-puss hearse driver included, were bobbing their heads up and down all in unison in response to my entirely fucked-up speech," Reverend Mr. Biggins woefully added. "After I finished my fucked-up spiel, I had a wicked panic attack and anxiously rushed into the anteroom in a state of absolute frenzy. A well-intentioned aged old maid approached me as I was breathing heavily into a white cloth church moneybag. The elderly maudlin bitch, who incidentally was also from Springfield, quite ruefully said, "Oh, oh, I'm so sorrowed that my friend Barnaby has passed on. I regret that I didn't have the opportunity to see him before he died of malaria and small pox. His sudden departure is oh so tragic!"

"You loved him then back in Springfield, even when he wasn't a streetcar passenger being savagely punched," I strangely answered. "I mean Madam, you had known him well before old Barnaby was a streetcar passenger having his ticket punched."

"Loved him? Loved who?" the confused elderly retired incontinent whore asked during a moment of pure short and long-term memory loss. "Who the hell are you talking about?"

"Why poor deceased Barnaby Hampton of course!" I exclaimed before again raising the empty white cloth moneybag up to my mouth for some additional improvised self-therapy.

"Oh him, yes, him, Barnaby Hampton," the old mentally deranged bitch replied. "Certainly I loved Barnaby, God rest his gentle soul. He did have a big dick! I hope that when St. Peter meets and greets him at the Pearly Gates, the main guard doesn't ask Barnaby for his ticket so that St. Peter can punch it in the presence of the eternal passenjare!" Reverend Mr. Biggins testily communicated to me exactly what the elderly retired bitch-whore had mentioned to him in the anteroom.

"Did the old retired bitch whore ask you if you had been present when Barnaby got pissed-off with the world and voluntarily gave up his ghost?" I facetiously asked my visitor.

"Yes, and I explicitly explained to her that she ought to find the nearest bag to breathe into before she fuckin' died from a lack of oxygen in the anteroom," Reverend Mr. Biggins explained. "I told the nosy bitch-whore, whose overall inquisitiveness was mercilessly annoying the hell out of me, 'Barnaby's last dramatic words to me were, 'Punch, brother, punch with care, punch in the presence of the goddamned passenjare'!"

"And what the hell did the old retired bitch-whore say in response to your most intelligent declaration?" I curiously inquired.

"She said," the Reverend Mr. Biggins whimpered and then coughed, "She fuckin' said, 'A blue trip slip for an eight-cent fare, a buff trip slip for a six-cent fare, a pink trip slip for a three-cent fare, punch in the presence of the passenjare!' That's exactly what the fuck the old retired dry cunt bitch replied."

I desired to get Reverend Mr. Biggins to step outside as soon as possible because my disturbed and fazed friend looked as if his frazzled brain needed an immediate enema or else his head would probably explode right off his neck and propel into the upper atmosphere. In the flickering hall gaslight his hopeless bloodshot eyes met mine for a pregnant moment and then the essence of his shallow thoughts were verbally revealed and conveyed.

"Mark, you've been rather reticent and laconic during my whole gut-wrenching revelation to you," Biggins angrily objected. "You offer me no solace or solution to my aggravating melody malady. It's just as fuckin' well, I suppose. You couldn't help me in a million years after spending ten millenniums being a dedicated student in a goddamned psychiatry university!"

"Well Reverend, your ugly tongue isn't doomed to wag that pathetic jingle for all eternity," I optimistically consoled. "I do have in my possession an adequate remedy for your gross condition if you have the patience and the wherewithal to listen to my special cure. It's really not too damned complicated after all, that is, once you exhibit some self-discipline and get the full hang of it!"

"I'll do anything short of divorce from my wife or castration of my genitals or decapitation by guillotine to resolve this fucked-up jingle crisis of mine!" Reverend Biggins sincerely exclaimed. "Cure me and I'll make you a goddamned saint once I become bishop!"

"Well, you don't have to go that far," I maintained with a degree of embarrassment. "Just put me in charge of your Sunday collection baskets, that's all I ask."

I then disclosed to the next ordained Connecticut Bishop how to rid himself of his debilitating-but-dispensable mental illness. The next week I arranged with a college professor acquaintance of mine for the afflicted Minister to give a vital seminar at the nearby university. Mr. Biggins, whom I had the distinct pleasure of introducing to the impressionable assemblage of college juniors seated in the huge lecture hall, performed his oral routine rather terrifically.

The man-of-the-cloth had inadvertently discharged the burden of his persecuting rhymes into the ears of the euphoric and receptive students, and naturally, they gladly accepted the profundity of his inspirational rhetoric and soon acquired mastery of the mantra-like poetic verses. The rhyming street trolley pestilence had been expertly transferred to several hundred ecstatic young asshole college recipients and Reverend Mr. Biggins was once again a sane American citizen ready to advance to bigger and better things.

Mark Twain (1835-1910)

Remarkably, Samuel Langhorne Clemens was both born and died the same years that Halley's Comet had made its seventy-five year revolution around the solar system. Clemens acquired his pen name "Mark Twain" from Mississippi River steamboat terminology of "twain" being a water depth of two fathoms (twelve feet), the allowable safe level for a riverboat to navigate over a reef or shoal, and the depth was measured by a leadsman who threw a heavy lead weight overboard and then after lifting it out of the river, would mark the twain.

Sam Clemens became a successful riverboat pilot under the direction of a captain named Horace Bixby, but after the Civil War broke out, the Mississippi River was closed to commercial traffic. Being unemployed, Clemens journeyed out west to try his hand at gold prospecting in Nevada and then at newspaper journalism in California. The writer gained international recognition with the publication of his classic humorous short story "The Celebrated Jumping Frog of Calaveras County," first published in 1865.

Mark Twain is generally regarded as a humorist but he is also understood by literary critics as being a serious philosopher and an astute analyzer of the antebellum and post-Civil War American societies of his time. Twain's most famous novels are *The Adventures of Tom Sawyer, The Adventures of Huckleberry Finn, The Prince and the Pauper* and *A Connecticut Yankee in King Arthur's Court*. Other important Mark Twain works are the books: *Roughing It, Life on the Mississippi* and *Innocents Abroad*.

In 1870 Mark Twain had married Olivia Langdon of Elmira, New York and the couple had two daughters, Susy and Jean. After becoming rich and famous, Clemens built a fabulous mansion in Hartford, Connecticut that had a porch and staircase that made the spectacular dwelling resemble a Mississippi riverboat.

"The Gay Tailor Who Became King"

"The Gay Tailor Who Became King" is an imaginative piece of children's literature based on a Polish folklore tale about the delusions of a jolly old homosexual clothes' adjuster whose wild and unrealistic expectations are told in such a manner that they seem almost logical and ordinary.

Once upon a time people wore so many clothes all year round that the imbeciles couldn't distinguish what sex they were and the general situation was just like today when folks wear so few clothes and still have the same problem identifying males from females from neuters. A gay, little thin tailor named Mr. Nodicka lived in those mysterious ancient times and the merry fellow had a scrawny beard that contained exactly three hundred and sixty-five hairs (representing the number of days in a year) and a rather sparse pubic patch with the same number of active growth follicles.

Mr. Nodicka was very gaunt, so slender that his appearance resembled a needle and thread and many of his most loyal customers attested that the tradesman could pass through the eye of a needle much easier than a pregnant camel could. And on holidays' and on special occasions' like anniversaries Mr. Nodicka braided his beard so that he could look as fucked-up as everyone else in the tiny village of Stitchylvania.

One gloomy dismal day a sinister-looking Gypsy entered the modest tailor shop and she specifically requested some important work to be performed. "I have no money to pay for your wonderful services but I'll gladly read your fortune in return for your work," she told the mild-mannered Nodicka.

"What has to be done?" the jolly tailor asked. "Do you need your crotch or asshole sewn up? What about zippers installed under your hairy armpits? I used to work at the hospital's emergency room you know!"

"You're actually on the right track," the old conniving Gypsy related. "I cut my left foot on a shattered mirror my ugly face had accidentally broken so I need a surgical *knit*wit like you to darn the damned wound. But be careful how you sew-up the flesh and don't leave any scar otherwise I'll return to this shop and fiercely suffocate you with my lousy smelly cunt!"

Mr. Nodicka rendered his essential services and two weeks later the Gypsy returned to his humble shop to fully compensate him. "Leave Stitchylvania this Sunday and walk due West," the fortuneteller advised the little gay tailor. "In time you'll arrive at a place where there is a shrinking nobility among the population and then you soon will be appointed King."

"I've heard some incredible bull shit in my time but this fantastic tale of yours appears to be the best," the gay tailor scoffed and laughed. "And since your extremely fucked-up story has made me even more cheerful than I usually am I'll accept it as a valid payment of debt. Ha, ha, ha, ha!" the faggot tailor chortled. "It's so humorous that I feel as if I'm about to grow a square dick with cubic balls! Ha, ha, ha, ha!"

The following morning Mr. Nodicka closed his nearly bankrupt tailor shop and left *his* debt-ridden place of business carrying a bundle that included a thousand needles (some of them from pine trees), a dozen brass thimbles, ten thousand kilometers of light-blue thread, seven lucky irons and three pairs of sharp scissors of various sizes.

"Which way is West?" Nodicka asked a fellow pedestrian that happened to be blind.

"The two-hundred year old senile gent wearing a ten gallon hat full of rye whiskey and matching brown cowboy boots with heavy spurs answered, "Over there' Asshole! West' is where the people say the sun sets'. But I warn ya' young fella' that there ain't too many saloons with swinging doors over in that fuckin' direction! And partner, make sure ya' don't fuckin' get shot at the *OK Corral*. That *OK* is not okay with me!"

Mr. Nodicka began walking in the direction that the old Polish whiskerando had recommended. Just outside Stitchylvania the jolly tailor encountered a strong gusty wind, and it was a good thing the happy-go-lucky gentleman was carrying his heavy bundle or else he would have been sucked away with real gusto. The merry gent laughed exceedingly as the blustery wind pushed him along until he heard someone shout: "Who the fuck are you' over there trespassing into my field?"

Nodicka looked around during the turbulent windstorm and noticed a frail Scarecrow standing in the middle of a wheat field. The elegantly dressed figure wearing an Abe Lincoln stovepipe hat and a navy blue jacket was composed of five sticks: two arms, two legs and a long erection upon which assorted blackbirds landed and pecked away at the figure's much abused pecker.

The traveling tailor momentarily dropped his heavy bundle, removed his tiny cap and bowed as if he were addressing high-browed Polish royalty. "Sorry to intrude on your territory," the gay tailor apologized to the Scarecrow. "But I too live just a *sew-sew* life!"

"I am very pleased to make the acquaintance of such a retarded asshole as yourself," the simple-minded Scarecrow answered. "I am Baron Scarecrow and I am genuinely bored out of my mind watching various birds fly overhead attempting to raid this precious wheat field. But I would prefer fighting tigers or panthers rather than simply scaring birds away," the figure divulged. "And besides that Mr. Nodicka, I'm the best in my field because as you can determine I'm the only Scarecrow in my field. Ha, ha, ha, ha! Where are you heading kind sir if I may ask?"

"Mr. Nodicka was entirely too courteous and naïve for his own good so he respectfully bowed and then hopped like a gay robin (or in this case like a silly jerk off) three steps backwards and inadvertently smashed against a tall oak tree. "That's the way well-bred men in Stitchylvania show their honor," the skinny tailor informed as he got up off the ground and dusted himself off. "All except the collision part with the tree is the customary acknowledgement. Baron Scarecrow," the traveling tailor continued, "I'm really on a bold journey to a distant place where I will become King. I suspect that you are a clairvoyant Scarecrow for you knew my name without me disclosing it to you."

"Is it possible that a complete insignificant fool like you could ascend the complicated bureaucratic aristocracy' ladder and ultimately become a King?" the Scarecrow rhetorically argued. "On the other hand most Kings I've ever heard about are indeed fucked-up Assholes just like you are."

"Of course I was born with a destiny and a propensity to become a King," Nodicka pompously stated, "and I believe that if you accompany me on my royal ramble you will be all the merrier. What do you say about my designs Mr. Strawbrains?"

"All right Mr. Nodicka, I wholeheartedly accept your stupid invitation to join your folly," Baron Scarecrow replied. "I am very weary of this monotonous job I have been maintaining for a century. But first you must mend my torn trousers," the good-natured Scarecrow requested. "I might meet someone prettier than you along the way and decide to marry him or her so I must appear handsome and debonair to everyone I encounter."

"I'll sew up your pants and even re-do your zipper despite the fact that you can't possibly piss out of a normal dick like ordinary male humans do," the tailor chuckled in a blithe tone of voice. "I can identify with what it's like being dick-less so don't feel so fuckin' sorry for yourself."

In an hour the jaunty tailor had mended the Scarecrow's hat and trousers, and after Mr. Nodicka completed his enterprise a dozen ravens showed up expressing their disdain for the two conversing idiots. The meddling black birds flew overhead and egregiously crapped on the two royal imposters' heads and also begrimed their colorful clothes.

On the arduous journey "West to Nowhere" the two companions gradually became close friends. The thin tailor tethered himself to the Scarecrow in various "Rest Stop Fields" along the way when it was time to sleep and when viciously attacked by wild rabid dogs. The loyal Scarecrow would protect Nodicka by kicking at the growling curs and yelling, "That'll be the last straw, you fuckin' beastly mangy mongrels!"

While passing near the hamlet of Slowvodka where all of the residents were chronic alcoholics Mr. Nodicka suggested to his itinerant colleague in an appropriate oxymoron, "There's a heavy light originating in that house. Let's knock on the door and perhaps the drunken resident will provide us with adequate food and shelter to pass the night."

"I sincerely agree," the now-chilly Scarecrow declared. "I know this place can't be Chicago because it's but a mere windy village and not a slum-laden *Windy City*. Say my good friend', what the hell's wrong with this fucked-up dwelling? It's slowly turning around and the structure must have legs, ankles and feet!"

"The owner of this house must also be gay like us because I see him dancing and jumping about inside," the tailor observed and related. "Let's wait until the front door makes a complete rotation and then we'll surreptitiously enter. I don't know if you've ever noticed it or not," Mr. Nodicka pontificated, "but it's pretty hard walking in through a damned window, especially when it's closed. That's why fuckin' houses have doors. I just figured that bull shit out!"

After the front door made a full revolution (without guns, rifles, muskets or cannons) the two interlopers furtively entered the abode without first knocking on the door. They viewed an exhausted elderly Nobleman warming himself next to a log-filled fireplace even though it was the height of summer and a hundred and ten degrees outside ever since the intense windstorm had passed through the area. Then the two trespassers were astonished when the Nobleman clearly and plainly articulated, "Welcome eminent

Mr. Nodicka and honorable Baron Scarecrow. Welcome to my humble domicile."

The tailor hopped back three times like a gay robin while Baron Scarecrow removed his tall stovepipe hat out of courtesy to their rather weird-looking host. The two guests then listened intently to the Nobleman's extraordinary oratory.

"Stay with me for dinner and tomorrow you two morons can continue your odyssey," the strange host deliberately suggested in a low tone of voice. "I will contact my wife, my daughter and my relatives and we could all participate in a major gang bang even though you gay Mr. Nodicka are impotent and devoid of a penis and you Baron Scarecrow should really be Barren Scarecrow because you only have a wooden stick for an erect dick. Ha, ha, ha, ha! What a pair of retards you two are!"

Then the bizarre Nobleman sternly clapped his hands and suddenly thirty new people appeared without ever entering the room through doorways, portals or windows. When the Nobleman's daughter talked she sounded exactly like a horse whinnying and neighing, and when the ugly young lady informed Mr. Nodicka that she'd like to have him for her husband the tailor humorously responded to the unattractive unpleasantly plump girl, "Quit horsing around because I'm both gay and dick-less! Find yourself another stud, preferably a stallion or a goddamned mustang."

A giant hanging cauldron with steaming soup inside was taken from the fireplace's metal rack and the hot foul food was served to everyone. The Nobleman then had something relevant to disclose to his two gullible guests. "Mr. Nodicka and Baron Scarecrow," the austere aristocrat prefaced, "for some inexplicable reason my family is always cold even during the height of summer. And so every evening we eat this ill-flavored hot soup for supper but we really get *stewed* by drinking hundred-proof-vodka from eight p.m. until midnight. Ha, ha, ha, ha! That's basically all we ever fuckin' do each and every evening in Slowvodka."

"I guess then you often resurface your walls and really get plastered too!" Mr. Nodicka cleverly added. "And next dear Nobleman you probably stick baked dough and sliced apples in your pupils and really get pie-eyed! Ha, ha, ha, ha!"

Soon a queer-looking servant resembling a macabre ghoulish zombie entered the dining room and brought a large dish of fried rats garnished in a rich black sauce and soon he returned with bowls of broiled locusts, baked worms and raunchy fillet of salamander. And for dessert the odd assemblage ravenously devoured sour ovary eggs and testicle' meatballs, but the gay tailor and the impotent barren Baron Scarecrow alternated tossing all of their hideous despicable food under the very long wide table.

"I'm quite impressed with your noteworthy ambition," the Nobleman said to the zany tailor. "I happen to be a proficient mind-reader and am quite aware that you desire to ascend from Gay Tailor to Gay King without even becoming a totally queer Gay Lord. Did you know Mr. Nodicka that King Hineymunch of Warsaw just passed away? He was killed by his subjects after the terrorist people *saw war* in Warsaw."

"I understand completely," Baron Scarecrow rudely interrupted. "Since Warsaw is the city where the country's central government is located the unsuspecting King was ludicrously killed by the administration of *capital* punishment. That's all very rational and logical. Now is Warsaw very far from Slowvodka?"

"A *crow* that is not *scared* can fly from here to Warsaw in two days Baron Scarecrow," the Nobleman joked. "And the bellicose people of Warsaw are all clamoring to elect a new King. And I must tell you Mr. Nodicka," the phony aristocrat emphasized, "anyone who marries *my* weirdo daughter and shares her bridal honeymoon suite will be nominated as the next Polish King of Warsaw."

When the Nobleman's daughter heard the word *"bridal"* she automatically thought *'bridle'* and again began neighing and whinnying like crazy. Then the hideous-looking lass amorously threw her arms around the tailor's neck and kept pretending to be and sounding like a filly from Philly' in heat.

"Let's run away from this preposterous madness!" barren Baron Scarecrow demanded to his traveling companion. "Now I definitely know that this loony unkempt house is really a barn when the owner's daughter acts and sounds like an absolute night *mare*!"

The befuddled tailor looked around the expansive dining room but could not see a door or a window from which to escape. The gent then lowly whispered to the neurotic Scarecrow that the two should jolly their hosts until the opportune moment arrived to swiftly hightail it out of the seemingly dangerous premises.

"We'll all now salute and drink to your good health dear tailor," the very-disciplined Nobleman insisted, "but do you know the lyrics and melody to any particular song?"

"Yes indeed!" Mr. Nodicka cooperatively answered. "I shall sing the first and worst verse and then have everyone in the room mimic my lunacy and poor taste." The very thin guest removed his cap and began inharmoniously singing a most terrible tune while saluting the Nobleman's daughter-equine-wannabe'.

> "Sing praise to the lovely Slowvodka whore,
> Sing praise to her wondrous snatch.
> Let her juicy slit pump and hump some more,
> And then I'll greedily eat her hairy patch!"

All of a sudden the entire insulted, perverted extended family arose and loudly cursed and then proceeded to wildly chase Mr. Nodicka and Baron Scarecrow twelve times around the long wide dining table and next out of the odd house. And upon exiting the queer place the two haunted escapees turned around and were astounded to see the house and its peculiar occupants instantly vanish out of sight.

The two journeymen trekked to a distant meadow to evaluate their circumstances and options. Both shared common opinions about the spectacular unnatural episode that had just transpired.

"I believe that the Nobleman and his fucked-up relatives were actually terrible transmigrating demons," the tailor said to Baron Scarecrow. "And his ugly fat daughter that falsely thought she was a horse that also wanted to be Queen of Warsaw was even more fucked-up than her totally fake father was!"

"If you had a dick and wore jockey shorts," the Scarecrow imaginatively responded to the gay tailor, "then you could have ridden the Nobleman's daughter all night without a friggin' saddle."

The two disenchanted adventurers continued on their' merry way and again sauntered West' for seven more days until they finally reached the outskirts of metropolitan downtown Warsaw. But inside the city limits the rain came down in torrents in what was aptly described by Mr. Nodicka as "a combination hurricane and monsoon."

"I refuse to enter the city because then my stovepipe hat will get wet," the Scarecrow confided to his already drenched companion. "Then the straw in my head will become saturated and I'll have a nasty case of water on the brain."

"And I refuse to enter the city and come into contact with so many people who are wet behind the ears," Mr. Nodicka confidentially conveyed to his associate. "This heavy rain has indubitably already dampened my spirits!"

A crowd of disgruntled irate Warsaw residents approached and quickly confronted and then accosted the two visitors. The city's temperamental Burgomaster next conducted a rather hasty and harsh interrogation.

"Who the hell are you and why have you' come to Warsaw?" the Mayor asked the perplexed intruders. "You both have unfortunately arrived during a very ominous time!"

"What the fuck has happened here?" Mr. Nodicka asked the volatile Burgomaster. "What's all of this bull shit deluge all about? Has the venerable Noah been reincarnated and is he coming to town in his acclaimed ark?"

"The city's destruction seems to be inevitable," the gloomy Mayor predicted. "King Hineymunch died a week ago and ever since his passing it has not stopped raining. The chimneys in our houses cannot sustain fires and soon our affected homes will be floating away all the way to the evil crack houses over in Krakow."

"That's too bad!" Mr. Nodicka exclaimed. "Jimmy cracks corn in Kansas and I don't care, and dope addicts crack houses in Kracow and I don't give a shit about that either."

"But the worst part of the dreadful situation involves the King's ugly fat daughter," the pathetic Burgomaster related as the miserable crowd of onlookers became even more rowdy and rambunctious. "The grotesque-looking Princess has promised to marry any man, native or visitor' who can stop the rain from falling."

"Baron Scarecrow!" the tailor yelled above the din of the increasingly hostile throng. "Let's go into Warsaw and stop this friggin' downpour from completely flooding the city. 'I think I know exactly how to stop this heavy rain and tame it into a *baby shower*! Ha, ha, ha, ha!"

After walking through savage torrential rain along with gusting gales the two dreamers finally arrived at the city's Royal Palace. The disconsolate Princess opened the door and reluctantly let the two do-gooders inside. "Oh what a handsome man you are!" the royal young ugly obese lady said to the likeable tailor. "But please don't turn sideways. You're so damned skinny that you're liable to disappear from sight!"

The slender Mr. Nodicka hopped backwards three times like a timid gay robin and then respectfully addressed his new regal acquaintance. "Is it true Your Grace that you will marry the one that stops the rain?"

"I publicly pledged that I would do precisely that!" the alarmed Princess conceded and verified.

"And if I do it?" the clever cunning tailor proposed while indirectly also proposing marriage.

"Then I will keep my promise no matter how tiny your dick or your balls might be!" the corpulent ugly girl confirmed.

"Very well Your Highness!" the determined tailor amiably agreed. "You will see beyond a shadow of a doubt that I shall stop the fuckin' rain and unilaterally salvage your city from despondency, ruin and eradication!"

The thrilled thin tailor nodded to his irascible Scarecrow confederate and the dynamic duo subsequently left the regal palace. As the pair privately conferred the entire pissed-off population crowded around them holding pebbles, stones and rocks to hurl and hammer the new arrivals with should the two fail in completing their proclaimed endeavor.

"How are you going to bring back pleasant weather amidst such a wet and unpleasant mob?" Baron Scarecrow apprehensively asked his confident mentor. "These nasty uncouth morons will light a match to my straw and set me on fire right out here in the middle of the fuckin' street!"

"I know where the rain comes from!" the tailor bragged. "From the damned sky! And I also know that it always falls down and does not ascend up!"

"No shit Sherlock!" the Scarecrow attested. "You're about as smart as your last wet fart!"

"I have a theory," Mr. Nodicka intellectually stated. "When the great King Hineymunch died he went directly to Heaven and made a hole in the sky to look down on his city. The Monarch felt saddened leaving his subjects and predicates and family down on Earth so he continually weeps like an infant. He chronically cries right through the dismal opening in the sky!"

Baron Scarecrow saw much merit in Mr. Nodicka's fantastic hypothesis. "You are either the smartest tailor that ever lived or the world's biggest fucked-up asshole!" the impractical straw-headed fellow commented. "Why can't we just initiate building a duplicate Warsaw ten miles East of here! Or we could even lead all of the city's ruffian residents to Stitchylvania and make the village a hundred times larger than it is now and call the new fuckin' place Warsaw!"

"Here's what we'll need from the fair citizens of Warsaw," the determined tailor instructed the Scarecrow without ever considering his partner's useful suggestions and opinions. "Have a hundred men carry a hundred ladders to the Warsaw Royal Palace. We'll tie them together and make a vertical path leading straight up to the sky. And then I'll use the needles, thimbles and thread from my bundle and I'll stitch up the opening that poor melancholy King Hineymunch had formed and consequently stop the troublesome rain from falling," the tailor predicted. "I believe we'll require only about two hundred kilometers of thread to successfully perform the difficult labor."

The wet disgruntled grumpy men helped assemble and lift the huge connected ladder and then the valiant Mr. Nodicka climbed up the myriad rungs with his bundle of useful materials. After two full wet days of assiduous sewing the badly torn piece of sky, the gap had been satisfactorily repaired and the now-jubilant Warsaw' citizens all rejoiced when the rains finally ceased. Finally the triumphant tailor descended the multiple-ladder to the applause of the appreciative peasant and serf' residents.

The now-ecstatic Princess exited her Royal Palace and wiped her eyes, forgetting all about wiping her fat ugly ass. She threw her arms around the blushing tailor's waist and repeatedly kissed his wet red face. Then the deceased King Hineymunch's daughter drew Mr. Nodicka's hands to her breasts and allowed the trembling tailor to massage and fondle her nipples and next his quivering hand was led to her bush and permitted to gently rub her smelly brown pubic garden.

Mr. Nodicka was extremely happy and almost became sexually aroused as numerous hormones surged throughout his skinny dickless body. Then the horny Princess made a rather shocking revelation. "Dear tailor from afar, it's a good thing you have no penis because I am very allergic to sperm juice," she disclosed. "Sperm juice rots my uterus and intestines from the inside out! I know this truth because sometimes I masquerade as an old fortune-telling Gypsy woman and other times I pretend to be a Nobleman's daughter with a terrible crotch infection living out in the country."

"What the fuck are ya' talkin' about ya' ugly fat bitch?" Mr. Nodicka boisterously exclaimed. "I thought that when King Hineymunch's *rain* stopped then my *reign* would begin!"

"That's what the fuck you think new Kingy!" the livid Princess' imperatively exclaimed. "I'm really a repugnant witch with supernatural powers. And so while you and Baron Scarecrow obey my every command and whim," the new Queen of Warsaw declared, "I'll just pretend that I'm a horse giving you plenty of fuckin' irrelevant instructions and directives."

And much to Mr. Nodicka and Baron Scarecrow's bewilderment, the new Queen began neighing and whinnying incessantly like a filly from Philly' in heat.

"All's Well That Ends Well"

Act I

The setting for "All's Well That Ends Well" is Rossillon, a section of southern France on the border with Spain not far from the *Pyrenees Mountains* and in proximity to the *Mediterranean*. The story takes place in the 1500s with the second Count of Rossillon dying and his son Bertram becoming the new Count. After the funeral young Count Bertram, his mother Countess of Rossillon and the inimitable Count LeFew (an emissary to the funeral from the King of France) were nostalgically reminiscing the past and slowly constructing the stage for the present and the future. Count Bertram was quite disturbed upon evaluating his current situation.

"Shit Mother!" the young Count Bertram exclaimed. "I'm now a damned ward of the King just like the waif wench Helen is a ward to you. These French jerk-off aristocratic rules really suck! Now against my will I must go away from good old familiar Rossillon and live in the King's court at Paris. My father's dead and I have to leave his estate and finally learn how to be a gentleman! Now if that doesn't really suck I don't know what the hell does!"

"How the hell do you think I feel Bertram about this unfortunate developing crap?" the Countess of Rossillon questioned her distraught too-big-for-his-britches son. "I've lost my second husband and now I'm losing you with your being away to learn how to properly dunk doughnuts into porcelain teacups and how to formally set silverware and gold-plated dishes on tables and also mastering where to place the silver candelabra. You dear Bertram could learn all of that picayune nonsense, if you haven't absorbed it already, right here in your native Rossillon."

"The King's court will teach young Count Rossillon a few important things," Count LeFew declared. "I trust Master Bertram that you show the King of France a few basic courtesies like honoring his curfews."

"And may I remind you Bertram that His Majesty is very sick suffering from the combination of a devastating venereal disease and a terrible chest and abdominal ulcer that's approximately three foot in length," the upset Countess of Rossillon added. "In fact young Bertram, my second husband, God rest his' ornery soul, who incidentally suffered from the same maladies as my first spouse was expected to outlive our revered King. Is there any hope Count

LeFew of His Majesty's recovery or am I being too damned optimistic here?"

"The revered King has abandoned a few of his more orthodox physicians," Count LeFew pointed out, "but a few remain at his disposal to diagnose and treat his few deadly maladies. But few realists actually believe that the King will ever recuperate in less than a few years."

"Allow me to introduce my fellow mourners to the young Lady Helen, whose father was an acclaimed alchemist and also a suspected sorcerer," the Countess sadly stated. "She has become my dependent ward but I staunchly refuse to keep her in the mansion's psycho' ward with you, my Bertram. I'm sure that if Lady Helen's father had lived he could've formulated a wonderful elixir that could've cured the King's terrible physical afflictions, of which only a few we are aware."

"I've known a few quack weirdo alchemists in my time," Count LeFew angrily indicated. "And of those few totally demented experimenters only a few of the few were engaged in legitimate and beneficial enterprises."

"Helen's recently deceased father was quite famous in his lowly alchemy profession, which as you know in this primitive and antiquated day and age is on a rung directly below the oldest profession, and I'll not prostitute myself to mention its inferior name," the Countess of Rossillon articulated. "But I'm sure Count LeFew that you've heard of the famous genius Gerard de Narbon, an amazing ingredient mixer who had possessed an international reputation."

"Yes Countess, I've heard a few complimentary remarks about Helen's renowned father Gerard de Narbon," Count LeFew confirmed to the grieving widow. "But if de Narbon knew a few things about finding an *immorality*, er, I meant to say finding an immortality formula, he could've lived a few years longer himself and actually outlived more than a few genetically inferior incest-created French kings."

"What is the King specifically anguishing and languishing from?" young Count Bertram asked LeFew.

"A few unspeakable communicable diseases along with a fistula, a chest and intestinal ulcer extending more than a few feet from his nipples to his testicles," LeFew recollected and stated. "Only a few noblemen and a few physicians at court know exactly what the hell's wrong with him."

"I never ever heard of a fistula before!" the inexperienced and immature Count Bertram asked. "It sounds a little like it's a musical instrument! On second thought one would imagine that a fistula is an inflammation or deformity of the fist!"

"I've heard a few asshole suppositions asked in my time but few have been more stupid than that one," LeFew chastised the upstart Bertram. "Now Countess, tell me a few things about this intriguing Lady Helen, the daughter of the hated wizard by more than a few, that deceased infamous fellow Gerard de Narbon," Count LeFew queried the sobbing grieving widow, who was entirely dressed and veiled in black.

"Dear Helen was de Narbon's sole soul child who likes fast music and the darling has sincere aspirations of becoming a soul child," the disconsolate Countess explained. "I intend to provide for her the best of educations and dear Helen shows a particular affinity to follow in her renowned father's small footsteps and become an alchemist, a most dangerous profession indeed for as you know many chemical wizards are burned at the stake by prejudiced narrow-minded mentally psycho' people professing to be devout Christians. Finally LeFew, I wish to keep young Helen honest, good and chaste so please be careful in her presence. Don't say anything obscene or lewd to offend her innocent ears."

"I'm sure that your continued warm praise Countess will produce a few tears cascading down dear Helen's cheeks," Count LeFew observed and remarked.

"I wonder if her ass's cheeks are sweating just like her facial one's usually are, ha, ha, ha!" young insensitive Bertram criticized and mocked.

"Bertram! Watch your tongue while you still have one wagging in your mouth!" the elderly Countess admonished her all-too-cynical son. "Pay no attention to my obnoxious son and heir," the Countess advised the mourning Helen. "Brash bungling Bertram really desperately needs to learn all the pleasantries and courtesies that the King's court has to offer."

"I do feel sorrow at your tremendous loss Countess, for it reminds me of my dear father's passing and of the King's terrible suffering also," young Helen de Narbon sobbed. "There's entirely too much misery and travail in this life, much too much for mere mortals to endure."

"A few pearls of wisdom originating from a babe's mouth," LeFew said. "A few moderate griefs are indeed the right of the dead but excessive sorrow is the enemy to more than a few of the privileged living."

"Mother," Bertram said to the Countess, "please bestow on me your' holy blessing even though you've never ever been ordained a deaconess or a witch. And I want my inheritance as soon as I get back from the King's ass-backwards all-too-snotty pompous pig aristocratic court. I desire to possess what is rightfully mine!"

"There are a few major disadvantages to being overly impetuous," Count LeFew scoffed at young Bertram, "so act the opposite of how the few of us know you normally abnormally behave!"

"Bertram, may you grow in wisdom as well as in height," the black veiled Countess prayed aloud, "and for the sake of French civilization may you exit puberty quicker than you had entered it. You hereby have your birthmark, er, I mean birthright Bertram, and my sage advice is to do wrong to no one otherwise you'll get your puny ass kicked and eliminated like your loudmouthed recently buried father did. Like father, like son, so the all-too-true maxim goes. Learn to be judicious, discreet and wise my son!"

"May young Bertram have few enemies and very few problems for the rest of his life although everyone present here in this room knows that with few exceptions that wishful thinking is impossible," Count LeFew reluctantly congratulated the heir to the vast and sprawling Rossillon estate. "Now Countess," LeFew graciously continued, "Bertram and I must be on our way to Paris and we'll stop at a few select inns along our journey for a few libations."

"Farewell Bertram, farewell LeFew!" the Countess said breathing a sigh of relief for her frivolous and sarcastic son's departure. "Have a safe trip Bertram and keep your dangling noodle limp and dry between your legs! That's the best way to stay out of trouble because believe me when I say that hungry lower class pussy is big dangerous trouble everywhere in France, let alone throughout the rest of Europe!"

"Farewell pretty Lady and good luck on your few studies and experiments," LeFew commented to the weeping Helen de Narbon. "And may few alchemists excel beyond your' future few accomplishments."

Bertram and LeFew promptly left the mansion's mourning chamber and mounted two horses with their ultimate destination Paris. The very relieved Countess soon exited the dismal room and then stepped to another section of the manor house. Through a window she observed the men climb upon their horses.

'Oh, I think I love the brash and arrogant Bertram,' Helen romanticized. 'But crap, I'm just a poor lass with a firm ass and the young Count's a man of wealth, title and nobility. Perhaps if I can concoct a magic potion I could gain the callow son-of-a-bitch, er, I mean upstart son-of-a-bastard Bertram's attention and then possibly he'll look more favorably on me. It's a long cannon ball shot, but what the hell? It's worth a try. Oh Christ! My slit is getting damp just thinking about him desiring me! I must change my dirty thoughts before dampness turns to embarrassing wetness resulting in reflexive rubbing and then I'll definitely have to change my very saturated underwear!'

Later Parolles, a knavish friend and disciple of Bertram entered the mourning room early that afternoon. Parolles, a scoundrel recently out of jail on parole, had a bad reputation for being an avid instigator and an uncouth insolent troublemaker.

"Hello fair chemistry queen," Parolles greeted the usually shy Helen. "Seldom am I in the presence of such majestic royalty."

"If I'm a queen," the impoverished Helen sullenly replied, "then you're the Czarina of Russia after undergoing a sex change operation. I understand from Rossillon gossip that you're a companion of handsome Count Bertram who has arrived here for the funeral and actually, that's the only reason I feel compelled to even speak with you."

"Precious Lady, are you presently meditating on losing your virginity?" Parolles vulgarly asked. "Is that why you're so sad?"

"Frankly, and I say *that* word because we're conversing here in France, I'm meditating on how the hell to successfully avoid you," Helen eloquently responded, endeavoring to articulate elegantly like a sophisticated noblewoman. "Men are indeed the enemy of women's chastity. Therefore, since you sound like a fellow of military background Parolles, how may I barricade my good spirit so that I can adequately protect it against you and your vile verbal bombardments?"

"If either Bertram or I use physical force against you, you' destitute country waif wench," the crude Parolles hypothesized and expressed, "then little lady the laws are on the side of male chauvinism and the male ego. I could rape you right this second and not worry one iota about suffering any legal consequences."

"You're a coarse brazen brute and how dare you insult my values and my religion with your indiscreet oral whorehouse rambling," the insulted sensitive girl chided. "You male animals are intolerable two-legged beasts and if you persist in your uncivil gross impertinence I'll loudly scream and summon the Countess of Rossillon."

"Your futile defense against my amorous advances would only represent a temporary obstacle," the discourteous and repugnant Parolles countered. "I'll take what I want when I want and you'll have little recourse other than to enjoy my penetration. Let's face facts you disillusioned village wench. Your lowlife virginity is worthless without any status or royal name to sufficiently protect you from an unsavory cad predator such as myself."

"If all men were like you' then I'd prefer dying in my old age as a frustrated virgin," the all-too-sensitive Helen protested. "Now I shall follow through on my insistence of summoning the Countess with a boisterous scream should you continue to speak to me like a rude noxious barbarian."

"If your filthy mother was a lousy virgin then you could've never been fuckin' born," the despicable Parolles ridiculed the already berated girl. "Virginity should be a sinful crime punishable by death I say. Chastity is a damned woman's way of saying 'screw you' while refusing to be screwed at all! And when you're lying on your lousy deathbed with a shriveled-up dry-welled cunt you'll finally understand wench that you' had lived your entire fucked-up life in pleasure-less vain!"

"You' tasteless inconsiderate monster!" Helen objected to her unsolicited treatment. "I'll scream and beckon the Countess this very second if you don't begin conducting yourself like a civilized gentleman instead of like a manner-less primitive savage. I detest the social disparity between you and me and if you represent what the suavity of French aristocratic culture is, then I'm truly glad that I'm just a poor uneducated pauper alchemist's daughter."

"Now that Bertram is away to Paris to learn how to hop into bed with dignified sophisticated women according to the rules of proper etiquette," Parolles disrespectfully stated, "then I suppose that I'll be porking and sodomizing you before he eventually returns and gets the opportunity for sloppy seconds. I predict that your delicious hair pie will be all mine, ha, ha, ha!"

"You rude reprehensible animal! Count Bertram is ten times the gentleman you'll ever be and I hardly even know you, you demented sex fiend," the pristine Helen volleyed back. "I trust that Count Bertram shall return and punish your uncouth insolence after he too learns how to treat a lady with respect and decency."

"The only thing that you can be trusting in Helen de Narbon is *him* thrusting his hard dick deep into your honey well just as I plan on doing soon when I too return from Paris," the obscene and whore-minded former soldier declared. "Now if you were a wealthy harlot instead of a poor beautiful virgin bitch, then there's a slim chance that I might act more honorably towards you and your desirable non-veteran pussy."

"Of all the unmitigated gall!" Helen chastised her relentlessly crude antagonist. "I hope your disgusting penis rots off your disgusting body and I pray that you must stand there watching a hungry rat chew, eat and swallow it!"

Much to the abused girl's relief a page entered the room and interrupted the intense argument. Fortunately Helen's threatened dignity had been temporarily salvaged.

"Monsieur Parolles, my Lord the distinguished Count calls for you. He demands that you meet him at the estate's entrance and accompany him to Paris. I have your horse ready for the journey."

"Farewell little Helen with the big virginity problem!" Parolles bade his most recent object of torment. "Some day either Count Bertram or I will return to snatch your snatch, or perhaps we can have a merry threesome going! Ha, ha, ha!"

"Monsieur Parolles, your black heart was born under a black star in a black universe I never wish to explore!" Helen cleverly answered.

"For your information Helen de Narbon I was born under Mars and I know it mars your day when I mention it," Parolles nastily replied. "All good soldiers are born under Mars so that when they're finished fighting the enemy wars they can then begin enjoying the whore wars."

"I'm not a promiscuous hooker and I vastly resent being referred to as one!" Helen vehemently protested as the suddenly aroused page stood there in the background rubbing his genitals and involuntarily licking his lips. "I hope your ugly rectum falls off your anatomy while you're riding your horse to Paris!"

"That'll never happen because I'm so full of shit that the great weight of my intestines will keep my ass attached to my body!" Parolles devilishly returned in a rare display of self-satire. "That's the principal difference between me and you fair damsel! I know my shit stinks and you pretend that shit doesn't exist either inside my ass or inside yours!"

Parolles reluctantly exited the room accompanied by the horny page while Helen reviewed in her mind the terrible insults to which she had just been exposed. 'Why was I ever born into this apathetic treacherous savage world?' the modest girl regretted. 'I must focus all my energies in a constructive pursuit to get my mind off of vile men and their evil habits and inclinations. I know exactly what I must do! I must occupy myself developing a wonderful formula to cure the King's chest ulcer and remedy his various mysterious venereal disease infections!'

* * * * * * * * * * * *

Young Count Bertram and his disreputable aide the dastardly knave Parolles (along with Count LeFew) finally arrived at the French King's palace and the Monarch impatiently awaited the Count of Rossillon's belated introduction. Cornets then announced the Count's presence but coincidentally the ailing King was preoccupied discussing current events with his narrow-minded political guidance counselors.

"I refuse to take sides in the war between Florence and Siena until it's perfectly damned clear who the victor is going to be," the King opined to his yes-men advisers. "As you know I hate to be on the losing side of anything, including life. I curse this son-of-a-bitchin' three-foot-long ulcer ornamenting my frail chest. I only wish that my erect dick were as long. And I totally abhor these confounded debilitating venereal maladies I have but I've found a degree of solace nostalgically recalling how I had contracted the son-of-a-bitchin' sex diseases."

"Your accurate analysis of your plight is most astute!" the First Lord praised his King. "The war in Italy is of little consequence unless its incivility spills over into France. At least that's my unbiased opinion on the matter!"

"My pompous cousin in Austria informs me by messenger that the Florentines are enlisting my support," the King confidentially divulged, "but if those pusillanimous pussies need support I'll send them a wagon load of bras for their wives' flabby tits," the demented King laughed.

"Your sense of humor is hilarious and it magnificently transcends your many potentially lethal afflictions!" the First Lord falsely lauded. "Have you ever fancifully considered an anonymous career in Vaudeville even though we all know that *that* unsavory activity is at least ten levels below your high status as Our Liege?"

"Let's see what the Tuscans do with their fleet of elephants in regard to the imminent Italian war," the King commented while ignoring the First Lord's zany remarks about him entering French Burlesque Vaudeville as a two-bit stand-up comedian.

"Let's hope that the Florentines and the Senoys kick the shit out of each other so that *our* cowardly armies can march into northern Italy and take over the Tuscan wasteland by default," the Second Lord suggested.

The cornets again sounded and a third more alert Lord escorted Count LeFew and Count Bertram (attended by the repulsive pest Parolles) to the throne. All eyes present in the opulent chamber stared at the new arrivals.

"May I present to Your Majesty the Count Bertram of Rossillon," the First Lord announced. "If you recall Your Majesty young Bertram's ninety-year-old father has recently died of complications resulting from venereal diseases contracted on various sexual escapades while he' had been accompanying you on several extended amorous adventures."

"Ah yes indeed," the forgetful weak King acknowledged and recollected. "Young Bertram, I trust that you've inherited your father's enviable genetics including his nationally acclaimed and notorious donkey dick."

"Yes Your Majesty," Bertram admitted with an uncharacteristic blush appearing on his normally pallid cheeks, "and I've memorized our secret French screwing motto, 'For God we thrust'!"

"Very good Count Bertram!" the King lauded and applauded. "Very good indeed! Your father and I had been dear friends for many decadent decades and we shared many loose whores and bitches in our random travels both at home and abroad on board all broads wherever we roamed, ha, ha, ha! Anyway Bertram," the King chortled much to the amusement of his mimicking court advisers, "it's too bad that the goddamned sand ran out of your father's hourglass. It's also too fuckin' bad that nature gives each of us only one hourglass to enjoy. It makes me mighty pissed-off Count Bertram that I may soon succumb to the same two VDs that plagued your father's health and besides that lousy horseshit I have an enormous ulcer that won't quit eating-up my chest and my abdomen. In fact I constantly experience widespread abominable abdominal pain!" the King winced as he farted excessively loud, nearly blasting the toupee right off of the First Lord's head. "But from your father I had learned humility, which in truth has taught me absolutely not a fuckin' thing! I've concluded young Bertram

145

that pride, ego, greed and sex are what keeps us male chauvinist pigs going, wouldn't you agree with my analysis?"

"Without a doubt Your Highness!" Bertram readily concurred. "Those cited motivations you've just mentioned are definitely what keeps my restless ass going! Your royal speech My King is so excellent that it should earn you royalties! Ha, ha, ha!"

"It does, you' young impulsive Asshole!" the King rebuked his wise-ass Count. "It's called taxes and tribute! They're the neat royalties that I collect each and every day! But I must tell you Bertram that your father's demise is a great catastrophe because it forewarns me of my own frail mortality and impending death. I shall courageously fight this unfair snuffing-out of my life!" the King shouted before inhaling a larger quantity of snuff. "That's enough snuff!" the Monarch yelled as he violently smashed the unclosed snuff box into the First Lord's stomach, thus releasing a cloud of powdery dust that made everyone standing around the throne start sneezing snot and prodigious-sized boogers all over the formerly immaculate regal chamber.

"This is great fabulous entertainment Your Excellency!" Count Bertram approved as Parolles and Count LeFew nodded their heads indicating their wholehearted appreciation and amusement.

"The King is always good for a few jolly laughs!" LeFew jested. "It's a good thing I'm not made out of ceramics because his few comments really crack me up! Ha, ha, ha! And for more than a few times too! Ha, ha, ha!"

"And for how long was that quack alchemist Gerard de Narbon at your father's side prior to your old man's passing?" the Second Lord curiously asked Bertram while the failing ailing King wiped his mouth and nose with his silk sleeves and the First Lord stooped over to retrieve his toupee from the white marble floor.

"About a half year," Bertram recalled and answered. "And when the old fart experimenter finally died, my father, lacking the old man's meticulous care, methods and diligence, well Your Majesty, Pop's vulnerable ass was trapped and promptly apprehended by the Grim Reaper too!"

"I truly wish that the renowned-but-indigent wizard Gerald de Neighbor, er, I mean to say Gerard de Narbon was still living so that he could treat me even though he was a poor destitute scoundrel and couldn't treat anyone to anything! Ha, ha, ha! What did the alchemist die from Bertram?"

"I'm not sure," the young Count of Rossillon said, "but I believe it sounded something like Narbon monoxide poisoning!"

* * * * * * * * * * *

The Countess of Rossillon was sitting in her mansion's drawing room sketching a picture of a well-endowed male nude on her easel's canvas when an alert Steward entered and told her a secret that she found to be rather disgusting.

"What I have alluded to is indubitably true," the gay Steward maintained while he stood there and admired the naked male sketch being artistically produced. "I've heard it with my own eyes and seen it with my own ears."

"Your character and reputation Steward are as suspect as those of the lowly Fool that has just entered my drawing room from his designated side door," the Countess stated as she noticed her inane impish Clown appear on the scene. "I also have good reason to believe that you two imbeciles are sleeping with and sodomizing each other! I can tell by the way you're presently screw-tinizing my artistic rendition!"

"I pardon the unfortunate intrusion Countess," the impish Clown began his brief narration. "But hear me out for I'm a poor asshole while many rich aristocratic assholes are being damned to hell by their frivolous antics. This is my humble entreaty! I wish to marry the servant girl Isbel and seek your distinguished permission."

"Why do you want to get married since you're a gay faggot perfectly happy porking my Steward as if he was actually my Stewardess!" the Countess challenged her Clown. "I believe you have your gender holes mixed-up although I think that to the best of my knowledge that both men and women possess exit hollows commonly known as assholes!"

"I need to get laid to determine if I'm a bona fide bisexual or just an ordinary homosexual," the Fool reasoned and honestly revealed. "The only thing worse than gender orientation is gender disorientation. Do you follow my gist Countess?"

"You Clown have been a wicked creature ever since I've employed your stupid moronic ass," the Countess of Rossillon admitted. "And I suppose that marrying a woman is a form of repentance and will increase the size of your family and relatives and allow you to have standard conventional sex with a wife or a real live woman for the first time. But be wary Clown that your all-too-queer friends are not also your enemies, nor your enemas. That's why it's a lot friggin' safer to have casual acquaintances than so-called close friends."

"I don't give a wet or hard shit if my best friends kiss and screw my future wife Isbel or not," the Fool asserted. "While they're busy with their' activities I'll be busy either pumping their wives silly or being behind the barn or in the hayloft shacking-up with your long-dicked Steward. I just gotta' find out Countess if I'd rather pump a woman or be porked up the yazoo by your well-endowed Steward. That's the principal reason why I, your dedicated Jester desire getting hitched to Isbel!"

"Stop pestering me you dirty-mouthed calumnious worthless knave!" the Countess yelled. "You're distracting me from my nude drawing of your muscular lover, the Steward."

"I thought that the person in the sketch looked mighty familiar, but I couldn't tell his exact identity for certain because you haven't yet completed outlining his enviable erection," the irascible Fool stated.

"Why have you come inside my mansion Fool?" the Countess impatiently rankled. "Can't you see you're rudely interrupting my artistic reverie?"

"If my name were Parson Monius I'd be a much richer man!" the Fool ridiculously uttered. "But my purpose in coming was to announce that Lady Helen wishes to speak with you, or you with her, I can't fuckin' remember which."

"Yes clumsy Fool, Helen's wizard father bequeathed her to me and I only wish that I could transfer my title and a portion of my wealth to her in my will," the Countess disclosed to the bungling blundering un-sanctimonious Clown. "I absolutely adore young Helen and will guard her chastity with a vengeance against any man trying to immorally pilfer it."

"Madam, if I may speak frankly," the gay Steward politely interrupted, "I was standing near young Helen de Narbon and overheard her speaking to herself expressing in perverted poetic verses how she had the hots for your aberrant son Bertram. She went-off the friggin' deep end when the whimsical girl romanticized about your fucked-up son Bertram being her knight in shining armor rescuing her from an evil tower of despair guarded by a thousand fire-breathing dragons. That's why I've rushed over here to report to you her sudden insanity!"

"Let's keep this tawdry secret between the three of us despite the truth that a secret is no longer a secret when told to a second party," the Countess implored her gossipy servants. "Now you two loony psychopaths leave me alone so that I may privately confer with Lady Helen before she accidentally kills herself in her imaginary Troy."

The oddball servants sauntered out of the mansion through their respective doors and a moment later Helen de Narbon entered the edifice's massive drawing room, which actually had never drawn anything of merit.

"Hello dear Helen," the Countess greeted from her leather-seated stool situated behind her easel. "I clearly remember when I was your age, so eager, so anxious and so energetic. I felt tingling rushes all over my curvaceous body and those fantastic sensations always settled in my clitoris, which then naturally throbbed and pulsated like an enormous male erection."

"Why have you summoned me to your drawing room?" Helen asked. "Do you want me to demonstrate discipline and listen to your sex life history?"

"I'm like a mother to you even though you've probably called me much worse appellations," the Countess coyly began her lecture. "I would adopt you if I were certain that Bertram wouldn't have conniptions and throw tirades and diatribes all over Rossillon. Now then," the concerned Countess proceeded to explain her purpose, "I have an inkling that you're in love with my selfish, ingrate, avaricious, jerk-off shit-brained son. Now how could I possibly make you my adopted daughter if you would then marry my son? The scandal would be unbearable with everyone in France prattling about how incest abounds in my family!"

"I don't want to be Count Bertram's sister," Helen stated, "because if *we* ever marry then it indeed would look and sound like incest. I'd rather remain poor little Helen de Narbon than to suffer public humiliation!"

"You're even more fucked-up than warped Bertram is!" the Countess marveled and accused. "Lots of luck Helen with your' silly naïve fantasy! Bertram is excessively wild, impulsive, covetous and ambitious. He wants to marry the daughter of someone in the King's court, not for love but for goddamned power and prestige," the Countess elucidated. "I truly admire your noble idealism and your far-fetched aspiration but quite candidly your dream is a living nightmare. My covetous son wants in a woman everything that you are not: wealth, power, authority, perverted sex, fellatio, cunnilingus, more fellatio and finally social status. I fear dear Helen that your magical fancy is but unattainable fantasy. Do you actually love my fucked-up son?"

"Yes Countess, with all my heart and with all my' inexperienced vagina," Helen intimated and revealed. "As you know I'm a pauperous, honest and vulnerable waif. And I'm aware that I futilely love in vain and that my devotion for Bertram is not reciprocal. I know so because for the first time in my life I desire to get laid right through the center of the strongest of mattresses."

"If I sent you to Paris to pursue your foolish fantasy," the Countess said to the grieving kneeling girl, "what will you accomplish from your escapade?"

"My father left behind some very special prescriptions for potent un-patented medicines," Helen shared with the influential Countess. "I must first focus my attention on curing the King of his debilitating ulcer and then healing his insidious venereal diseases and my next goal would be to develop an aphrodisiac that will make Bertram want to screw the hell out of me, with or without the strongest mattress in the world. Those particular desires dear Countess would be my primary ambitions after arriving in Paris."

"You'll be amply castigated and mocked by the King's ruthless physicians and surgeons," the Countess predicted. "They'll debunk and describe you' as a poor uneducated virgin girl who doesn't know her cunt from her asshole and who wipes one orifice for the other! Beware of those jealous wipers, er, vipers who are so indoctrinated into their fucked-up materialistic sciences that the inflexible bastards shun and abhor the simple truths that you'll be genuinely presenting and recommending!"

"The lucky stars in heaven along with your blessing and my father's good records will guide me through the men's prejudiced staunch opposition," Helen ascertained and related. "I promise to cure His Grace's out-of-control ulcer and also his malignant VD problems so that he can screw his kinky high-society women with complete confidence once again along with everybody else in the whole goddamned country."

"Well my precious Helen, contrary to conventional logic you've convinced me to wholeheartedly endorse your expedition to Paris and your stay at the King's court," the Countess decided and declared. "You have my leave and my love. But I insist that you remain a pure and chaste virgin or else your ingenious experiments might all end in total disaster! If you lose your asshole virginity then I predict that disastrous consequences are sure to result! Heed my sage advice dear Helen! Keep your cunt out of the hunt!"

Act II

The King of France sat squirming and wriggling about (because of enlarged hemorrhoids from sitting and shitting too long and too often) in his throne room when cornets flourished to gain his attention. Soon the Ruler spoke with several glory-seeking courtiers ready to depart and then participate on opposite sides in the Florentine War.

"Farewell my good Lords foolishly seeking glory while leaving the comforts and luxuries of my elegant court," the King cavilierly addressed the young cavaliers as he vigorously scratched his ass. "And I don't give a shit if you both get killed because either Florence or Siena will think that I've sent forces to defend them and thus I'll gain their separate favor, regardless whoever the hell wins the damned war."

"On the contrary Your Worship," the First Lord said, "I hope that all your brave young knights will return alive so that they may witness and cherish your speedy recovery from your maladies."

"Succeed in Italy my fine knights so that my wimpy army can storm into that foreign country and rape the cities and pillage the women, er, I mean you oughta' just reverse my last fucked-up statement to fully comprehend my intent! And when problems flare up," the King said while gingerly massaging his inflated piles, "be equal to the task and rub them off, er, I mean rub them out whenever you can. Do not shrink, er I mean shirk from your duties, you *paris*-sitic ass kissers!"

"And fair knights," the First Lord sanctimoniously added, "watch out for those flirting Italian broads. It's hard to tell an Italian lady from an Italian whore. Don't lose the battle of love before you go into combat fighting and knocking the shit out of each other!"

The naïve glory-seeking knights proudly exited the throne room and Bertram and Parolles soon entered while the King instructed his Second Lord to get his bath ready so that he could soak his hurting ass in hot steaming water.

"Are you two gentlemen going into the war too?" the First Lord asked Count Bertram and his aide Parolles who incidentally had AIDS. "If so don't forget to pillage the villages!"

"War is hell and I oppose doing that stupid bullshit all over again!" Parolles answered out of turn and out of rank. "Who needs to have your ass and testicles blown off by an errant cannonball?"

"I want to go but the King insists that I'm too young and too inexperienced to get my ass kicked and my balls blown off!" Bertram spoke up. "Maybe by next year my ass and balls will be big enough to venture over to Italy', screw some horny broads there and then during a moment of weakness allow the enemy the opportunity to blow my balls and ass off!"

"There is honor and courage in your indecipherable words!" the First Lord commended. "You two assholes sound like you deserve to be ass-less!"

"I'm thinking about sending you off to the Florentine War just to break your stones Monsieur Parolles," the King grumpily stated. "You're a veteran of such childish bullshit and stand a good chance of coming back to France alive. And besides, I hear that Mars dotes on you when he doesn't occasionally suck you off!"

"Yes Your Majesty, I'll be ready to leave for combat duty upon command," Parolles replied. "I know for a fact that the best sex, either straight or gay is in Italy and I'll gladly serve you there."

"Until I call for either of you two imbeciles, get the fuck out of here!" the King hollered at Count Bertram and Parolles as *his* royal piles encircling his anal ring piled even higher. "What's next on my goddamned agenda before my steaming hot bath is ready?"

Count LeFew stepped forward to cordially address the King. The nobleman's demeanor was very formal and straight-laced, just like his pink panties that were neatly camouflaged from the court's scrutiny and amusement.

"May I say a few words to Your Majesty," LeFew began. "I have come before you to ask your blessing and mercy on a fellow, a deceased gentleman that has served France well in developing a few exotic formulas in the controversial science area of alchemy."

"How the fuck can I bless a dead person?" the King yelled. "LeFew, are you trying to say that this man's prescriptions will cure my ulcer, my VD cases and my blazing hemorrhoids all at the same fuckin' time? If so, bring the fuckin' bastard back to life and I'll gladly grant him an audience!"

"I've seen with my own two eyes a few medicines that can bring a few stones to life," LeFew claimed. "These few medicines will make you dance around like a proud peacock and sing like a hyperactive canary. But I must tell you that this remarkable man with a few cures that I'm referring to happens to be a she!"

"What the fuck are you talking about?" the King wrangled. "I don't want any bi-gender asshole experimenting with my gonads!"

"No Your Majesty, you don't understand a few things," LeFew clarified. "The famous alchemist Gerard de Narbon recently died a few months back, leaving his daughter a few of the secrets of his groundbreaking research, although poor de Narbon had few coins to build and labor in a normal laboratory. Now don't underestimate young Helen de Narbon, who knows a few significant things about chemistry and a few about Narbon monoxide poisoning too."

"Bring in this lady trickster so that I may evaluate her knowledge of an obscure subject I don't know shit about," the King ordered LeFew. "I don't know a damned thing about the science of art or the art of science, but since my friggin' life and health are suspended here in the balance you'd better damned sure allow the industrious bitch an audience while I put my soothing hot steam bath on hold."

"It'll only take a few minutes to get her in here," Count LeFew promised the royal pain-in-the-ass.

"LeFew is more full of shit than even I am!" the King told his First Lord. "He's even more full of shit than you are!"

LeFew re-entered the throne room with the nervous and anxious peasant girl. "Here she is, Helen de Narbon to say a few words to you!" the Count introduced his newfound healer.

"This inventive young lady must've created wings to get here so swiftly," the King said to LeFew. "I hope she's not going to wing it through her presentation!"

"Tell the King a few of the things you've told me," LeFew coaxed Helen. "Be careful Child, for the King has executed more than a few quacks that have made promises they couldn't deliver. I'll leave you here a few minutes while I attend to a few important matters in the adjoining room." Count LeFew exited the throne room and the King gazed upon his newly discovered "charlatan miracle worker."

"Now tell me young Helen, tell me a little about your father and his final clandestine experiments," the King insisted. "For example, did he have a remedy for my' hemorrhoids, which at the moment are more troublesome and more painful than either my tremendous-sized ulcer or my bothersome venereal disease discomforts."

"My kind father gave me many recipes, er I mean prescriptions on his deathbed," Helen nervously explained. "I've boldly come to your court with the gift of his notes to cure you of your ulcer, your hemorrhoids and your sexually acquired diseases. But if prevention is always better than cure perhaps you should first watch what you eat and what you screw," Helen advised the Monarch. "Now I would love to use you as a guinea pig to learn all about the science of alchemy despite the fact that I have no degree in apothecary."

"Your statements are so crazy to believe that I have trouble doubting your exceptional claims or your marvelous veracity," the King assessed and said. "But please tell me more of your fascinating bullshit. For example, how can you be better versed in pharmacy than my physicians when the best learned and prestigious

153

doctors in all of France can't shrink my mammoth ulcer or decrease my king-sized hemorrhoids?"

"Doctors don't know shit about apothecary or about alchemy," Helen effectively argued. "Physicians only know how to treat patients while tricking them into believing that they know what the hell they're doing."

"Are you sure you aren't perpetuating a cruel and unusual hoax here?" the King angrily ranted. "I absolutely despise fucked-up quacks pretending to be professional healers who have in the past had their noggins decapitated for public exhibition."

"It won't hurt to try my unproven cures," Helen answered the unpredictable tyrant. "The worst that can happen is nothing, which has been the result of all your King's doctors and all your King's physicians. Trust in my experimental ability Your Highness and perhaps you'll cease your suffering, escape death's relentless clutches and be able to eat, sleep, shit, screw and suck like a young virile trooper again."

"Don't get my hopes up only to be deflated!" the King upbraided the industrious maiden. "I'll call for you should I feel I have to trust and solicit your services. I must consider all aspects and potential consequences before I reluctantly surrender my chest, dick and ass to your suspect practices."

"Look My King! I have confidence in what the hell I'm doing even though I've never cured a single person or a ham of a single disease," Helen intrepidly maintained. "I'm a chaste virgin and have the aid of Heaven on my side so I don't screw around when I treat someone, even a bizarre King like you. Judge me as an impostor if you like but please remember, I claim I can solve your medical problems when your asshole doctors claim they can not!"

"How long will it take for me to be cured according to your timetable?" the King curiously asked Helen. "Do I have to hang suspended in a smokehouse like a cured ham?"

"To quote Count LeFew," the girl valiantly stated, "it will take only a few days. And if I fail or if you die from my malpractice, er, I mean specialized treatment, I shall accept for my disgrace the punishment of execution."

"You seem to be possessed by either a blessed or an evil spirit that gives you uncanny confidence to make such extravagant claims," the King replied with a dumbfounded look on his face. "You seem to know your shit. Perhaps I should have you designing a new palace sewer system instead of placing credence in your competence as an aspiring alchemist. Forget the chemistry for a moment. Perhaps you can give me a physics formula instead so that I can finally take a non-bloody crap!"

"My father left me no such magic formula!" Helen confessed.

"And if you succeed in your crazy experiments and I am healed of all my fucked-up maladies," the King wondered and related, "then what should your reward be my fair chaste maiden?"

"Allow me to marry any palace Courtier or Lord of my choosing," Helen daringly and resolutely requested. "I wish to have my choice among the royal young studs of France so that my low and humble name can be proudly catapulted into cultural prominence. I wish to become a highly respected member of French aristocratic society."

"Take my trembling hand as proof of my word, for my word is my seal, and my seal is laying somewhere in the archive library room," the King informed his newly appointed employee. "Now for some remote inexplicable reason I trust you regardless that you've shown me no particular talent or demonstration to substantiate your wild promises. But if I die because of you Helen de Narbon," the King stressed, "then you don't have much of a fuckin' future to either think or worry about! And you'd better know your shit because half my dick has already rotted away!"

* * * * * * * * * * * *

The Countess of Rossillon urgently called for her Fool to dispatch the zany ignoramus on an important mission to Paris, not with-standing the fact that the awkward idiot had never left that isolated region of southern France.

"Listen-up you impudent wise-ass and go easy on the ludicrous bullshit equivocations," the Countess said to the Clown after he had entered the mansion from his personal side door. "If it weren't for my need for recreation you'd be a street mendicant begging for crumbs and wearing burlap for clothes. Now then freak-face, I'm dispatching you to the King's Court in Paris to deliver this vital letter to Helen, my undomesticated domestic ward."

"I might get lucky, entertain the King and get a high paying service commission as the official Court Jester," the Clown imagined and stated.

"I don't think so!" the Countess abruptly dismissed the Fool's unattainable ambition. "The King's suffering from some life-threatening illnesses and he doesn't want to put-up with your nonsensical frivolities. Does my explanation fit and synchronize with your lowbrow mentality?"

"Just like a barber's chair accommodates all size asses and all varieties of assholes and just like a kinky nun's lips fit against a horny Cardinal's throbbing pecker," the Clown creatively responded. "One size fits all!"

"I think you require about three centuries of charm school breeding and long-term discipline training to elevate yourself from asshole up to the rank of junior jerk-off!" the Countess chided her silly Fool. "You probably use your grimy clothes to wipe your fat ass, you gay cad!"

"Be careful how you address me for I might actually be an envelope in disguise," the simpleton Fool bantered. "And who the hell knows? Perhaps I shall return to Rossillon as a newly appointed King's courtier, the esteemed Lord Dumbass!"

"Fool, I've always been amused by your idiotic phraseology and by your jestering gesturing," the lady aristocrat said with a scowl on the Countess's countenance, "but keep aggravating me and your dumpy ass will wind-up in either a prison or in an insane asylum. And if those mediocre institutions reject you," the on-a-tear widow said, "I'll savagely whip you and pour vinegar onto all of your exposed lash wounds! In fact after my loyal Steward churns and whips the butter I'll simply have him churn and whip you!"

"What a novel way to have my tender ass whipped!" the Fool ridiculously quipped. "That oughta' whip me into shape!"

"Now stop acting like the fucked-up Fool that you are and take this essential letter to the King's Court in Paris and convey it to the charming Lady Helen de Narbon. And I want you to take this assignment seriously because I'm not blowing smoke up your ass but if you fail in completing it, I'll shove a chimney into your throat and blow billows of smoke down your trachea and into your already contaminated lungs, thus choking your ass to death."

"Anything else Countess?" the Joker joked.

"Yes!" the woman of means very audibly yelled. "Bring back a written response from my ward Helen and make sure it's not the same goddamned letter I had entrusted you with to take from Rossillon to Paris. Now Clown, haste makes waste so kindly take your good old time the next occasion you feel an intense need to take a wicked dump!"

* * * * * * * * * * * *

Count LeFew and the flamboyant-but-contemptible Parolles were debating the issue of miracles in one of the palace's parlors not far from the ostentatious King's throne room. LeFew was optimistic about the prospect of success regarding Helen's mysterious formulas but Parolles was a negative cynic and was totally skeptical of her "quack claims and endeavors."

"I agree that there have been few recorded or documented miracles in the last millennium and a half," LeFew conceded to Parolles, "and more than a few disbelieving atheists and apostates place credence in that supernatural stuff. Only a few of us staunch advocates still have faith in the wonders of the Almighty."

"Galen was the father of ancient medicine and Paracelus the pioneer researcher of modern anatomy and neither of those academic jerk-offs placed any validity in miracles and both of those acclaimed geniuses assessed the notion of miracles as unequivocal bullshit," Parolles equivocated. "Now *that* discourse just about exhausts my knowledge of medical history!"

"A few undocumented miracles still occur away from the scrutiny of the scientific community," Count LeFew disagreed, "but few scholars have over the course of history had the courage to author a few papers about them out of fear of a few decapitations that have happened to a few practitioners of divine healing in the past."

"Those that wait for miracles to happen fuckin' ignore reality and are blind to the goddamned truth," Parolles stubbornly argued. "Miracles are for narrow-minded religious zealots like you and not for an open-minded sophisticated philosopher and intellectual like me. Diogenes, as fucked-up as *he* was LeFew," the rogue said, "that' cynic happened to be the true founder of modern day knowledge."

"I speak in respect to a few saints and on behalf of the Almighty," the Count maintained. "A few of us still belief that the spiritual words presented in the *Bible* constitute a divine mystery that transcends both science and your malignant cynical bullshit."

"Poppycock and gibberish!" Parolles stubbornly countered.

"Be careful of a few things you say Parolles or else you'll burn for more than a few millennia in Hell. There' are but a few Christian ministers and a few Catholic priests that still believe in the phenomena of miracles. All the rest of the fools save but a few are blatant garrulous heretics," LeFew insisted.

"Let's get real LeFew! The King I'm sorry to predict will not recover from his grave medical problems because of a harebrained formula concocted by Helen's stupid old man," Parolles doubted and declared, "and if I fuckin' sound like a damned dubious atheist then I take pleasure in being the apostate you accuse me of being.

Oh shit! Here comes the King and your miracle worker Helen. Let's follow them and hear all about the girl's impending execution, ha, ha, ha!"

The pair' of side chamber kibitzers joined the procession of the King, Helen and the royal lords into the regal main throne room. Naturally LeFew expected the best and Parolles the worst for the diminutive and naïve Helen de Narbon.

"As all you skeptical self-aggrandizing imbeciles are my witnesses," the King began his sugarcoated praise of the common country girl, "I'm now fully cured of all my diseases and my dick is no longer decaying and rotting away. A spectacular miracle truly has happened. So before you gathered dunces ask me some irrelevant questions, let me express that I've promised young Helen de Narbon a husband and she may select a man, I hope, from the assembled courtiers. Thank God I'm a king and am fully excluded from the wench's choice because I prefer indulging in same-sex relationships," the King joked. "Now then Fair Maiden, scrutinize the noble bachelors standing before thine eyes and excretely, er, I mean discreetly take your husband. I emphasize that your power and authority to choose cannot be rejected by your selected candidate."

"I'd give anything to be the lucky nominee from among these few upstart lads," Count LeFew whispered to the still-in-shock Parolles. "A few of these little thin-bearded assholes should measure-up to Helen's few demanding qualifications, whatever the hell those few undefined criteria may be."

"Heaven's help has assisted me in restoring our King's good health," Helen prefaced her revelation. "I'm just a sincere and simple countryside damsel and I've already decided whom my lucky husband shall be."

"I wish the choice were me but there are few chances of that possibility because I'm more than a few decades older than Helen and I have few hairs on my head, under my armpits and around my almost non-existent dick," LeFew whispered to the still shocked Parolles, who was stunned at learning that the King had been cured.

"My wish being granted but not taken for granted by me," Helen diplomatically appraised her emotional decision, "I'll keep you all in suspense for a moment for I have a flair for the dramatic ensconced in my heart. Essentially I'm a frustrated thespian!"

"If anyone from the few nominees assembled should deny Helen," LeFew whispered to the still-incredulous Parolles, "then the

King should have one more dumb ass punk eunuch added to the few specimens that he already possesses."

"What the fuck did you say you old insane coot?" Parolles whispered back, finally snapping out of his stupor.

"I said that all but a few of these young bastards lined-up here are worthy of Helen's love not to mention her warm inviting bed," LeFew descriptively qualified and reiterated. "And more than a few of the bizarre bastards are pissed-off because Helen is not the bitch they each deeply desire for a cheating wealthy wife."

"I choose Bertram of Rossillon as my husband, a cad who when he dies will certainly become a cadaver," Helen stated much to the elation of all of the other candidates and much to the dismay of the momentarily flabbergasted Count Bertram.

"Well young Bertram," the King gleefully acknowledged as he scratched his hemorrhoid-free ass from force of habit, "it looks like you're the man and certainly not the best man at your not-yet-planned wedding, ha, ha, ha!"

"Your Highness, I have good blood flowing in my royal French veins and excellent semen being produced in my very potent testicles," Bertram claimed. "Yet Your' Majesty, I must marry a meager country wench who is nearly my sister by adoption at her insistence. Is not this a form of accidental incest?"

"Look Bertram, Helen has like a saint raised me from my sickbed just like the Lord had raised Lazarus from the tomb," the King lauded the girl. "Now you must agree to marry Helen under my authorization or else you're gonna' fuckin' be the next Lazarus without a resurrection! In your case Bertram, 'Incest is best'!"

"But this skinny waif is the daughter of a poor untitled weirdo wacko deceased alchemist!" Bertram strenuously objected. "She comes from an inferior origin, a low stock indeed, and the dame lacks the fine graces and bed skills of a cultured French lady!"

"Strange is your disdain for gorgeous Helen," the King publicly chastised the ungrateful opinionated Count. "Everybody's brown shit smells including both yours and hers. Great deeds often spring forth from those of little means, Joan of Arc being a prime example. Elevate yourself above *selfish* vileness young Bertram if you don't want to sell fish for the rest of your damned life, you ingrate dolt!" the King bellowed so all could hear. "Helen is fair, wise and pristine, and consequently she's so unlike your' tattered disreputable past. Now either consent to marrying her or else you'll be the victim of the first public castration and official male neutering at my court. Do I make myself clear or do your fucked-up hazy eyes still have cataracts?"

"But the destitute wench has no dowry to offer!" Bertram protested. "I need a nice payoff from a rich living father-in-law!"

"Virtue and kindness constitute Helen's dowry, you materialistic slime ball," the King admonished the unhappy dissenter. "Now either marry Helen or accept the ramifications of being a eunuch for the remainder of your sex-deprived life!"

"This is absolute total bullshit I'm being subjected to as your royal subject," Bertram demonstratively complained to His Majesty. "I'm being persecuted unjustly and I'm being regally screwed!" the Count balked as the other young courtiers all laughed their balls off at his predicament. "I can't possibly love this spaghetti-legged wench nor do I intend to. If I need be married then it'll be in title only, and merely as a legal bond. I'd rather screw a whore chicken than have intercourse with this homely-looking wallflower chick!"

"You've no choice or freedom in the matter you insubordinate bratty asshole!" the thoroughly upset perfectly healthy King ordered. "Now Bertram, either marry Helen or marry life-imprisonment. Those are your limited options you wet-behind-the-ears gigolo!"

"But I'm a rich aristocrat and this skinny bitch is a poor girl from the uncultured uncivilized boondocks!" Bertram protested.

"Look you lack-of-account Count," the agitated King commanded, "I insist that you stop being such a scornful kumquat. There's nothing defective about this comely girl who has benevolently saved my life. Learn honor and obey your King or die and then obey no one but Satan. Be loyal to your duty or, frankly speaking Bertram, I'll personally ban you from France without pity and you can spend the rest of your days in England or in some other totally fucked-up country like that," the livid King yelled. "Now Helen, take this radical youth by the gland, er, I mean by the hand and get the hell out of here before I lose my goddamned temper!"

"Your Majesty, haven't you forgotten to mention a few parting words!" Count LeFew reminded the aggravated Monarch.

"Yes, thank you LeFew," the Ruler acknowledged. "The favor of the King smiles upon this glorious marital contract and I command that an official church ceremony be conducted later this night by one of our senile pedophile priests," the King said, officially blessing the marriage bond Helen had stipulated. "Now let us go in peace and dili*gently* if not gently prepare for the anticipated wedding feast, which by my royal edict will be Dutch treat of course. And will one of my stable boys please groom the groom!"

After all parties concerned and all of the lords and counts left the throne room LeFew and Parolles stayed behind to review the extraordinary proceedings thst they had just witnessed.

"Monsieur," LeFew cheerfully commented, "your Rossillon buddy made a few errors but in the end it was wise of Count Bertram to recant his few objections to marrying Helen. Many were called to screw Helen but less than a few had been chosen, namely that doomed hedonistic scoundrel friend of yours."

"I admit I'm a stouthearted companion of Count Rossillon who as you know plans to inherit a whole county," Parolles academically explained. "But you're too old of a fart LeFew to realize that Count Bertram desires his absolute freedom and does not want to marry Helen or any other ambitious wench right now. This fucked-up marriage vow contract was performed all-too-expediently and was made to pacify the King's corrupt absolute will."

"Your few succinct words both speak and reek of virtual treason!" Count LeFew determined and criticized. "Life is full of more than a few travails and disappointments, especially a few appointments that turn-out to be disappointments. Learn to adjust to a few deviations and willingly accept a few travesties that the King renders upon your shoulders or else my dear fellow you'll die prematurely a disillusioned young buck that ain't worth a fuck!"

"My Lord LeFew, you bestow upon me a most egregious indignity, you moody grumpy pissed-off cantankerous old coot!" Parolles said and ridiculed. "You resent my youth and my energy and you're extremely jealous of my handsome virile physique."

"You're totally fucked-up Parolles, more than a few degrees above normal body temperature," Count LeFew firmly reproached the supercilious and haughty young snot. "You should be vexed with the fires of Hell on Earth in order to satisfactorily correct your more than a few errant ways. I don't know which is more fucked-up, your attitude or your philosophy! I do believe that you require both a few attitude adjustments and a few philosophy adjustments."

"Well you scurvy pock-faced antiquated Lord," the arrogant disdainful Parolles defiantly answered his good-intentioned elder, "I'll beat the shit out of you in a duel should you attempt to lecture me again on proper etiquette and expected behavior. And I won't pity your' goddamned age LeFew when I gladly slice your throat open with my trusty sword, you pathetic Methuselah-aged swine!

Stop perpetually berating me with all of your superfluous nonsense or else you'll surely die!"

But the wily LeFew had several high-value cards up his sleeve with which to play and the ball-breaker further antagonized the already steaming Parolles. "Now that your lord and master Count Bertram is just about officially married, being selected from a few qualified courtiers," LeFew said, "I understand that you have a new mistress you're going to screw through a few mattresses and much to your public embarrassment she no longer remains anonymous."

"What the fuck are you' driveling about now LeFew?" Parolles threatened reaching for his sword. "You're fuckin' pushing me to the threshold of committing murder! You must have a desire to die, a real death wish you old gimpy fuck!"

"The Devil and a few of his demons are your masters and lords and not the distastefully brash Count Bertram as you might think," LeFew cleverly remarked. "By my honor if I were your age again Parolles I'd smash and mash your face into flesh pulp a few times and your asshole would be wearing your nose after a few pretzel maneuvers that I had once studied and employed in other in-my-face altercations. You're nothing but a nauseating offense and an absolute disgrace to humanity, you feuding adolescent punk bully. You deserve to have a few of your bowels removed for I believe that you immediately require a few urgent brain operations."

"Tell me who my new mistress is or I'll barbarically kill you on the spot and feel no guilt about your passing to the after-world," Parolles vehemently yelled while partially removing his sword from its sheath.

"You're indeed an aimless loser vagabond Parolles," LeFew charged and insulted, "and I know few less deplorable individuals than thee. Now as for your mistress, she bears the name Florentine War. If you want to get laid she'll fuck you good before taking your last few breaths away!"

"Get the hell out of my sight you old cowardly codger before you die as if you yourself were participating in the goddamned Florentine War!" Parolles said and intimidated as he fully drew his sword and wielded it over his head.

As Count LeFew hastily scampered out of the chamber Count Bertram came in from the opposite direction to commiserate with his colleague in sin and frolic, the dastardly Parolles.

"I'm undone, unraveled and thoroughly pissed-off!" Bertram lamented and griped to his friend. "My reputation for being a lover has been ruined."

"What's the matter sweetheart?" Parolles joked as he skillfully imitated Helen's sweet innocent alto voice.

"Although I just swore marital vows with Helen in front of a solemn and sanctimonious pedophile priest and his seven gay altar boys," Bertram explained, "I'll not sleep with and screw the goody-goody-two-shoes Pollyanna wench. I'll turn homo' before I ever pork that studious female egghead."

"What are you going to do?" Parolles asked. "Offend the King's intentions? That faux pas wouldn't be a wise decision! His Majesty will have a fuckin' French hemorrhage!"

"I have an idea Parolles," Bertram facetiously suggested. "I'll secretly marry you and we'll elope to fight the Florentine War together. I think I'd rather sodomize you than break that childish Helen's microscopic cherry."

"I have news for you Count Bertram," Parolles replied. "I have no goddamned cherry inside my tight asshole!"

"I've heard that my mother has sent me important letters from Rossillon," Bertram remembered and revealed. "I wonder what their contents are? Maybe they're a fortunate series of suicide notes?"

"Probably more of *her* stupid shit that sounds quite much a facsimile to Count LeFew's stupid shit!" the pessimistic Parolles theorized and shared.

"Here's my plan my Confederate that might sound like a fucked-up caprice," Bertram whispered. "I'll send Helen back to my mother where she'll live a lonely child-like existence just like she had done before coming here to Paris. Then I'll run away to war with you in protest of the King's decision, for he definitely owes me a prize for consenting to marry Helen de Narbon and that gift he'll bestow upon me will be the liberty to fight in Italy."

"You're a marred married fool Count Bertram," Parolles ascertained and declared, "and you *have* been done wrong by your King, who has screwed you good by affording you a string-bean teenage wife whom you don't want to screw at all!"

* * * * * * * * * * * *

Helen had received a letter from the Countess of Rossillon that had been delivered by the sometimes-efficient Fool. The new bride anxiously opened the sealed envelope and discussed the missive's content with the imbecilic messenger.

"Oh Fool," Helen joyfully said, "my prospective mother and new mother-in-law greets me warmly. The Countess states in this letter that she's bundled and wrapped in three woolen afghans even though it's now the height of summer."

"She's dreadfully ill and is pretending that she's well so as not to upset you," the Fool told Helen. "The Countess is ill because she's sick and tired of her detestable son's bullshit antics!"

"My eccentric husband does exhibit some rather peculiar behaviors that I find both intriguing and disturbing," Helen revealed. "For instance what heterosexual man in his right mind has no desire to screw his newly begotten bride?"

"You got me on that one Lady Helen," the Fool amiably acknowledged. "I'll gladly volunteer to be your substitute husband in the honeymoon suite."

"No thanks you horny toad pecker head," Helen laughed. "I think I'd rather have sex with that son-of-a-bitch Parolles on a spiked board than share a comfortable mattress with you."

No sooner had Helen uttered those regrettable prophetic words that Parolles stepped into the palace chamber. "Bless you and your precious ovaries my Lady Helen," the chronic insulter nastily said. "Oh knavish Fool, how's the old lady doing back in Rossillon?"

"She's wrinkled but always manages to add several new wrinkles to any given situation," the Fool smartly and cleverly answered. "The Countess plans to leave me a small portion of her estate and to you nothing, *no thing*, nada, not a thing, get it you asshole bully!"

"Away with you witty knave moron or else Lady Helen will be wearing your tiny balls for earrings!" Parolles threatened as he quickly reached for his sword.

"You must find some aspect of me when you honestly examine your own flawed personality," the perceptive Fool countered. "The major difference between you' and me' Parolles is that I'm merely an everyday asshole and you're just a pompous snot-bag pig wannabe' aristocrat asshole!"

"You mock me one more time jaded knave and I shall have my rewarding bloody retribution on you," Parolles predicted before grinding his teeth. "And forget hearsay; I say here and now that you're a fucked-up gay blade without a razor shaft to hold."

"Forget about the gay faggot dimension of my personality! Everyone is a fool and you're no damned exception to that all-too-truthful axiom of life," the Clown mercilessly hammered away at his chosen target. "Fools make the world laugh! Have you no sense of humor Master Parolles?"

"Listen carefully Lady Helen," Parolles said while ignoring the Fool's general bravado, "tonight Master Bertram is going away to engage in necessary personal business. That's really why he didn't want to marry you because he had other urgent matters to attend to but was reluctant to tell the King. Since Count Bertram is leaving immediately for Tuscany," Parolles added, "he strongly recommends that you get permission from the King to return at once to Rossillon and attend to his ailing mother, who is, as you quite well know, your prospective mother and also your current mother-in-law. And I actually thought that the world was fucked-up after I had entered it! Anyway Lady Helen," the always scheming villain paused and then proceeded, "the predisposed Count Bertram sincerely apologizes for any inconvenience his current important responsibilities may have caused you."

"Does this astonishing news sound like unbelievable bullshit?" Helen asked the Fool.

"Yes My Lady. Like bullshit, horseshit and chicken shit all rolled and wrapped into one massive dung ball!" the Fool aptly and congenially verified.

* * * * * * * * * * * *

Count LeFew located young Bertram meditating in the palace smoke and mirrors' room, reflecting on *his* present marital problem. LeFew had difficulty believing that Parolles was a true-blue friend worthy of the young Count's trust and confidence.

"That dastardly bastard Parolles, a scumbag few cards short of a full deck, that status-hungry prick is beyond a few shadows of doubt a yellow-bellied belligerent snake that'll betray you the first few times a soldier's obligation to his fighting partner is needed," Count LeFew un-persuasively argued and exaggerated his point. "Your so-called assistant is no more of a dedicated soldier of character than that craven son-of-a-bitch Judas Iscariot was a reliable colleague to chaste Jesus Christ, and if you want me to provide a few more classic examples from history or religion, or from religious history, I most certainly will because I happen to know a few more."

"On the contrary Count LeFew'," Bertram adamantly disagreed, "Parolles is a valiant crusader even in light of the fact that the crusades had been fought hundreds of years ago. That assertion kind of makes my distinguished friend a sort of living anachronism, now doesn't it?"

"If I am wrong, and I have been a few times in my lengthy life," Count LeFew aptly stated, "then your chum Parolles is an onerous vociferous fake and a loudmouthed diabolical fraud who'll pull a few fast ones on you when you require his allegiance the most. I say these few critical things because my moral compass has only been wrong a few times in judging the character of a few perceived nefarious characters."

"Parolles is truly a loyal genius and not disingenuous as you've erroneously argued," Bertram professed in defense of his craven fiendish associate. "My trusty friend is not half as fucked-up as you erroneously accuse him of being."

"If you think that I've transgressed against and traduced his valor a few times," LeFew volleyed back to Count Bertram, "then I cannot find the heart to repent my oral sins and I'll soon retire to my quarters and down a few shots of delicious hard liquor. Here comes that treacherous skunk taking a few strident steps in our direction. Try a few times to make us friends Bertram, for Parolles has promised and threatened to shave my cherished tufty goatee off my pointed chin and then violently shove it down my choking throat."

"Ah kind Parolles," the sugar-mouthed two-faced LeFew greeted, "tell me a few things about your talented tailor. The few clothes I've seen you wearing can only be described as high-class haberdashery. I figured that a few words of compliment would improve our contentious enmity."

"Has Helen gone to speak with the King about returning to Rossillon?" Bertram asked Parolles without paying any attention to LeFew's shoddy rambling flattery.

"She'll be leaving on the eight o' clock coach tonight back to Rossillon!" Parolles matter-of-factly answered. "She's taking some theatrical lessons from a stage coach on how to act as a nonchalant passenger as we speak."

"I see," Bertram understood and mechanically nodded his head like a bobbing head dog. "I've already written my sad 'Dear Helen' letter, and I've arranged for our speedy horses to be ready for our exciting journey to Italy so that I don't have to sleep and screw my bride's tight honey well on my honeymoon night."

"The few words I have to say are God save you captain," LeFew succinctly uttered. "Marital bliss belongs only to a lucky few!"

"Is there any particular conflict between Count LeFew and you?" Bertram asked the bully Parolles, who was at that particular moment' preoccupied snarling directly into the old man's face.

"This fucked-up old man verbally abuses me to the hilt every time we meet and I have an inclination to dispose of him rapidly and efficiently," Parolles indicated, gripping his sword.

"You've acted more than a few times like the Countess Rossillon's Fool who once had leaped into a vat containing a few tons of sizzling-hot whipped cream last carnival season for our amusement," Count LeFew *count*ered. "And Lord Bertram, I have no further desire to have a few additional quarrels with Monsieur Parolles and quite bluntly I have a few better things to occupy my full attention. Good day Monsieurs!"

Count LeFew hastily departed, fearing the reprisal of the skilled swordsman Parolles, who had twice gestured grabbing his weapon from its sheath with the implied intent of dismembering and butchering the pesky old fart on the spot.

"He's an idle gossiping old jerk-off!" Parolles concluded and told Bertram. "I swear I'll cut his tiny nuts off if he has any."

"I've known the old fellow all my life and I think that Count LeFew is an honorable man who is just a little bit too gregarious for his own good," Bertram maintained. "Unfortunately the poor old decrepit guy never shuts the fuck up!"

"If you like old farts that much, then I suggest that you should work in a thriving geriatric shit-house!" Parolles laughed.

Helen then appeared in the corridor and was rapidly heading in the men's direction. The newlywed had a concerned and worrisome expression on her acne-free adolescent face.

"Here comes my virgin queen nemesis!" Bertram satirically whispered to Parolles as the Count's puzzled wife approached.

"I've spoken to the King and he's granted me permission to return to Rossillon to act as a hospice and tend to the dying Countess's needs," Helen informed her momentarily reticent husband. "Now that *your* mother is also my dear mother-in-law and my prospective mother too, I've volunteered my nursing services although I'd rather have you Bertram nursing on my succulent breasts now that we're officially married by that old boring senile pedophile priest that spoke to us of cardinal sins during his thirty-second sermon, which he later falsely indicated was really his ninety-ninth sermon."

"I shall obey the King's intentions and meet with him privately about your redeployment," Bertram insincerely pledged. "I'm awfully sorry Wife that I've been secretly assigned to report to duty in Italy to participate in the no-holds-barred Florentine War. Here's a letter I wish for you to deliver to my mother, er, I meant to say *our* mother back in Rossillon. I might stop in to see you at the estate before Parolles and I head out to Italy to kick some wop ass!"

"I shall faithfully fulfill your honorable wishes and present the letter to the Countess," Helen sobbed and cried. "But I can't fathom why we can't share the same bed and sleep together on our wedding night like normal married couples do. I mean Bertram, for the first time in my life I want to get laid."

"My haste to travel to Italy is very great but first I must appease and placate the King," Bertram answered before feigning a frown. "But right now I have to take a long crap so I must depart and find the nearest soundproof outhouse. Farewell Helen and say 'hi' to Dearest Mommy for me!"

"Oh Bertram, I'm but a country waif, the daughter of a bankrupt alchemist and although I've been through much adversity, in my troubled heart I feel that I'm not worthy of your fabulous title and great wealth. But I solemnly pledge to be an obedient wife and even though the notion of sixty-nine is totally repugnant to me, I promise I'll diligently perform it on demand if you will *that* awful dread upon me! Will you not kiss me?"

"I already told you Bitch that I have to piss and have no time to kiss!" Bertram inadvertently rhymed. "And tonight I must again shit and have no time for clit! Then I must ride my horse to Rossillon on my way to Italy and have no time to ride you tonight in Paris or tomorrow night in Rossillon either!"

"Goodbye Bertram and I hope to see you at Rossillon!" Helen replied, alternately weeping and sobbing. "This is indeed the beginning of a strange marriage relationship! I had more fun doing nothing but imagining and dreaming of having sex with you when I was still single!"

After Helen sadly proceeded down the palace corridor Bertram had some pertinent rhetoric to relate to Parolles. "Let us have flight before we fight!"

"Bravo friend Bertram! Save your energy and your sex juices for the dusty musty Florentine Wars and for the lusty busty Italian whores!" the ignominious Parolles loquaciously articulated.

Act III

The Duke of Florence appreciatively and cordially welcomed the two French Lords that had shown-up in Italy to voluntarily fight in the developing war pitting two Italian city-states against one another, Florence and Siena.

"Greetings noble Frenchmen," the very stiff and stuffy Duke of Florence formally said to the new arrivals sent by the King of France. "It's not our custom here in this cultural city for men to kiss men unless they're active in an underground organization we Italians call the Mafia. That French-kissing practice looks so damned gay! So please don't slobber all over my impeccable recently shaved face and respectfully refrain from kissing other men while the hell you're here in Tuscany waiting to fight in the war."

"Your Majesty, glad to be of service to your service," the First French Lord directly said from his kisser. "And Your Grace, I hope you have some nice big breasted hairy-crotched wenches residing here in Florence for us flirtatious Lords with yeoman's sexual appetites to service and kiss too."

"Indeed, you can start your amorous sex-seeking campaign with my grotesque-looking wife Florence!" the Duke joked. "And after my famed city emerges victorious in the war with Siena you two mercenaries can have any single dolls named Flossie in Florence that you might want to screw and shack-up with."

"Our Roman ancestors spoke Latin so the French and the Italians all share a common cultural heritage," the Second Lord observed and prattled to the Duke. "In fact Your Worship, it's really hard to distinguish French dressing from Italians undressing, ha, ha, ha!"

"Very good stupid-assed pun!" the Duke of Florence commended and applauded, leaning over splitting a gut and almost falling off his wobbly throne. "Both of these naïve silly visiting assholes must reside in the northern French Vaudeville Valley, judging by your fucked-up burlesque-style humor. But I'm glad to see that you're speaking Italian, or fuckin' trying anyway."

"Many of our native Frenchmen grow fat and lazy but we two gentlemen thirst and lust for adventure and glory," the First Soldier interrupted the Duke's merriment. "Two better volunteer assholes you'll not find anywhere no matter how hard you search. We humbly offer our service to your noble cause and we can't wait to become involved in the whores, I mean in the Florentine Wars."

"Tomorrow you shall enter into combat and if you know any other aristocratic French idiots please write and tell them they're welcome to fight for Florence or for any other bitches living in my fair city," the ridiculous Duke guffawed and slapped his knees. "Tonight you two inbred retards can get laid in our popular haystack fields and tomorrow you can get mortally wounded in our killing fields! Ha, ha, ha!"

* * * * * * * * * * * *

The buffoon Fool quickly returned from Paris back to somnolent Rossillon with letters from both Bertram and Helen to read to the ill Countess, who still possessed her sharp tongue in spite of her debilitating illnesses.

"I'm surprised to see you coming back to Rossillon so soon," the Countess quipped to her Fool. "If you couldn't get a job as a jester at the King's Court then you could've tried an audition for Vaudeville or become a glamorous male prostitute at a sophisticated Parisian gay clown bar and inn!" the very dignified Lady stated. "I think that the word 'taverns' is what they call those new perverted bawdy dens of iniquity."

"I must tell you My Lady that Count Bertram seems to have become a very surly, sullen and melancholy fellow whose face looks a little like a cross between a melon and a collie. Anyway," the mentally disorganized Fool went on, "your weird son would have a lugubrious expression on his countenance one minute and two minutes later be singing, and then Bertram would continue that fucked-up behavior pattern alternating between the two emotional terminals continuously until the objective observer hypothesizes that your mood-vacillating son has some sort of peculiar *acute* terminal illness that's not a cute illness at all."

The Countess opened Bertram's letter and (since she did not trust the Fool's literacy or intellectual honesty) silently read that her son was sending a new daughter-in-law Helen de Narbon home to Rossillon because she had cured the King of his manifold diseases and had won the right to choose the young Count as her husband. "But Mother, I have wedded but not bedded with Helen and I've sworn not to ever sleep with the pristine little country waif. I've run away from my dismal reality to fight in the Florentine War with my good friend and buddy Parolles, who as you know is a reckless iconoclastic soldier of fortune always looking for some frivolous feud or frolic." Signed: "Your unfortunate stigmatized son, Bertram."

'This is not right for my stubborn ass-backwards Bertram to disobey the King's wishes and go to war and not stay in Paris and sleep and screw the virgin Lady Helen,' the sick Countess thought with great disappointment. 'My asshole son is so full of contempt and defiance that he's liable to explode from the internal pressure and blast his blood, urine and sperm all over my majestic rolling hills Rossillon county.'

"Don't worry Countless, er, I mean Countess!" the absurd Fool awkwardly comforted his employer. "The very capable Parolles, I say that description because the snidely fellow wears a black cape, will diligently protect Bertram from harm. And don't be surprised my Countess if Parolles tries stealing several pay rollies from the theft-vulnerable Italian army, ha, ha, ha," the goofball servant jollied. "Perchance Madam the two playboys have fled to Florence to merely cavort around with loose and risque women and to escape tedious responsibilities and obligations here in France," the facetious Clown hypothesized and commented. "Screwing around with whores and not getting screwed in dangerous wars is their forte." With those oddball words the unscrupulous Fool retired from the classic mansion to his humble barn quarters, exiting the edifice through his personal side door.

Two Gentlemen that had been escorting Helen from Paris arrived later that day at Rossillon manor to turn the young blushing bride over to the Countess's protective custody. "Here's your daughter, er, I mean your new daughter-in-law Countess!" the eminent First Gentleman said.

"Madam, my husband is gone forever and will never sleep with me and knock me up!" Helen sobbed and cried to her ailing mother-in-law. "What the hell should I do?"

"Gentlemen, where is my derelict delinquent irresponsible son?" the Countess asked her guests, trying to confirm the Fool's sketchy information (and the letter's content) while putting Helen's tearful outburst temporarily on hold.

"He's off to serve the Duke of Florence, who incidentally does not resemble a tennis ball, as if the Duke doesn't have enough servants or problems already," the Second Gentleman relevantly disclosed. "Your careless son is a reckless maverick and indeed a sociopath and his pal Parolles is an exceptionally bad influence that'll most certainly place Count Bertram's life in jeopardy on the wheel of fortune."

"Read the postscript of Bertram's letter Countess that'll reveal some additional queer details to this sordid puzzle," Helen implored. "My strange estranged situation can only be characterized as a complete and utter mess."

"It says here at the bottom and I quote what my son had expressed to you," the Countess read squinting her weary eyes, "when you Helen can get the ring off my finger, which I guarantee will never happen, and when you are pregnant carrying my child then and only then will I sleep with you." The Countess reflected on the weird details for a moment and then commented, "Those crazy conditions are impossible. I'm afraid my dear Helen that my contemptible son never desires sleeping with you ever, so I advise that you save your cherry for some other more civil and more mature gullible sucker that happens to stumble across your path."

"That main sentence is a dreadful sentence I've been cruelly sentenced to, judging by your last poignant sentence," Helen somberly told the very alarmed and distressed Countess. "Such stupid bullshit should only happen in tragic plays."

"We're sorry about all the happy horseshit-type grief we've brought you dear Countess, but as the King often utters, se la vie," the Second Gentleman escort summarized. "And I myself' always say 'la vie' and it matters little to me. To tell you the honest-to-God's truth I can't comprehend why the King places so much credence in that utterly silly redundant phrase!"

"Oh Helen, you're truly more of a daughter to me than Bertram was ever a son," the Countess lauded the skinny-but-likeable country waif. "The contemptible bastard's defied my wishes and has defiantly run away to become a soldier having his ass in Florence while his dick ought to be in you somewhere here in France. If I could legally disown the unruly asshole, I most certainly would! But regrettably my precious ward, the chauvinistic laws created by men dictate that I must give my prosperous thriving estate to my carefree irresponsible son, that reprehensible, disrespectful and totally greedy pecker-head."

"Well Countess, it's time for us to return to Paris so that we can pray at the *Cathedral of Notre Dame* and then rob the left bank," the First Gentleman joked. "And if we leave now we can also catch the striptease couch dancers at the Palace, er, I mean performing at the Palace Burlesque Theater!"

"Damn it!" the Countess angrily exclaimed and cursed. "My son and I are playing mental chess here and I intend to win. I'll strategically move to block Bertram's inheritance, right up until my dying breath, which the way I feel right now might be before midnight. Anyway kind Sirs," the elegant-but-ill wealthy Rossillon widow continued, "Helen deserves a Lord equal to her virtue and I believe that my lousy son Bertram does not qualify. You Gentlemen say that the thug rogue Parolles was with Bertram and that the two renegades are heading to Florence?"

"Yes My Lady!" the First Gentleman confirmed. "And Parolles is just as much fucked-up as your juvenile delinquent offspring Bertram is!"

"Well then," the Countess assessed and concluded, "tell my son whenever you next see the egotistical narcissistic bastard that his war sword can never win the honor that his overall negligence has lost. Only his erect pecker inside Helen's luscious pink love tunnel can resolve this serious escalating family crisis!"

"We'll tell the flippant young hooligan precisely that if we ever have the misfortune of encountering the idiot again!" the Second Gentleman promised.

"Good, I'll see you Gentlemen to the door since my lazy Steward is busy reading pornographic literature and jerking-off in the stables. He does the same damned thing the same damned time every damned day of the week."

Grief-stricken Helen mentally reviewed the weird circumstances that crazily became included in her very distressing wedding day. 'Yesterday should've been a happy occasion but instead it evolved into a hideous nightmare. Maybe if I masturbate that'll make me feel better and improve my self-esteem! It seems peculiar dear Bertram that I want to own you while the Countess desires to disown you!' the girl evaluated the odd coincidence. 'I suppose that life's full of such contradictory ironies and paradoxes! Oh well, I'll start by massaging my nipples and then slowly work my hands and fingers down to my bush!'

* * * * * * * * * * * *

The very next morning the rejuvenated Countess retrieved the unstable Steward from his stable enterprises and then pulled the hedonistic pervert into the mansion by his ear.

"If you were an innocent girl like Helen de Narbon is," the Countess hollered at her red-faced Steward, "where would you go? Travel to London to rob meat from a Beefeater? To Florence to seek-out her husband Count Bertram? To hell to visit the Devil?"

"Knowing Helen's shy clandestine character and personality, if I were she I would definitely make a secret *retreat* to the Shrine of St. James over in Italy, although I would be walking forward and not backwards," the Steward intelligently answered the Countess's riddle with a stupid bit of levity.

"Yes, you've hit the fingernail right on the head, you blundering hammerhead," the amazed Countess marveled and praised her Steward. "She's probably going to walk barefooted on the cold damp ground and then catch pneumonia. This note that Helen left states she's going someplace far away to meditate on her ever-proliferating problems. She's going to steadfastly pray for Bertram's safe return from the Florentine War so that she could steal his ring, drug him up in order for him to get her pregnant and then sleep with the lazy dolt every night for the rest of her doomed life!" the Countess told the uncaring Steward. "At least that's what the hell I'm surmising from the gist of her scribbling."

"This is heavy esoteric bullshit, no doubt about it!" the Steward agreed. "Now Countess, can I return to the stables and finish my important business?"

"Shit! Had I spoken more extensively with Helen I could've dissuaded her from undertaking such a perilous journey to the Shrine of St. James!" the Countess regretted and remarked. "But then again I've done some stupid things in my life too like marrying twice and giving birth to that pinhead Bertram. I forget which of my deceased derelict husbands was the true goddamned father!"

"If you adopt me as your son and chief beneficiary," the delusional Steward said to his already depressed lady boss, "then I promise to stop doing my stuff in the stables and I'll cease my infatuations about molesting and raping the Fool," the depraved servant seriously and candidly pledged. "Then I would marry my half-sister Helen to whom you will have adopted too, and after all that happy bullshit we'll all live happily ever after just like in those grim Grimm fairy tales I used to read before I got into ultra-dirty hardcore porn'."

"That's not such a bad idea Rinaldo!" the Countess said calling the Steward by his first name for the first time. "I see merit and commendation in your recommendation. But first I'll dictate a letter to my insolent son stating that if he doesn't get his goddamned act together soon I'm disowning the worthless bastard and adopting you and Helen as my legal rightful heirs!"

"I'll get pen, ink and paper right away!" the Steward euphorically exclaimed. "At last I'll be an heir to a substantial fortune! Status is just around the corner!"

"With an excessive amount of debits and debts!" the Countess clarified. "I'm not nearly as rich as every poor bastard and bitch in Rossillon County thinks!"

* * * * * * * * * * *

Perplexed Helen (dressed as a devout religious pilgrim) had haphazardly hitchhiked from Rossillon, France all the way to Florence, Italy and was conscientiously looking for affordable lodging on her way to pray at the Shrine of St. James. 'God! I'm really glad that the shrine's not in Spain,' the girl thought. 'I'd have to walk across the steep treacherous Pyrenees Mountains to get there and life's too full of treacherous mountains and valleys as it is!'

It was on the outskirts of Florence (and not on the petticoats of Florence) that Helen met a Widow and her daughter Diana along with their busybody neighbor Mariana at a bustling and congested marketplace where almost everyone and anyone were sneezing their sinuses out.

"We're almost near the city and there are fuckin' soldiers all over the place looking for easy whores to fuck!" the Widow told her two companions. "And must I remind you two young girls that my husband had died from venereal disease complications and was not killed on the goddamned battlefield by enemy soldiers or by cannon blasts as his obituary had falsely stated."

"Look Mother, even some French courtiers have shown-up in town to screw Italian whores while pretending to be chivalrously fighting in the war," the Widow's daughter Diana added. "And all of this amorous activity is occurring while we're heading to pray at the Shrine of St. James. Where is St. James Place anyway? It is said that we Catholics have a monopoly on it!"

"It's rumored that the Duke's brother has been brutally slain by enemy soldiers and not killed by venereal diseases as has been originally and inaccurately reported," the Widow sobbed and related. "I only hope that there aren't any predatory pedophile priests or any brutal bishop and cardinal womanizers worshiping at the shrine while looking for prospective victims. I can't stand when the men of the cloth rape the clothes off of innocent children and widows and their unsuspecting daughters too."

"Yes ladies," their neighbor Mariana butted-in as she examined some freshly grown tomatoes belonging to a marketplace vendor, "let's beware of several handsome Frenchmen that are wandering about, or should I say scouring this region of Italy searching-out well-endowed Florentine women to rape, screw and sodomize. These retarded Frenchmen always add to a developing dilemma by cleverly mixing love and war!"

"Diana," the Widow said to her very discerning daughter, "I've already told Mariana how a certain Frenchman tried seducing you the other night and I think that his obnoxious companion is no better than he is when it comes to soliciting delicate Italian ladies. Beware of these sex-starved Frenchmen wearing woman's perfume!"

"I've heard of the infamous Count Bertram and his villainous sidekick Parolles," Mariana mentioned to her fellow fruit, vegetable and bread shoppers. "The two rogues are indeed lusty cheaters that aggressively screw everything walking around with a beaver slit and an accompanying butt hole."

"And the egomaniac French men wrongfully think that all women are filthy sluts with hungry bushes. We respectable ladies don't have to worry about the soldiers of Siena raping and sodomizing us. It's our contemptible Frenchmen allies we have to be wary of," the perceptive Widow opined. "And when there are no females to be screwed and sodomized I've confidentially heard from dependable sources that Bertram and Parolles industriously pork each other up the old yazoo."

"Don't fear for me Mother!" Diana assured the Widow. "Each night when I'm not having my period I cut my hand and smear blood all over my crotch and asshole to discourage men like Bertram and Parolles from taking savage advantage of me with their abundant charms and their avaricious arms."

"Look Diana and Mariana," the Widow' gestured and impolitely pointed like a well-trained hunting hound dog. "Here comes a lost pilgrim looking for the Shrine of St. James. I can tell by her dress and by her anxious and curious demeanor that she's baffled and searching for appropriate lodging. Let's approach the girl and find out some juicy gossip."

Helen took the initiative by asking the three women where the traveling palmers visiting the local religious places were lodged.

"At the most excellent St. Francis over near the river," the informative Widow revealed. "But be careful young lady because the St. Francis is in reality a bawdy inn and not a religious shrine like the grotto of St. James is. Come now with us fair maiden and we'll take you there, for that's our current residence. So many soldiers and French Casanovas are in Florence that I fear for your safety and for your suspected virginity."

"I'll hang-out with you ladies until I can continue my journey back home," Helen de Narbon confided to her new acquaintances in broken Italian.

"You have a distinct French accent," the Widow recognized and stated. "Beware of several disreputable Frenchmen that are raping and pumping every woman in sight. Their distrustful names are Count Rossillon and his deputy Parolles, whom we understand is just out of prison."

"I've vaguely heard of those vile notorious gentlemen," Helen graciously lied, "but I don't know what they look like."

"We've learned through the local grapevine that the French King had made Count Bertram of Rossillon marry an ugly fat wench that was not to his liking," the scuttle-butting big-butted Diana disclosed to Helen. "By any chance do you know this fat ugly French woman? Have you come across her in your travels?"

"No, but I did hear that the lady is very delicate, bashful and attractive," Helen reported to the contrary. "She's a fine beautiful thin virgin and not a whoring ugly horny harlot as has been widely and falsely publicized."

"A Frenchman, namely this Parolles jerk-off, he's been badmouthing the Count's wife all over Florence," Diana disclosed to the suddenly disconsolate Helen. "He says that the lady is the opposite of the famous and legendary Helen of Troy. Instead of having a face that launched a thousand ships the Count's wife has a face that launches a thousand Frenchmen in the direction of Italy to die in the damned Florentine War."

"This random chatter is actually unfounded gossip that's detrimentally impugning the chaste reputation of the Lady Helen, who is a most honest and fair damsel, and her impeccable character should not be recklessly smeared and tarnished," Lady Helen expressed in defense of herself. "I've heard from reliable sources that Count Bertram's wife is still in cherry condition."

"We've been informed that she's a fat ugly witch that denies Count Bertram all his assumed pleasures, both declining oral and regular sex," Mariana said, repeating marketplace hearsay she had heard and was now perpetuating.

The Florentine army led by Antonio, the Duke's eldest son along with Count Rossillon and Parolles slowly rode on horseback by the marketplace in an improvised military parade.

"Young Woman," the Widow pointed out to Helen, "there is Escalus, the Duke's eldest son who is always looking for ways of ascending to higher heights in Florentine society. Isn't he especially handsome?"

"Which idiot, or should I say soldier is the infamous French Count?" Helen asked feigning ignorance of the matter. "Is he riding alongside that opportunistic rascal you've described as Parolles?"

"The egocentric jerk-off wearing the plume on his helmet is the French Count," Diana indicated, "and the arrogant-looking asshole riding beside him is Parolles. Beware Pilgrim Helen, for the Count of Rossillon is a handsome cad who thinks he's a valiant cavalier.

But his sinister and wily purpose is to womanize every doll in Florence while imitating and masquerading as a loyal soldier of fortune, or in the women's case, a soldier of misfortune who screws like a trooper, a storm trooper."

"Well ladies, the French Count looks like an absolute full-fledged asshole to me!" Helen opined while shocking the three impressed ladies with her unexpected vulgarity. "He couldn't charm a dog with a bone and the snobbish smug knave couldn't possibly charm me with his bone."

"Louder with the drums!" Parolles yelled in broken Italian. "My deaf eardrums have trouble hearing them! Ha, ha, ha!"

"The Count is truly vexed and depressed or else he's horny as hell," Diana chattered to her three observant companions. "He's checking us out as if we're spies-in-heat with grandiose designs of whoring around with him."

"Be gone panderers!" Diana shouted at the amorous haughty Count and the diabolical Parolles. "Ride your horses because you certainly aren't going to ride me into a goddamned mattress!"

The military procession soon passed and the women again engaged in bantering anecdotes and bartering gossip. The Widow was the first to pipe-up a suggestion.

"Come Lady Pilgrim, come to the St. Francis with us!" the Widow implored. "There're already five penitents like yourself lodged there and you'll make six. I'll try my best to preserve your sacred virginity for at least one more day!"

"I humbly thank you," Helen replied to the non-grieving Widow. "I'm a confused traveler in a strange land where apparently harmful strange things happen to virgin strangers like me. I hope you have an excellent wooden outhouse there at the St. Francis! God do I have to piss and shit badly!"

* * * * * * * * * * * *

At the Duke of Florence's resplendent palace Bertram of Rossillon and other more gallant French counts and lords entered the throne room to have an audience with the ruler, when in reality they themselves were the audience.

"This Parolles fellow is a craven coward," the chatty First French Lord whispered to the second one. "He brags about past military accomplishments but has shown me nothing but his venereal warts and crabs. That's what the fuck happens when a man carelessly goes fishing in women rather than in the sea or ocean. Instead of fish he instead catches crabs!"

"Do you believe that Parolles has deceived me about his impeccable record of combat service?" Bertram challenged the dominant opinion being gossiped among the French and Florentine lords. "True Gentlemen, I fully agree that the rambunctious fellow does screw around with women but he doesn't screw around when essential military discipline is required."

"This criminal-minded fellow Parolles is in my estimation a most notable coward, as much as I despise criticizing my own kinsman," the First French Lord insisted. "He's an infinite liar, a deft promise breaker and an adroit ball-breaker. The conscienceless queer-bait asshole doesn't possess one decent attribute worthy of your entertainment, Count Bertram."

"You can't rely on that womanizing jerk-off to come to your aid when you most need him," the Second French Lord rendered his biased opinion. "How can this incompetent knave Parolles show you any balls on the battlefield when his erect dick is always stuck in some whore's bottomless snatch?"

"How can I test his loyalty to me as weighed against his infidelity to women?" Bertram asked and challenged the other assembled French counts and lords.

"He's lost his drum and that's why he must beat his meat instead," the Second Lord shared and laughed. "And don't be surprised if your close pal the jerk-off Parolles eats drumsticks at supper tonight and keeps the damned bones while searching for the rest of his beating instrument, ha, ha, ha!"

"I'll enlist the help of a few frivolous Florentine troops I know," the First French Lord volunteered. "We'll collaborate on a nifty plan and hoodwink Parolles, catching his duped ass by surprise. Leave it to me, the always dependable Lord Beaver."

"What do you intend to do?" Count Bertram curiously asked Lord Beaver.

"We'll disguise ourselves as enemy soldiers, capture and kidnap your colleague Parolles, blindfold the detestable cock sucker and then take him into what he believes is an enemy tent," Lord Beaver disclosed. "Next we'll interrogate and promise him escape and safe passage to the Florentine lines if he betrays you and gives us intelligence about the maneuvers of the Florentine army."

"Then we'll tell the shit-head that we have his drum, which naturally we've already pilfered, or should I say already borrowed," the Second French Lord added to the very interesting yet-to-happen escapade. "Now Gentlemen, let's be reticent about this ruse for here comes that coward Parolles now. First we'll tantalize the gutless asshole bully with his missing drum, just for the love of laughter."

"How's it going Monsieur?" Lord Beaver asked the seemingly robust and confident Parolles. "Does this drum I'm holding look familiar to you?"

"No My Lord, I have my own goddamned drum and I'll proudly use it instead of the one in your hands when I enter the fray against Siena," Parolles lied. "I tend to march to the tune of another drum, so stop fuckin' trying to drum-up laughter at my expense."

"But there's one drum missing from our supply," Bertram added to the controversy, "and it must be found, presented and accounted for Parolles, since it had been entrusted to you and was your personal responsibility."

"Perhaps your missing drum has already been recovered and has not been noticed or especially accounted for," the lying fiend replied. "I know that I have my fuckin' drum safely in my possession inside my tent so the one in question here must've been lost by some delinquent asshole drummer not paying any particular attention to his assigned property. But I promise I'll search for this missing drum if you insist on it Count Bertram."

"I'll assign you to the high-level-duty of retrieving this alluded to valuable missing drum and I'll faithfully report your progress directly to the Duke," Bertram emphatically told Parolles while the alert Lords surrounding them snickered and chuckled. "Fuck-up this assignment my loyal aide and you'll be demoted to either a potato peeler or a dish washer."

"I shall undertake your assignment My Count and shall retrieve said missing drum expeditiously," the lying scoundrel Parolles pledged. "And when I discover it I'll return the lost object to your care by rook or by crook."

"Get on the assignment right away or else everyone in authority will consider you a lying prevaricating asshole!" Bertram ordered tongue-in-cheek.

"I'll get started on the top-priority detail early this evening!" Parolles cockily vowed. "I have an important scheduled appointment to get laid at nine o'clock so I'll be free to explore the missing drum situation after I closely explore my new lady companion's pink juicy love tunnel."

"Well, I'm going to tell the Duke all about your upcoming missing drum and re-acquisition exploit," Bertram joshed, "so my good friend make sure you're assiduously screwing some disease infected bitch and not the Duke's constantly bitching old bag wife! Ha, ha, ha!"

"This is no time to be joking around when a key military drum is missing," the always-conniving Parolles returned. "I predict that I'll be successful in performing the top-secret mission, no matter how fucked-up it presently sounds."

"I know you'll put forth a very dedicated effort," Count Bertram said to his aide with a contrived austere expression evident on his facial features. "Stop bullshitting Parolles and get that important drum back into our' possession in a hurry or you'll be beating your meat on a prison toilet seat and not beating your indispensable drum on the march into battle."

Parolles left swiftly, his worried mind in a quandary as the aristocratic schemers waited for their dupe to vanish from sight before finally guffawing loudly.

"What a fucked-up devious deceiver!" Count Beaver evaluated and related. "The dumb snake-like bastard acts so confident about performing a service that he in fact knows cannot be completed, just to cover his ass. The brusque felonious fiend persists in damning himself and he'll be trying to convince us later on that he's personally innocent of any negligence in losing the friggin' drum."

"Your confidante' Parolles is a surreptitious wolf in sheep's clothing that's slyly attempting to pull the wool over our eyes," the Second French Lord told Bertram. "He's a sneaky tricky bastard from the word 'Go'."

"He'll probably try making a duplicate drum or stealing one from our supply tent to support his statement that his registered drum is accounted for," a Third French Lord stated. "The supply tent should be guarded at all costs."

"Yes Count Bertram, our mutual friend Count LeFew had a few nasty words to say to us about your devious associate Parolles!" Count Beaver informed the humored Count of Rossillon. "And few lords can deny LeFew's character and veracity. Tonight your man Parolles will be separated from his rogue disguise and from his continuous overt and covert treachery."

"The ornery evasive asshole will be caught like a wily fox in a trap," Lord Beaver (an international expert on animal traps) affirmed. "The sooner the better for that most shifty and exceedingly mendacious swindler."

Count Beaver and other French lords left the rapidly dispersing assembly cackling and joking amongst themselves' while Bertram and the Second Lord remained behind to consult with each other.

"Now I shall lead you to a lodge called St. Francis and show you this wench Diana I had spoken to you about," the playboy Bertram told his playboy lord friend. "I saw her but once during the parade and later met her on the street and immediately was turned on. She was so cold to my pick-up lines that I instantly became all hot and bothered. I just have to screw her!"

"You say her name is Diana?" the impressed Second Lord asked. "That's the Roman name for Artemis, the sacred Greek virgin goddess of hunting. How ironic it is my Count that you're fuckin' hunting her!"

"That's what the fuck happens when my dick gets straight as an arrow!" Bertram indulgently laughed.

* * * * * * * * * * * *

Meanwhile at the notorious St. Francis Inn and Whorehouse the Widow and Helen were having an enlightened conversation while an intense lightning storm was in progress outside the popular suburban brothel.

"I must confess to you dear Widow that I *am* the much-talked-about maligned and shunned Count Bertram of Rossillon's rejected wife and I'm here in Florence seeking retribution for my crazy husband's denial of our nuptial vows," Helen confided to the gossipy woman. "Can you and your daughter Diana help me in fulfilling the two outrageous conditions that my husband has bragged about for us to sleep and screw together?"

"What are those weird stipulations?" the nosy newsy Widow asked.

"The outlandish warped conditions are that I somehow must obtain my husband's personal ancestral diamond ring to wear and that he makes me pregnant," Helen conveyed, "but I don't see how those two insurmountable provisions can be met or satisfied with me not ever sleeping with him! I mean to say dear Widow', I'm not the Blessed Virgin Mary about to have a miraculous Immaculate Conception! This whole fucked-up conun*drum* constitutes quite an imaginative project on my behalf and I trust Widow that you can conceive of a viable creative plan that'll materialize those two specified impossibilities I've just mentioned."

"Don't despair fair Helen!" the shrewd Widow answered. "Unlike you, I was well born into the Italian aristocracy, for all of the good it has done for me," Diana's mother sadly explained. "I'm fully acquainted with what inbred blue blood is and how it produces fucked-up ingrates like your husband and my unfaithful ex. I'll certainly help you achieve your honorable goals by employing some imaginative stealth I have in mind. Now my kind Helen, since I've fallen into difficult straits, I demand a stipend in gold. Can you accommodate my expenses for my unique services rendered?"

"I have this purse filled with gold coins given to me by my mother, er, I mean by my mother-in-law the Countess of Rossillon," Helen all-too-hastily declared to the Widow. "Now I understand that Count Bertram, my philandering husband that has not given me the pleasure or opportunity of screwing with him," the flustered girl editorialized, "I understand that my cheating spouse wants to screw your cold frigid virgin daughter Diana. Take this gold and devise for me a feasible plan that'll trick my unwary husband into getting me knocked up and then me victoriously wearing his precious cherished diamond ring."

"Indeed this outlandish canard will require much ingenuity and good timing," the old hag Widow evaluated as she counted the gold coin bonanza now in her possession. "Sometimes I wish I had more education so that I could become a renowned playwright. I think I would prefer comedy over tragedy!"

"Forget the small talk!" Helen insisted. "Now what's your damned expensive strategy?"

"Okay vengeful Bitch er, I mean Helen, here's my goddamned plan for what it's worth," the Widow whispered so that no one around in the otherwise empty room could hear. "I'll persuade Diana to sleep with your playboy husband Count Bertram and possibly losing her valued pristine virginity in the process. But she'll allow him to screw her on only one condition. Your husband must surrender his prized diamond ring to her, which she'll then give to you," the Widow schemed and told Helen. "You're coming out way ahead in this deal my dear because the lustrous diamond ring is worth ten times as much as the sack of French gold coins you've graciously paid me."

"Well that unique jargon all sounds quite terrific in theory," Helen complimented, "but how the hell do I get pregnant from a diamond ring? It all sounds like some enigmatic fairy tale fantasy! It just doesn't seem logically possible!"

"Listen you dumb thick-headed Cunt!" the avaricious Widow chastised the chaste girl. "After your louse of a spouse Count Husband screws my daughter he'll probably fall asleep. Then you trade places in the dark with Diana and get your husband all hot and horny again and have him screw your eager beaver right through the fuckin' mattress. That's precisely how the hell you'll get knocked-up by your uncooperative and obstructive husband and how the hell you'll wind-up with his favorite ring too!"

"That's a most fabulous plan!" Helen congratulated the Widow. "It borders on the spectacular! The heirloom diamond ring is worth three thousand crowns and only the very rich King of France could ever afford owning an identical one. Congratulations! What a fantastic conniving old bitch you are! I can't believe I'm going to finally get laid by my lunatic husband!"

"Yes my Helen, you'll probably get knocked-up when your lazy vagabond husband is too damned drunk and too damned incoherent to know what the fuck he's doing or who the fuck he's fucking in the dark!" the slick Widow cackled. "He'll definitely think that you're my hot-to-trot daughter Diana! That's the most expeditious way for you to lose your goddamned virginity Helen de Narbon and as a delightful bona fide bonus get knocked-up at the same time. It's the finest scheme that I can *conceive* of! Actually, the finest scheme that *you* can conceive of! Ha, ha, ha!"

Act IV

Persistent Count Beaver was determined to capture and detain the villainous Parolles and teach the notorious scoundrel much needed lessons in civility, in military obedience and in honor. The resolute French Lord was organizing a bevy of army personnel to ambush the thug and strip away *his* pleasant-but-lying façade.

"The bastard will approach the camp from no other way except along this hedgerow," Count Beaver told a soldier that was in on the imaginative prank. "Surely sally upon him quickly even though his name's Parolles and not Shirley or Sally. Speak harshly and cruelly to him in a slightly different Italian dialect so that the creep thinks the enemy army from Siena has apprehended him. And one of you imbeciles must act as an interpreter from Italian to French so that our targeted dupe will get the wrong idea about the true nature of what the fuck's actually happening to him."

"I'll volunteer for that duty," a highly motivated Captain said. "I used to interpret tarot cards for women who sought new sexual partners so this queer novel assignment ought to be a piece of cake."

"Do you know this man Parolles and will he recognize your distinctive voice?" Count Beaver asked the adventurous volunteer.

"No Sir, but to be safe and sure I have a degree in ventriloquism from a liberal arts college in a French puppet state," the Captain jested. "I'll speak Italian gibberish in Italian and this Parolles jerk-off won't suspect a single nonsensical word I'm articulating."

"Just speak in Italian like you're speaking to me in French and the blindfolded bastard will be thoroughly confused and disoriented," Beaver joked. "Parolles must believe that we're his avowed adversaries seeking some sort of entertainment pleasure from his hostage situation. For example, speak politics to the fucked-up Frenchman and nobody including myself will fuckin' understand a syllable of your inane chatter. Now here comes that French jerk-off who has insulted the revered Count LeFew more than a few times," Beaver observed and said. "Let's seize and capture him and then scare the shit out of the prick until he finally spiels-out the truth."

Unassuming Parolles had been strolling along the hedgerow in the dark looking and feeling for his lost drum. 'It's nearly ten o'clock and I'll have to find that cheap piece of shit drum or a good facsimile or my ass is grass without any gas,' the desperate fiend thought. 'I need to concoct a suitable excuse for not having it otherwise the abstraction known as disgrace will knock my door down and my shiny varnish will be removed and I'll be quite exposed, symbolically speaking.'

"Get ready to jump the fork-tongued toad," Count Beaver advised and spoke softly to his men. "And you Captain, make sure you lay plenty of jabberwocky on the silly-assed hedonistic bastard that has mocked venerable Count LeFew more than a few fuckin' times. Speak poppycock to this cocky no good bastard."

"All this worry over a cheap piece of shit drum!" Parolles grumbled to himself. "I'll smack my face and arms until I bleed and then tell Count Beaver and the other shit-faced lords that I got into a scuffle protecting my drum that had been violently seized by drunken fanatical enemy troops."

"Ahora!" Count Beaver commanded in Spanish even though he was supposed to be an Italian officer thinking 'a whore a!'

The eight accomplices leaped from the shadowy foliage, first surrounding the astonished Parolles and next pouncing on him until the startled victim was violently wrestled to the wet ground. Soon the designated Frenchman was tied-up and blindfolded by the well-trained commando attackers.

"What the fuck's going on?" Parolles screamed. "If you want ransom I'll get it from Count Bertram!"

"Throca movonus, cargo cargo, villianda par corbo carbo carbohydrates!" the multilingual Captain interpreter yelled into Parolles' dirt-smeared face.

"Look assholes!" Parolles vehemently protested. "Do any of you craven jerk-offs know any Dane, German, Low Dutch, Swahili or French? Those are the languages that I'm proficient and fluid in!"

"Lowinko, Monica, towaddo kreetrencho," the Captain answered.

"Look creeps, if any of you assholes speak English or Florentine along with a smattering of French we can communicate and negotiate a satisfactory settlement!" Parolles yelled to no avail.

"Boskos thromuldo ergotiempo!" the competent grim-faced Captain eloquently answered.

"What the fuck are you' jabbering?" Parolles hollered. "I speak at least five different languages and can't understand a fuckin' consonant of what the hell you're saying! Find me an experienced interpreter! Find me a goddamned capable interpreter!"

"Bentavi bon jovi muskos kerllybonto!" the astute Captain promptly uttered.

"What the fuck are you' exhaling!" Parolles balked. "Are you smoking opium or drinking an excess of vodka?"

"Manka reuania oschrbidulchos voliuorco vodka glucose," the creative Captain firmly and professionally replied.

"The General is content to spare your life but you must say something pertinent and informative to save your hide from being tanned," the Captain acting as an interpreter proceeded by changing his voice to sound like a gay faggot vociferating.

"I'll tell you all the secrets of the Florentine camp including their ranks, positions and numbers," Parolles pleaded. "And if that's not enough to placate *you* militant General, I'll give you the address of the St. Francis Inn and Brothel and every other functioning whorehouse and bordello on either side of the Florentine lines."

"Acordo meeka linto lento lentil soupo!" the Captain cryptically answered. "Ipso factore ravioli, lasagna spaghetti!"

"You guys are even more fucked-up and bigger assholes than the warped Florentines are!" Parolles exclaimed before being dragged away against his will into the nearby rendezvous tent.

"We've trapped the wily woodcock (who flashes and sports a fleshy red cock) and will keep him muzzled," Count Beaver instructed and reviewed for the sake of the mentally challenged commando team. "Go tell Count Bertram of Rossillon that the skunk is in the cage. In case you're wondering, those are the code words for 'we've trapped, molested and kidnapped the heinous Parolles'."

"Aye, aye' Count Beaver of Rottendamton!" the highly qualified Captain saluted. "This thrilling caper's actually more fun and delightful than eating and licking neglected unwashed pussy!"

* * * * * * * * * * *

Count Bertram soon visited the popular St. Francis Inn and Brothel and met-up with the frigid Diana, whose breasts were as cold as Arctic icebergs. The young lady's aloofness and cold disposition made Bertram's demeanor all the meaner and him wanting to get laid to triumphantly conquer another uncooperative resisting maiden.

"They told me down in the pimp's lounge that your name was Fontibell but you look more like a tinker-bell," Bertram analyzed and described to his desired prey. "It's not easy being a medieval sexual predator in this unpredictable day and age."

"My name's Diana," the girl answered a little too truthfully. "Why do you think you're still in the hunt for me when I don't give a crap about sex and abhor the idea of becoming a whore?"

"Because you have a fine hourglass-type figure that I figure needs some internal lubrication," Bertram crudely and crassly replied. "I know there's some quality sex hidden behind those two icebergs, er, I mean gorgeous breasts that are sticking out from your very adorable frame."

"I am a monument to virginity!" Diana maintained.

"You might be a monument to virginity but I possess a monumental sex drive that won't fuckin' quit," the aristocratic hoodlum emphasized. "But you're right about the monument part. You're colder than an ancient Siberian gravestone and harder than the Egyptian Pyramids. But I'm sure that your mother was warm and fuzzy the night your ass was conceived in her womb."

"My mother simply performed her marital duty, which I'm not obligated to render because I'm not wed to you, you filthy slimy dirt ball!" Diana wrangled and reproached her disreputable wooer.

"Look you raunchy Bitch!" the perturbed Count ridiculed the obstinate virgin. "My dick stick needs to be licked by a girl hick like you and right now you're the only game in town! I love thee Virgin Witch and will not be satisfied until I'm satisfied!"

"You desire for me to commit an unholy act and think nothing of it," Diana objected. "Your oath is not hallow but hollow and shallow too, and I see right through you as if you have no soul in your transparent anatomy, you relentless insidious totally foul Pervert!"

"Your opinion of me is quite inaccurate, for I insist that sex *is* love and that love is true expression of feeling that you're afraid to exhibit either in private or in *pubic*, er, I mean public," the molester claimed. "Love is wholly holy and you lack it. That's why the fuck you're a frigid wench afraid to have sex and openly and genuinely express your latent feelings!"

"I shall not surrender my conscience and discretion to your sick lusty desires," Diana squawked. "But if you're that determined to steal my maidenhead and bust my cherry, then I demand that you give me that tawdry ring on your finger as a token of your so-called love. I'll call your bluff even though you don't own, lease or rent any goddamned mountain!"

"This diamond ring doesn't shine for me anymore, that is to say, if I stupidly give it to you," Bertram the garrulous playboy argued. "It's an heirloom handed-down from my ancient greedy ancestors whom I really don't give a shit about."

"When you do surrender it to me you persistent Asshole," Diana countered, "you' should remember that my virginity is *my* precious jewel that you want to seize. I figure it's a fair trade, my valued gem for your family jewel, and I'm not referring to one of your non-golden nuggets hanging beneath your dangle either! If you want to claim my chastity then you'll have to barter your cheap ring."

"Okay you miserable Bitch, you win!" Bertram conceded as he removed the ring from his finger and handed it to Diana. "This is definitely the most exorbitantly expensive piece of ass I've ever paid for and I've hung out at the most prestigious bordellos in all of Europe during my brief tenure in Paris."

"Look you sex-starved buck, when midnight chimes on the central square clock knock at my chamber window," the slick-minded girl calling the shots directed. "My mother will be in bed soundly asleep with her arms draped around her male manikin so she won't hear us humping and pumping in the room above. You can only screw me once and then we'll go to sleep and wake-up in the middle of the night, and as soon as I shove a substitute maraschino cherry up my slit you can screw me again."

"But I'll be out a wonderful diamond ring for simply two lousy screws!" Bertram realized and exclaimed.

"Well, before I wake you up from your slumber between fucks I'll place a second ring belonging to me on the proper finger of your left hand as a token of my affection for your astounding animalistic nature."

"Now you're talking!" Bertram agreed. "We get it on at the stroke of midnight! That's when I start stroking and stoking you?"

"Precisely Tiger!" Diana verified and then lowly growled like a mother cat about to relinquish her lone pussy. "Until the magic hour I bid you adieu!"

"Holy fish smell!" Bertram joyfully responded. "I shall indeed experience a virtual Heaven on Earth. I hope an unexpected blizzard doesn't blow the roof off the St. Francis while I'm taking your virginity and ravenously feeling your icy cold body and iceberg-like tits."

"You must've worked in the back room of a candy store because you say the sweetest things!" Diana exaggerated.

"I'll see you at midnight," Bertram affirmed. "When the clock strikes twelve I'll ring your chimes!"

The suitor hastily exited the girl's modest bedchamber all flushed (even though they didn't have toilets with handles way back then) and flustered.

'My mother told me just how to arouse, woo and trick the dumb bastard!' Diana recollected with a smile. 'Bertram has sworn to marry me when his wife is dead. Little does the asshole know that I've met and befriended the innocent Helen de Narbon'. She and I will pull the old switcheroo before he gets to my snatcheroo a second time. And the half share of the gold in my mother's purse will give me enough money to buy in as a partner in the very profitable St. Francis Inn and Brothel. Then I'll parlay my initial investment by building a St. James Lodge and Brothel right adjacent to the historic religious shrine. Jesus Christ! Medieval capitalism is really great!'

* * * * * * * * * * * *

Count Beaver and other top-notch French lords were discussing Parolles but the gist of their conversation soon switched to the temporarily distracted and preoccupied Count of Rossillon.

"Have you given Count Bertram the letter from his ill mother?" Beaver questioned the French Count of Catalina.

"I delivered it earlier today and the news it contains stings his nature like a swarm of wasps," Catalina reported. "It's like Bertram has transformed into a hideous surly monster."

"His mother's probably busting his chops good for baling-out on his new virgin wife," Beaver inferred and stated. "The imbecile probably doesn't realize that Helen could easily formulate a potent aphrodisiac that'll allow the pervert to screw horny women right to the perimeter of his own grave-site."

"And Helen has the blessing of the King, which ultimately will be a curse to the moody mercurial Bertram," a third lord Count Trilogy chimed in. "But local gossip has it that Bertram is shacking-up with a Florentine wench that stuffs cherries up her crotch before she has sex to convince her lover that she's a chaste virgin. Anyway," Trilogy proceeded with his misinformation, "I heard from someone staying at the iniquitous St. Francis Inn and Brothel that the ubiquitous Count of Rossillon has given the strange lady his cherished diamond ring in exchange for a tin one! Is that guy fucked-up or what?"

"We must rebel against this young maniac and his pervert friend Parolles or the specters of sin and scandal shall envelop our good reputations," Beaver asserted. "If we don't mutiny against those two punk whippersnappers then we're condoning their misconduct and we're guilty of apathy in the eyes of the normally don't-give-a-shit court of public opinion."

"Let's ostracize the two fanatical assholes from our company," Lord Catalina suggested. "Their preposterous misbehavior is as counterfeit as Parolles counterfeit missing drum! Ha, ha, ha! Any of you men have a solution involving how to dispose of that scumbag Parolles? On second thought, let's leave it to Beaver."

"Forget those two juvenile morons!" Count Trilogy insisted. "What the hell's going on with the war? Has there been a skirmish yet or is everybody dancing around in dumb circles shadowboxing?"

"I hear that there's an overture of peace being written by the conductor of the Florence Symphony Orchestra!" Count Beaver divulged and then laughed. "And what will Bertram do once the war's finished without it even beginning? Will he return to France?"

"Sir, it might be best for Count Bertram to return to Rossillon before his mother dies because I hear that Helen has come to Italy in pursuit of the on-the-lam bastard," Catalina informed his counterparts. "Rumor has it that she's doing a pilgrimage to the sacred Shrine of St. James but in reality the wench is staying at the bawdy and disreputable St. Francis Inn and Brothel. This is a horrible scandal of major magnitude if it ever gets back to France!"

"Well my dear French Catalina, how have you learned this tabloid-type bullshit?" Trilogy questioned his colleague.

"Well Lord Trilogy," Catalina responded, "neither Bertram nor Helen can keep secrets long and word's gotten out in the barber shop gossip mills that all of the aforementioned facts have been written in letters sent by the dying Countess of Rossillon to both Helen and her son, the fucked-up Count."

"I never suspected that *that* dolt Count Bertram was a man of letters," Beaver said and chuckled to his amused colleagues, "but now the rotten bastard's about to get the third degree."

"Our lives are caught in a tangled spider's web and it's a good thing that the Countess is fair-skinned and not a black widow!" Catalina stupidly remarked.

A courier interrupted the silly bull session with an oral message of paramount importance. He repeated the intelligence to Count Beaver, who then shared it with Catalina and Trilogy, who had heard the same dispatch just as clearly as Beaver originally had.

"Holy smoking chimneys!" Beaver exclaimed. "The Duke thinks that Count Bertram's unneeded services are unneeded and His Majesty is sending the frisky lad back to France with a letter of commendation bureaucratically praising and congratulating his contribution to the war that never happened. I'll be Beaver damned! Holy shitoli! Here comes the inimitable Count Bertram now!"

"I've had a busy fucked-up day Gentlemen!" Bertram confessed to his disinterested lordly audience. "I've written and dispatched a nasty missive to my mother, I've bullshitted with the Duke, who wants my lazy ass out of Italy, and I've gotten laid twice and the crazy broad had two separate cherries busted. This has been an extraordinary twenty-four hours!"

"You must be tired from all of that strenuous activity," Count Beaver (an expert on female genitalia) injected into the discussion. "Now you ought to rest up to prepare for your long trek back to France."

"I'll not go until I learn of what has happened to that traitorous knave Parolles! Is he into stocks and bonds or is he stealing some lady's mutual funds?" Bertram inquired.

"He's in deep shit presently sitting shackled on a mound of horse manure!" Trilogy informed the vernal virile Count. "He's sunken down all the way to his nostrils so now we all know from verification that the tricky weasel is a goddamned brown-noser."

"The mental wreck, *your* former best friend, weeps like a cheerless wench still clinging to her chastity," Beaver analogized to Bertram. "He's confessed his guilty shenanigans to a superior officer after being afraid of suffocating in the stinking seven-foot-high animal dung mound."

"He hasn't implicated me in any of the outrageous lying fiction he's been squealing about, has he?" Bertram asked the French officers with a rather concerned look on his now-ashen face. "A pox upon Parolles! May he' die from the blue bonnet, er, I mean the bubonic plague! Here comes that lying betraying scum-wagon right now! Two soldiers are escorting the blindfolded dung-laden shit-faced son-of-a-bitch over to us."

"What the fuck do you mean communicating all of this crazy nomenclature?" the blindfolded and shit-stained Parolles yelled at the talented and versatile Captain interpreter.

"Portotarttarossa denitomoogers!" the Captain humorously answered.

"Speak plain German, Low Dutch, English or French please! I even know a little Russian and the prick's only four-foot-tall!"

"What are the charges against soldier Parolles?" Count Beaver asked the clever Florentine Captain.

"Bosko Chimurco and Boblibindo Chicmurcoco!" the Captain eloquently answered.

"I see! Very grave allegations indeed!" Beaver ascertained.

"Count Beaver! I discern your feminine staccato voice! What the fuck's going on here?" the blindfolded Parolles yelled before spitting a lump of horse manure from his mouth.

"Are you deaf Parolles? Bosko Chimurcho! Didn't you hear the words Boblibindo Chicmurcoco, you mentally challenged Ignoramus!" Beaver hollered and chastised the indicted conniver and wanton traitor.

"We've captured Count Beaver too!" the intelligent ventriloquist Captain lied to the blindfolded and shit-laden nearly paralyzed Parolles. "Now tell us upon threat of being beheaded and then hung upside down by your ankles, how many troops does the Florentine Duke have?"

"Five or six thousand but they're very weak and hungry," Parolles confessed. "And the fucked-up soldiers are scattered all over Florence and vicinity futilely looking for the infamous St. Francis Inn and Brothel."

"Are you ready for the anointing oils of Extreme Unction?" the Captain austerely declared to the shocked Parolles. "I'm not a priest so pretend you're speaking to an audience of bishops so do the next best thing and contritely and not tritely shrive yourself before us."

"I demand an honest trial and not this impromptu wallaby court farce!" Parolles futilely protested.

"You've deceived all of us and put our lives in jeopardy just to save your own cutthroat neck!" Count Bertram piped-up as Parolles recognized his master's voice.

"Bertram!" Parolles yelled, inadvertently spitting dung into his boss's face. "They've captured you too!"

"No you knavish repulsive traitor! No you pathetic shit-head!" the heir of Rossillon hollered back. "You've been duped by the old 'schoolboy missing drum scam' and now you've voluntarily betrayed the Duke, your officers and your fellow soldiers in an attempt to lie and salvage your own skin. What a poor excuse for a human being you are, you contemptible demonic vitriolic vituperative pretentious mercenary!"

"Please let me account for each interrogative separately!" the usually cavalier Parolles begged. "I have cash stashed away that I've stolen from all of you from one time or another to ransom my ass."

"What's this letter in your coat pocket?" Bertram noticed and asked his former pal. The Count opened the contrived and planted envelope and read the autobiographical note aloud. "Young Bertram is a dangerous and lascivious and vicious juvenile delinquent who relishes screwing and knocking-up defenseless virgins anywhere between Paris and Florence." Then Bertram asked the devious and detestable girl user and abuser, "Parolles, did you author this damnable document?"

"Parolles ought to be whipped by Helen's miracle whip she has brought from the gay Steward in Rossillon stable!" Count Beaver constructively suggested.

"This vile Wretch was your friend and ally, the antithesis of all that is honorable and noble in soldiery," Trilogy reminded Bertram. "With friends like him' who needs barbarians to brawl with?"

"By our Commander's discouraging looks," Catalina informed the still blindfolded and dumbfounded captive, "there will be no parole this time for you Parolles. You're going to be castrated by the army butcher and then hanged on a sturdy clothesline by the army launderer."

"Look fellas', I'm not afraid to die but since my offenses are too innumerable, can't I just be allowed to live and repent all of my transgressions in a dungeon or even in stocks and bonds sitting in a horse dung mound up to my chin?" the apprehensive prisoner requested.

"Tell me something about the captured trilingual French Captain Dumane!" the accomplished ventriloquist Captain Dumane asked the hostage, whose sole aspiration in life was to be a knavish rogue. "What about the French Captain Dumane?" Dumane interrogated.

"He's a super asshole who will rob the eyes off of a blind man," Parolles attested, not realizing he was addressing the very adept Captain Dumane. "As far as rapes, ravishments, swindling and stealing from fellow officers is concerned, his deportment parallels that of the legendary mythological Centaur Nessus. Mundane, er, I mean Dumane does not keep his oaths and promises and is so fucked-up in his brain that he's unreliable and as untrustworthy as a viper. Drunkenness is his best virtue besides sodomizing every man or woman his eyes and dick could detect," Parolles unknowingly testified against himself. "Not even his night pajamas are safe on the prick because the uncouth jerk-off might steal them from himself in his sleep. Dumane is everything that an honest man should not be and that unscrupulous asshole deserves *my* sentence and not me."

"What about Captain Dumane's expertise in war?" Captain Dumane asked the blindfolded turncoat. "Was he valiant?"

"That arrogant fuck-head was always taking a shit in the woods or jerking-off or sucking some infected whore's asshole rather than setting a good example by leading his doomed troops into battle," the befuddled Parolles continued indicting himself'. "I wouldn't trust Dumane any further than I can throw the Pyramids of Egypt from Africa into Europe, both main objects at the same time. In fact Dumane has often stolen other officers' drums but has never been accused of it like I'm now being prosecuted and persecuted for that felony."

"A pox on you Parolles and I hope it is more than small!" Bertram wished and uttered in a disguised voice. "You have two assholes and one of them is situated above your chin."

"What about the other Captain Dumane, the first Captain Dumane's twin brother?" the second Captain Dumane asked the unsavory hostage, who still believed he was speaking with tough interrogating officers from the Siena Army.

"He's just as fucked-up as his twin brother is!" Parolles falsely testified to save his own skin. "The only significant question at hand is which' of the two craven pricks is more of a goddamned coward. Whenever the enemy is sighted, that younger Captain Dumane retreats to the nearest monastery and sometimes disguises himself' as a nun and then retreats to the nearest convent to deliberately and desperately avoid the thrill and glory of military conflict."

"Will you consider becoming a Florentine or a citizen of Siena and abandon your life's registry as a Frenchman?" Bertram asked his former sidekick in a queer-sounding (here gay-sounding) muffled voice. "What's your preference? Where's your allegiance?"

"Yes, Siena it is, and I'll convince my shit-head boss Count Bertram of Rossillon to do the same," Parolles told Count Bertram.

"And how about your' battle drum?" Count Beaver asked.

"I'll do no more drumming! A plague on all drums and their drummers!" Parolles yelled, not knowing he was speaking to a lot of pissed-off drummers. "I blame Count Bertram for getting me into this fucked-up war in the first place because by nature I'm a passive tranquil fellow who loathes violence and military actions of any kind. I suppose I'm what in the future might be described as a peace-loving conscientious objector!"

"There's no known remedy for your cowardly mental sickness but death!" the first Captain Dumane ordered. "Parolles, you've dishonestly belied and besmirched your French King, your Italian Duke, your admirable Count Bertram and the entire French contingent of the Florentine army. You sir are undeniably an insult to decency, a disgusting vermin that must be exterminated."

"Oh kind Sir," the blindfolded Parolles begged, "let me live so that I may again casually tour the world and see all of the wonderful children that I've fathered out of wedlock," the no good bastard pleaded.

"Look about you and take your leave of all your former friends that you've abused and lied about!" the first Captain Dumane said as he roughly removed the blindfold from Parolles' shit-stained face.

"You die tomorrow morning and your hanging will be dedicated to the noble Count LeFew along with a few of your former friends," Bertram conveyed to the shocked traitor.

"It's true that I'm a psychopathic liar and a treacherous lecherous braggart," Parolles confessed to his former colleagues. "And I'll never be able to achieve the high rank of Captain. I've learned too late that every braggart shall eventually be found to be an ass. In the end I've been fooled and tricked by my own wily methods. You're all right Gentlemen. I am truly fucked-up and do deserve to die!"

* * * * * * * * * * * *

The following morning Helen and her new friend Diana (the two self-proclaimed former virgins) along with the merry Widow set-out by coach to Marseilles where the totally *cured* French King was vacationing and enjoying sitting in a smoke-house he had mistaken for a sauna. The three women were enjoying a jolly conversation as the coach bounced and rambled along a bumpy country dirt road.

"As you can determine ladies," Helen said to the Widow and her daughter Diana, "I've not wronged you but have made you two bitches rich. We've circulated a wild rumor all throughout Florence that I'm dead and Count Bertram has probably heard such gruesome news and will be rejoicing all the way back to Rossillon. But first we'll stop at Marseilles and update the King on all my recent adventures concerning my strange husband."

"Gentle Helen, my daughter and I will be your dedicated servants until you're officially sleeping with that repugnant prick Bertram," the Widow vowed as she counted the shiny gold coins in her newly acquired leather purse.

"And all Diana and I had to do was lose our stupid virginities in order to hoodwink foolish Bertram into surrendering his ring and perhaps knocking me up besides," Helen laughed and shared with her newfound allies. "It is too bad Mariana was in another room of the St. Francis whoring around with another client or else she could've gotten into some of the fun too. And after I sell the Count's fantastic diamond to a reputable pawnbroker," Helen speculated and announced, "I'll then finance a whole network of whorehouse franchises all over Europe and possibly all the way to America. You two bitches will again be rewarded at that fortuitous time as my business partners, no doubt about it!"

"Yes Helen," the traveling Widow confirmed, "and when you switched places with Diana while Count Bertram was snoring away, that was a really splendid ruse. When he screwed you in the dark he didn't even realize who the hell you were. This is the most entertaining and inspiring gossip I've ever shared, ha, ha, ha!"

"I'll gladly shove maraschino cherries up my vagina and lose my virginity over and over again for you dear Helen," Diana vowed, "and I've even taught my Mother how the hell to do it too! And I'm even planning to buy a smooth lengthy thick cherry-wood dildo to practice with when there aren't any fucked-up men around to screw me right through the mattress."

"Well you happy Bitches," Helen cheerfully said to Diana and *her* deliriously elated Mother, "All's well that ends well!"

* * * * * * * * * * *

The Countess of Rossillon had heard of Helen's death caused by *her* overwhelming grief and by *her* being sexually rejected by Bertram and then the old woman's health declined even more. Count LeFew, who had also learned about Helen's reported death' arrived at the feeble woman's estate with a very interesting proposition.

"I have a few topics to discuss with you," Count LeFew said to the ailing-but-resilient Countess of Rossillon. "Bertram has made a few mistakes, one of which was hanging around with that villainous creep Parolles and another was rejecting Helen more than a few times and thus gaining the King's disfavor. I pity you Countess for young Bertram has given you more than a few headaches."

"I wish the hell I had given birth to a girl instead of that saucy son-of-a-bitch, er, I mean son-of-a-bastard," the grieving Countess curtly answered. "My ungrateful selfish son is responsible for gentle Helen's death and I wish I never knew the fucked-up son-of-a-bitch, er, I meant to say fucked-up son-of-a-bastard."

"Helen was a good young lady and there are few others like her," LeFew opined. "Yes, only a few choice vegetables in the finest of salads and Helen was one of the few sweetest tomatoes in the mix."

"Why are you here LeFew?" the Countess finally asked.

"I specifically came to make a few reasonable requests," the Count slyly indicated. "True, it's hard distinguishing Bertram from the Prince of Darkness and a few other prominent demons residing in and terrorizing Hell. Your son knows and hangs-out with a few naughty rascals, Parolles being the major one," LeFew reviewed. "Now Countess, I have a few items I wish to confer with you about. Now that Helen is deceased I've gotten a few permissions from the King, one of which is to arrange a marriage between your Count Bertram and my daughter, I can't remember her goddamned name at the present. Anyway dear Countess," LeFew said, "the King is going to forget the few displeasures he has developed towards your hapless irresponsible son if your Bertram consents to marrying my anonymous daughter."

"That sounds like a most marvelous arrangement and now that Helen's dead I'll wholeheartedly endorse its enactment," the Countess concurred. "But LeFew, I can't guarantee that Bertram will only faithfully sleep with your unnamed daughter."

"Tomorrow morning the King will be riding with his entourage the few miles from Marseilles to Rossillon to approve of the wedding pact," LeFew added, "and our Monarch thinks that he's still a thirty year old buck despite the fact that he's more than a few decades beyond forty."

"Bertram has written me that he's arriving here tonight and I hope to live to see our noble King visiting Rossillon tomorrow," the Countess declared, "and also I hope I never see my bastard son Bertram again after he marries your daughter, because to share a little secret between *us*, Bertram was born out of wedlock and both of my husbands were impotent, suffering from erectile dysfunction."

"Should I stay here a few days after the wedding?" LeFew asked.

"Certainly gracious Count," the ill-but-genial lady agreed. "You can sleep in the barn with the stable boy. Rank has its privileges you know, so LeFew, you can sleep in the uppermost bunk bed."

The Fool entered the mansion via his side door with a brief announcement to make. "Countess, your erratic son Bertram has just ridden into the estate and has a patch of scarlet on his forehead. I hope he doesn't have a case of scarlet fever."

"Probably a scar that appears scarlet he had deservedly received in a barroom brawl or from an enraged whore with long fingernails," the Countess evaluated and uttered. "I'm sure the lustful bastard didn't receive the mark from bravely participating in combat."

"Yes, come to think of it," Count LeFew said while examining the letter that Bertram had sent to his mother, "this missive contains a few discernible crimson stains. It's no doubt a scarlet letter to match the few purported lacerations on your son's forehead!"

"I wish the hell LeFew that Bertram wasn't showing-up until tomorrow. Then he could get the frig' out of Rossillon to honeymoon with your daughter somewhere else far, far away!"

Act V

Helen, Diana and the merry Widow arrived in Marseilles but the itinerant girl was unable to petition the King, who had on the spur of the moment ridden on horseback (with his attendants far behind) west to rustic Rossillon. Helen soon became quite disappointed but not totally disheartened upon learning of "His Impulsive Majesty's hasty departure."

"Where is the King?" Helen asked a familiar-looking guard she had known in Paris. "Is he still vacationing here at his summer residence? Has he gone to Florence to search for me? Has His Majesty ever mentioned me to anyone?"

"Hello my fine Lady!" the guard amicably answered the sweet young woman. "I recall seeing you at the palace in Paris several times. You're the alchemist girl that cured the King of his many illnesses. Maybe in the future you can get rid of my terrible gout. What's your pleasure besides sex with that scurrilous wandering playboy Count Bertram?"

"I've already told you I wish to meet with the King to confer with him about some urgent matters," Helen clearly communicated without revealing her specific purpose. "Is the gregarious King available for a consultation?"

"No Lady Helen!" the guard reported, much to the girl's discouragement. "He's ridden-off leading a large entourage to Rossillon, I believe. The party left in haste like happy convicts escaping from the *Bastille*! Who the hell knows what those fickle royal crazies are ever up to?"

"Well Sir," the saddened and frustrated girl said from inside her rented coach, "here's a document, well actually only a mere letter that I would like to petition to the King for his perusal and assistance. Please make him cognizant of it when he returns to Marseilles, whenever that obscure event will be."

"I'll see that he receives it whenever he returns to Marseilles, if he ever returns," the guard promised. "Sometimes not even the King knows where the hell he's at or what the hell he's doing!"

"I must leave now," Helen said without giving any hint as to her destination (being the same as the King's). "Farewell good Sir."

"Farewell Helen and friends!" the courteous guard replied. "Good luck to you ladies wherever the hell you're going!"

As the coach pulled away from the gates of the King's Marseilles palace Helen said a few sentences to Diana and the Widow. "We're going to Rossillon to make a surprise visit to the forgetful King. Holy Shit ladies! I forget to tell the driver where the hell we're going! Driver!" Helen screamed out the open window. "Stop this damned coach so that I can give you your directions!"

* * * * * * * * * * * *

Parolles, who had just been released from custody with a dishonorable discharge (after Bertram disowned and humiliated him in front of the other French officers and soldiers), rode on horseback from Florence all the way to Rossillon with a forged document to give to the gullible and partially senile Count LeFew.

Upon arriving at the enormous estate the fiend had several words with the Countess's gay Steward appropriately nicknamed "Stewart," who' was presently quite preoccupied watching two large horses in heat frantically having sex in a small stable stall.

"I have a letter from good Monsieur Lavatch to personally deliver to Count LeFew," Parolles told the gay Steward and the gay stable boy, who was also idly hanging-out at the Rossillon red barn/outhouse. "Now where the hell can I find the old fart Count? I understand that he's here somewhere on the property."

"He's inside the mansion incessantly bullshitting with the Countess," the faggot Steward reluctantly and apathetically revealed. "You can meet him there in the parlor room. But perhaps you might want to first wash-up at the well because confidentially Monsieur Parolles, you smell like shit!"

Parolles washed himself up at the aforementioned well, borrowed some clean work clothes from the cooperative stable boy and then confronted and surprised LeFew at the mansion's front door just before the Count was about to go out to the crap house and take a healthy hour-long constipation dump.

"Count LeFew," Parolles prefaced, "I'm a man that fortune has frowned upon. My luck couldn't get any worse if I were a naked penniless tramp. I solicit your confidence in what I consider to be an urgent matter that might interest you."

"Why do you' wish to have a few words with me, you horrendous loser!" LeFew chastised his rude tormentor as the Count squirmed and held his legs together at the doorway. "You've insulted me on more than a few occasions when you thought you were high and mighty and acting mighty high after smoking a few joints of marijuana. It serves you right to be scratched a few times on your forehead where a few scars are evident, and also as I understand a few times on your ass and balls by Mother Fortune, or should I say Mother Miss Fortune, ha, ha, ha!"

"Hear me out LeFew because we're not standing inside," Parolles begged. "Why the hell are you squirming around? Do you have ants in your pants?"

"How have your few war drumming exercises gone?" LeFew deliberately insulted his dastardly acquaintance as the old man continued his distracting wriggling. "You're indeed a most cowardly asshole and that's the alpha and the omega of your fucked-up scurrilous existence that's seen more than a few feuds."

"I'd like to work for you kind erudite Count and erase all of my past transgressions and trespasses," Parolles pleaded, going down to his knees. "Appoint me to your personal pleasure service and I'll even melodramatically perform intense fellatio on your limp flaccid dick if necessary. Say now, I don't know if it's you or me that smells like shit."

"There's a few distinct blasts from the King's few trumpeters sounding in the distance," LeFew replied without directly answering his chief nemesis. "I must go and clean up a bit for a few minutes. We'll talk about a few pertinent details a little later on. It's difficult being sentimental about you Parolles because of a few malicious things you've done to me in the past not to mention your reputation of being a lazy procrastinator for more than a few years. Although you're a jerked off jerk-off and a fucked-up knave perhaps we can exchange a few ideas and reminisce a few unsavory events after supper. But first I must attend to a few private business matters inside my rickety outside office."

* * * * * * * * * * * *

The neurotic King and his Lords and landlords entered Rossillon Mansion followed by their bevy of lethargic attendants. Trumpets (and French horns) flourished to announce their unexpected surprise arrival.

"Dear Countess," the imperial King said as the resident woman courteously curtsied, "we lost a lustrous jewel in Helen de Narbon and we all are much the worse for it, although I must say that I've been miraculously and permanently cured of my terrible ulcer, of my inflamed hemorrhoids and of my nasty irritating sex-related itching problems that had been prevalent mostly in my personal areas. May Helen's immortal soul rest in peace."

"It is indeed a terrible shame My Liege!" the not-too-nimble Countess sympathetically sobbed. "And with no body ever being found poor Helen could not even be afforded a decent Christian burial. Yet amazingly, you and I live despite enduring our seemingly fatal afflictions."

"I've already forgiven and forgotten young Count Bertram's shortcomings mostly because I no longer have a conscience or a functioning brain!" the King lamented and pontificated without realizing the significance or truth of his commentary. "The loss of your daughter, er excuse me, the loss of your daughter-in-law has sorrowed me greatly."

"May I say a few words," the underwear-less naked Count LeFew (who had just returned from the outhouse) butted in' as was his bad habit. "Young and brazen Count Bertram had committed more than a few offenses that grieved us all but I must emphasize that the upstart's biggest abuse that he had actually performed unto himself on more than a few occasions had been his maligning of his own good family name. And now Count Bertram has made more than a few of us disconsolate because the guiltless shameless bastard had aggrieved Helen so much that she has perished as a result of his selfish demeanor, which got all the meaner a few times over in Florence."

"Call Bertram of Rossillon hither from thither, or wherever the hell else he's hiding!" the King ordered. "Let him come forth and face the music although no hired musicians are playing any melody in this rather dilapidated mansion right now! I mean, I must have harmony among my noblemen!"

"I shall fetch the wretch My Royal Liege!" the crippled Lord Bawlbraker volunteered. "Count Bertram had hastily entered the outhouse right after Count LeFew had exited!"

"Now Count LeFew," the King asked the feeble old man, "has Bertram been introduced to your daughter, I forget her name, and has he proposed marriage?"

"They had casually met a few times in some tenement slum in Paris," the fuzzy-minded Count recollected and stated, "although I can't verify if they've already hopped into the sack a few times and if they're quite familiar with each other's anatomy."

"That's wonderful and excellent news!" the easily influenced King of France exclaimed. "I've recently received for the notorious gigolo Count Bertram a letter of commendation from the Duke of Florence attesting to *his* valor and his relentless audacity that had been exhibited in battle. He and Count LeFew's anonymous daughter will certainly make a model-couple match."

"Yes Your Majesty," the ecstatic LeFew confirmed, "a real match just like a few pinches of potash and phosphorus in a bed of tinder and the two youngsters should generate more than a few displays of friction and heat in the sack," the nude Count laughed, bending over and smacking his bony knees with his palms.

Bertram hesitantly entered, respectfully bowed to the King and immediately apologized for his "self-centered conduct" leading to his wife Helen's demise.

"All is whole again!" the King said to Bertram for all in the mirrored parlor room to hear. "Let thy myriad emotional scars be healed, you young heel! Now then, to get down to brass tax, er, I mean brass tacks," the confused Monarch continued, "does your recollection recall the name of the hard-to-remember daughter of Count LeFew?"

"Yes, my eyes laid upon her before I laid her," Bertram anxiously admitted. "I sacked the raunchy Bitch more than once in the sack back in a rear alley Paris shanty."

"It sounds like you loved this anonymous wench more than you had scorned the pristine Helen," the King rebuked his often wayward subject. "At any rate Bertram, let bygones be bygones and since you presently show a small degree of remorse, you have my imperial pardon for your failures as a husband to Helen. In the future I hereby warn you, don't make a trivial price of your serious obligations to your King and to your spouse. Learn to temper your fucked-up rash biological inclinations and balance your abundant faults with compassion for wife and for country. Now hear me Bertram, will you marry fair….."

"Maudlin, I knew it was a few syllable name!" naked LeFew remembered and contributed in more than a few words. "I still remember a few things despite my many mental infirmities."

"Yes, thank you LeFew!" the King commended. "Now Bertram of Rossillon, will you consent to marring, er, I meant to say marrying Maud Madeline, LeFew's heavyweight buxom daughter?"

"Kindly hand me a ring so that I may fetch my daughter in a few minutes and then re-enter this exquisite improvised wedding chamber," Count LeFew excitedly urged Bertram.

Thinking about possible negative consequences should he' refuse the King's command, Bertram reached his right hand into his pocket and produced the cheap tin ring that Diana had placed on his finger while he was sleeping in her bedroom at the St. Francis Inn and Brothel in Florence.

"Is this the ring you had originally given Helen in Paris?" the King inquired as he momentarily examined the cheap piece of merchandise. "It looks rather commonplace."

"No Your Majesty, I obtained the object in Florence as a good luck charm," Bertram instinctively lied. "And I must admit that my fortune has changed for the better ever since arriving back home here in Rossillon twenty or so minutes ago."

"But where did you obtain this tawdry tin piece of crap unworthy of a royal lady of aristocratic breeding such as the beautiful Maud Madeline or whatever the fuck her fucked-up name is?" the King orally blundered.

"I was casually strolling down an alleyway and a lady from a balcony threw it down to get my attention and the damned thing hit me on the head and then bounced directly into my hand," Bertram again fibbed. "I refused to surrender to her entreaty and I sauntered away keeping her cheap overture as a good luck token."

"Look Count Bertram," the perturbed King said raising his voice, "just pretend that Helen had given you this ordinary tin ring and make everything simple and easy so that we can commence with the goddamned wedding ceremony. Why must you always make the most elementary task so fuckin' painful and so ass-backwards difficult?"

"No Your Majesty," Bertram declared while being honest for the first time (at the wrong time). "Helen never saw this cheesy ring I'm offering Count LeFew to give to his daughter Maud Madeline, er, I think I mean Maudlin."

"This is unprecedented bullshit that's completely overwhelming my patience!" the distraught King shrilly screamed. "You speak falsely, insulting the integrity of Count LeFew, along with your mother's and mine honor. Why must you persist in still abusing your chaste dead wife? I must glean more actionable facts and testimony and sift this matter through. Guards, remove this lying young bastard from my mist, er, I mean from my midst!"

* * * * * * * * * * * *

No sooner had Count Bertram of Rossillon been escorted from the chamber to the temporary jail (the rickety smelly outhouse) that Count Beaver, returning from the strange military campaign in Florence, entered the mansion's grand room. The new arrival bowed and then politely addressed the King.

"Your Majesty, I have a petition from a Florentine woman who seeks justice in France for wrongdoing done to her by the brash and abrasive Count Bertram. May I respectfully read the letter's contents?"

"Stop being such an eager Beaver, my dear Count. Just tell me what the damned letter states in a nutshell that I hope is smaller than your diminutive scrotum nut shell," the King rankled. "I don't have all day to resolve picayune grievances from foreign whore wenches. It is only because Sir Bertram's character is in doubt here that I entertain your fucked-up request."

"The lady states in this less-than-tender note that she has recently learned of Helen's untimely death and that Count Bertram is now officially a merry widower," Count Beaver recounted. "The Count has given the lady his diamond ring in exchange for sex," Beaver accurately quoted and also paraphrased from the letter, "and after he screwed me five times the dirty bastard split out of town while I mourned for my lost virginity."

"This seducer should not flourish in your kingdom and with few exceptions not wreck my daughter's future too," Count LeFew argued to the thoroughly flustered King. "Bertram has sabotaged and ruined more than a few female lives, and his heinous traducing must be stopped. I'll randomly search out a son-in-law stranger at a few carnivals or at a few circuses rather than have fucked-up Bertram marry my vulnerable very emotional daughter Maud Madeline, er, I mean Maudlin!

"This latest piece of evidence we've discovered today in the form of the whore's letter definitely shows and proves Bertram of Rossillon's extremely arrogant and sinful nature," the extremely perturbed King declared. "Guards, go fetch Count Bertram and bring him here to orally confront his latest accuser face-to-face. That dastardly punk prick has eagerly snatched enough ladies' snatches to last him five lifetimes!"

Five minutes later the guards escorted Bertram back into the mansion's main chamber where Lady Diana, a resident of the St. Francis Inn and Brothel in Florence stepped forward and confronted the guiltless philanderer. Diana curtsied and addressed the wary-but-weary King.

"Your Majesty, I'm a wretched impoverished Florentine wench who humbly seeks your divine counsel and fair justice," Diana began her entreaty in stilted French. "I do have aristocratic blood in my veins and arteries for I am a descendant of the noble Capilet family of Italian distinction. Now then," Diana said while clearing her throat and glancing over at her mother tacitly coaxing her to speak. "Your Majesty, others have accompanied me to Rossillon."

"I am the Lady Diana's widowed mother and I too have greatly suffered under the complaint being presented by my dear daughter," the woman testified in French with an Italian accent.

"Count Bertram, do you know either of these women?" the very intrigued King asked.

"Yes, I met them both in Florence," Bertram acknowledged under duress. "What specific charges do these vociferous covetous hags advance against me?"

"Don't you recognize your lovely wife?" Diana exclaimed. "Don't you recall? You screwed me five times and sodomized me once in my room at the luxurious recently renovated St. Francis Hotel and Spa and then you fled Florence to screw and sodomize more innocent virgins here in France!"

205

"Your corrupt reputation with more than a few whores and sluts is not worthy of my daughter's attention!" the still nude Count LeFew yelled into Count Bertram's face. "You aren't fit to be a few giant furry gorillas' husband let alone my precious Maudlin's louse of a spouse!"

"Your Majesty," Bertram petitioned the King, "you've known me for some time, well, for several days while I was in Paris and you must know about the letter of commendation sent to you by the Duke of Florence. I'm not such a savage monster as this pathetic gold-digging wench claims I am, now am I?"

"This ravenous bastard had stolen my virginity after I insisted that he propose to me before screwing me!" Diana charged. "Ask the oaf about his oath!"

"How do you call yourself on this grievous matter?" the impatient King asked Bertram.

"The Italian Bitch is both impudent and imprudent," Bertram claimed, "and she whored around with many officers and even with common soldiers in the Florentine camp, which in the final analysis was not too campy!"

"Don't believe his shallow prattle Your Majesty!" Diana strongly maintained. "That lowly cunt-lapper, and I speak from experience on that sensitive matter, he has grossly abused my honor and my virginity. Here's undeniable proof, his sparkling diamond ring the asshole gave me as a combined engagement and wedding gift!"

"That dazzling gem is a treasured family heirloom and I would identify it anywhere as authentic!" the Countess of Rossillon disbelievingly gasped.

"And this man's knave associate Parolles knows all about this prestigious ring and its purpose in wooing me into marriage," Diana eloquently attested.

"I saw the scoundrel Parolles a few minutes ago washing a few horseshit stains from his face and arms at the well behind the stables," the naked Count LeFew chimed in. "A few birds of a feather have flocked together."

"Fetch the knave and bring the incorrigible disgusting son-of-a-bitch here!" the King commanded his inattentive guards. "Now comely Lady Diana, I hereby order that you may keep Count Bertram's ancestral ring!"

"I protest your premature decision!" the Countess of Rossillon balked. "You need more evidence that is not so circumstantial before rendering that kind of rash judgment!"

"Okay Countess, I retract my last statement and it is restricted from the official record," the King conceded. "Do you admit Bertram that you gave Lady Diana the ring at the newly renovated St. Francis Hotel and Spa in Florence?"

"Why certainly yes Your Majesty," the defensive heir to Rossillon affirmed, "but she seduced it from me promising me heavenly sex like I had never experienced before. I was duped, set up! How could I resist the great temptation?"

"You're beyond a doubt a virtue-less fanatical fiend who lacks an ounce of decency or shame," Diana yelled, wagging her finger at Bertram. "I no longer give a shit about the damned ring. All I seek is swift justice and *your* imminent punishment, which I shall relish and savor right to my deathbed."

"Do you recognize the tin ring that Count LeFew has in his hand?" the King interrogated the theatrical Florentine girl.

"Yes, but that's another story, a donkey of a different hue!" Diana strangely answered. "The tin ring was given by me to Bertram in my bedroom."

"Then you did not throw it down to him from the balcony of the recently renovated St. Francis Hotel and Spa?" the Monarch asked.

"Hell no! He received it in the bedroom to consummate our consentual marriage!" Diana insisted.

"This fascinating-but-warped story is getting more and more complex by the minute, wouldn't you agree Count LeFew?" the King queried.

"With more than a few twists and turns," LeFew confirmed. "I have seen few like it in my lifetime!"

The king's guards then roughly escorted the villain Parolles into the mansion's grand room to testify before His Excellency. Bertram and Parolles indignantly stared at each other.

"My Lord, I do confess that the heirloom diamond ring was given to Lady Diana," Bertram admitted upon seeing his archenemy's appearance.

"What do you know about Count Bertram's relationship with this attractive Florentine woman, Lady Diana?" the King asked the ignoble noble wannabe' Parolles.

"I admit that Count Bertram did love this saucy Bitch like a country gentleman loves a sophisticated woman of good standing," Parolles orally conveyed for all to hear inside the overly ornate parlor. "But he said he loved her but loved her not, just as if he were picking the petals off a daisy one at a time. This Florentine Bitch standing over yonder really had enticed and obsessed him for a while until Count Bertram finally decided to scram out of Florence."

"You must've known other secrets that smutty Count Bertram had shared with you?" the King asked the atrocious raper and sodomizer. "Reveal them and I might adjust *your* penalty!"

"Yes," Parolles affirmatively answered, "I do know that Count Bertram bragged about screwing Lady Diana on their wedding night and that he sodomized her at least once. That's the honest-to-God truth so help me Jesus Iscariot, er, I mean Jesus Christ!"

"Now Lady Diana, where did you happen to purchase the tin ring that you supposedly gave to Count Bertram? From which marketplace vendor did you procure it?" the inquisitive King nervously inquired.

"I did not buy or borrow it from anyone!" Diana nonchalantly exclaimed with a trace of guilt as if she were withholding certain important facts.

"Well then Lady Diana, if the tin ring never belonged to you where did you get it?" the perceptive King questioned the now nervous witness.

"This vacillating woman has made a few arbitrary remarks and is off and on like a cheap shabby used glove," Count LeFew argued. "Her testimony, all but a few irrelevant sentences, is full of a few large holes and appears to be quite erroneous!"

"Look you lying sleazy Italian Bitch," the incensed King threatened the now-horrified Diana, "you'll be hung in less than an hour if you don't tell me the truth about this less-than-mediocre tin ring. I suspect it belonged to Lady Helen, given to her by her indigent alchemist father!"

"I'll never reveal to you whom I had acquired it from, truth or dare!" Diana defiantly scolded the King. "Believe me Your Majesty. I am no whoring strumpet!"

"This Italian Bitch abuses my ears and nauseates my stomach!" the King bellowed. "Take her away out of my sight! Rip her tits off for all I care!"

"Good Mother!" Diana shouted to the now non-merry Widow. "Fetch my bail!"

"What do you mean by that nonsensical outburst?" the King bellowed.

"Helen de Narbon still lives and will testify in my defense!" Diana theatrically disclosed to her very appalled and shocked audience. "She has earned possession of the Count's ancestral ring, which she had later lent to me for good keeping. And to boot, Lady Helen is carrying Count Bertram's child in her womb!"

"This travesty is absolute bullshit that's positively too incredible to be ordinary horse shit!" Bertram protested.

* * * * * * * * * * * *

"Is there no exorcist present to cast-out the demons swimming in Lady Diana's spirit?" the King asked his bewildered subjects. "What goes here now?"

The Widow (Diana's money-hungry Mother) and the delicate Lady Helen entered the parlor chamber, much to the astonishment of all the eyewitnesses including addled Count Bertram. The pair methodically stepped toward and eventually approached the totally flabbergasted and awestruck King of France.

"Oh King, I confirm all that Diana has said is true," Helen lucidly articulated. "And here is a statement written by Count Bertram attesting that whenever I should have possession of his ring and bear his child in my body, then he would gladly sleep with me, his devoted wife Helen!"

"Such incredible bullshit ought to be organized into a really terrific stage play!" the King, an aspiring thespian dramatically said. "And thank goodness this fiasco is more of a comedy farce than a terrible tragedy! I think I'll become a playwright to finally get this damned play right!"

"Oh Mother, please accept me as your charmed daughter-in-law!" Helen wildly double-talked to the more-than-surprised Countess of Rossillon, who thought she was entering cardiac arrest for the final time.

"Even the smell of a few rotting onions couldn't bring a few more tears to my eyes," Count LeFew panted as if he too (like the venerable Countess) was entering into a coronary seizure. "I'm in such a sentimental mood that I want to hire that evil fiend Parolles to perform for me a few random errands and a few random chores."

"Latch onto thy wife Helen's hand Count Bertram and I'll gladly pay her dowry from the coffers of my imperial treasury, thanks to the generosity of our fine French taxpayers," the now euphoric King chortled and giggled. "But enjoy long sexual intervals with her Bertram of Rossillon because Helen no longer wishes to be a minute maid, ha, ha, ha! Needless to say my distinguished spectators, 'All's well that ends well'."

William Shakespeare (1564-1616)

William Shakespeare was born (just like the rest of us fragile mortals) in Stratford-on-Avon, England, situated about eighty miles northwest of London. The registers at the Holy Trinity Church indicate that Shakespeare was baptized (and nearly drowned) on April 26, 1564, probably three days after the future playwright popped out of his mother Mary's snatcheroo. William was the third of eight children born to John and Mary Shakespeare (maiden name Arden), and *his* merchant father was once mayor of the somnolent community who would knock on residents' doors and humorously and ridiculously announce, "Stratford-on-Avon calling! Ha, ha, ha!"

William courted and dated an attractive girl named Anne Hathaway, who lived in Shottery, a village around a half-mile (half-a-way) from Stratford-on-Avon. Anne was actually robbing the cradle since she was twenty-six and William was a mere eighteen when the pair wed in 1582 and even though Shakespeare never took drugs and seldom got drunk, as a horny youth he was often seen entering the "half-a-way house" in Shottery with a huge bulge in his pants. The couple had three children, Susana in 1583 and twins Hamnet and Judith in 1585. All three raunchy kids had to sleep in twin beds even though only Hamnet and Judith were bona fide twins.

After moving from the countryside to London, Shakespeare soon became an actor, playwright, poet and businessman, becoming a partner in the ownership of the now-famous *Globe Theater*. His acting company The King's Men often performed at the *Globe* and it is frequently and accurately said, "All the King's horses and all The King's Men, couldn't put Humpty Dumpty together again!"

William Shakespeare is reputed to have written thirty-seven plays and since he died at age fifty-two it is believed that he regularly wrote at "super-sonnet speed." Shakespeare often had trouble holding his sword or spear steady while standing on stage and hence his physical appearance and trembling mannerisms often matched the structure of his last name. In his work the playwright demonstrates a tremendous knowledge of a variety of subjects such as music, history, politics, sports, law', the *Bible* along with other remarkable assorted bullshit. In 1611 William became pissed-off and bored with the *Globe Theater* so he lived the last five years of his life as a country gentleman in Stratford-on-Avon where he resided in the second largest house in the town. W.S. was buried in Trinity Church where he had been violently baptized fifty-two years earlier.

"Dr. Heidegger's Experiment"

That very erudite and eccentric chemical-mixing scientist, Dr. Ludwig Heidegger, who had migrated to the United States from Heidelberg, Germany in his youth, invited four old friends to his dark secluded New Hampshire mansion. The purpose for the hastily arranged assemblage was to formally conduct a secret seminar inside the Professor's spacious study. Although the good doctor strongly wished to reminisce past events with his venerable acquaintances and also nostalgically review old times, his principal motivation was to gradually expose his aged comrades to the radical idea of becoming central subjects in a "marvelous miraculous experiment."

Three white-bearded gentlemen that attended the oddball consultation were Mr. Melvin Melbourne from Australia, Mr. Gaston Gascoigne from Paris, France and Colonel Kile Killigrew from Western Pennsylvania. One elderly wrinkle-faced woman was also in the visiting geriatrics contingent, Miss Wilma Whyknot from the New York City Battery District, where the indigent woman' now sleeps as a hapless bag-lady mendicant in the battery's terminals, either bus, subway or train.

Each of the carefully selected guests to Dr. Ludwig Heidegger's secluded laboratory had encountered bad luck in life and certainly would have been much happier at age ninety-five if the decrepit foursome had died two decades before.

Especially Miss Wilma Whyknot, who presently looked like Cleopatra does right now. In her younger days the former spitfire had been a daring promiscuous bitch who had had intense love affairs with Mr. Melbourne, with Mr. Gascoigne, with Colonel Killigrew and last but not least, with the eminent Dr. Heidegger when the hag had lived in Mass-a-two-shits.

It had been gossiped around all of Puritanical Protestant New England that Wilma Whyknot was indeed an ancient slutty hoary whore who had myriad romantic love affairs with Thomas Jefferson, with Alexander Hamilton and also with nefarious Aaron Burr, and that the jilted Burr had brutally shot and killed Hamilton in a Weehawken, New Jersey pistol duel that had been waged over Wilma Whyknot's then voluptuous body.

In Australia Mr. Melvin Melbourne had once been a well-to-do grocery store distributor but then "the mate" became involved in a crazy business investment, selling kangaroo meat to vegetarian-style supermarket chains. Melbourne soon lost his entire fortune and is now officially bankrupt, unhappily living in a Melbourne, Florida hippie commune, the failed entrepreneur harshly being relegated to the status of a more-than-desperate food stamps and welfare recipient.

Mr. Gaston Gascoigne has chronically suffered from gastritis and colitis ever since he had first plopped his fat ass on a toilet seat. Wilma Whyknot recalls that the gaseous jerk would fart relentless every time the amorous pair would engage in crazy frenetic sex. Even though Wilma would tell Gaston "Stop farting around," the poor fellow had no control over his spastic intestines, and the unfortunate "French hemorrhage" asshole always had the sorest anus around.

Colonel Kile Killigrew, whose many belligerent ancestors represented the Union during the bloody Civil War, hated any rebel or Confederate descendant born south of the historic Mason-Dixon Line. But in his perverted youth, the Colonel regarded himself as a veritable sex machine, bragging that he carried in his system a dozen sexually transmitted diseases including syphilis, gonorrhea, chancroid and nymphomania lymphogranuloma, but over the years, the antebellum erection champion had gained immunity to all of the potentially lethal maladies. Occasionally the now-sperm-less retired Army officer avoids the traditional V.A. Hospitals and goes for special treatment directly to the government's highly acclaimed National V.D. Medical Center.

"My dear valued old friends," Dr. Heidegger began his extemporaneous salutation, "welcome to my humble haunted house, er, I meant to say, 'modest home'. I urgently need your help in participating in one of my favorite experiments that I often use to amuse myself, frequently performing and perfecting the demonstration right here in my comfortable study. Oh now, I'm so awfully sorry," the absent-minded Alzheimer's candidate apologized. "My study is the adjoining room. This friggn' part of my mansion is the fuckin' foyer!"

"What is your mysterious study like?" Mr. Melvin Melbourne curiously asked. "Is it similar to a university library loaded with empty book shelves?"

"My study is actually an old-fashioned room that features tremendous spider webs and cob-webs all over the friggin' walls and ceiling, and I must admit that it is a veritable paradise for voracious insects and mice, and besides *that* dull stupid shit, the entire damned place has plenty of dust along with scads of accumulated filth in every corner," Heidegger calmly admitted and confessed. "And although I had been born in Hamburg, Germany, and then growing-up in Heidelberg, I only know a little German, and his name is Gunther Fadorkenbender, living way up in Dixville Notch. And regrettably," the garrulous Professor finished, "all of my books are in German and in Austrian, but to my frustration, I only know how to speak and read English and Mandarin Chinese."

Dr. Ludwig Heidegger next led his four very impressed guests from the massive foyer and then down the long drafty corridor serving as a portal into the aforementioned Grand Study, which also alternated as the scientist's personal laboratory, the exact setting where the fanatic intensively labored day and night on myriad obscure and insignificant projects.

The century-old guide next proudly showed his almost-blind visitors an immense marble statue of the Greek physician Hippocrates, seen peering intently into a naked woman's vagina with his left hand shoved inside the lady patient's sex tunnel all the way up to the kinky examiner's elbow.

Then quirky Dr. Heidegger opened the squeaky panel doors to a seven-foot-high wooden storage closet and to everyone witnessing the intriguing spectacle, the four visitors were instantly shocked viewing two skeletons incessantly rattling back and forth against each other in what truly constituted a very entertaining anatomical sex orgy.

"When I open the study's windows during a hurricane or blizzard," the unorthodox Professor explained to his now-fascinated audience, "the skeletons really move much better with the wicked wind blowing the dangling sons-a-bitches around in a frenzy. The only problem I have with the cute closet display is that both skeletons are males. I mean, I could have a gigantic gender lawsuit on my hands from the litigious gay and lesbian community, wherever the hell *that* fucked-up town is located! I mean, even the fucked-up trans-gender freaks will take me to court over this totally dumb-ass homosexual bullshit!"

Between two of the more grimy vertical bookcases was situated an enormous mirror with a faded gold-gilt frame. It had been rumored throughout the whole New England region that all of the Professor's dead former patrons were now spooky goblins and ghouls, all arcanely stashed inside the black magic looking glass, and that the trapped spirits would occasionally stick their ghostly heads outside the frame whenever stragglers into the dilapidated mansion would be glancing away from the bizarre-looking ominous mirror.

On the opposite side of the peculiar "museum" was a young lady's portrait, the said female wearing a dull dress emblematic of a previous century, and the attractive apparel had been woven from imported silk along with an expensive satin fabric.

Melvin Melbourne, Gaston Gascoigne, Colonel Kile Killigrew and Miss Wilma Whyknot all noticed in sheer amazement that when the sunshine shafts penetrated the dirty windows and then shone directly into the eerie library/study, the young woman's wedding dress would transform from being opaque to being transparent, and the beautiful woman would be exposed stark naked with all of her pubic hairs and her fine succulent breasts and nipples being fully on display. And then conversely, when the drifting clouds took control of the sky and obscured the sun's radiant rays, the comely woman in the painting would be respectably fully clothed once again.

"That's not me up there!" Miss Whyknot observed and exclaimed. "That's the knockout bitch you dumped me for, isn't it Ludwig!"

"Yes Wilma," Dr. Heidegger confirmed. "That lady portrayed in the painting is my' former fiancee, Sylvia Ward. The night before our wedding, my love felt ill, so I gave her a medicinal formula I had been assiduously working on, but delicate Sylvia reacted negatively to the medication and died within an hour," the Professor lamented. "I've since sold the toxic formula to several state penitentiaries, who now use the special chemical solution to execute Death Row prisoners instead of utilizing costly electric chairs that incidentally are not environmentally-friendly, using too much voltage energy and thus, egregiously polluting the pristine atmosphere."

"Doctor, what's that huge volume over there?" Gaston Gascoigne wanted to know. "I've never seen a book quite that enormous anywhere!"

Just then the sunshine shone through the south-side windows and Sylvia Ward instantly again became naked. Also, the two male closet skeletons were now facing in the same direction and engaging in humpty-rumpty sodomy, and in addition, noble Hippocrates was now sniffing his stinky middle finger with a broad snarky smile evident upon his ancient Greek countenance.

Then the seemingly enchanted study became rather shadowy again when the sun retreated behind a dark cloud, and everything in the creepy room returned to its original appearance, including the hanging wall portrait, the homosexual skeletons and the weird marble "Hippocrates and Female Patient" life-size figures.

"Is that gargantuan book sitting there on the table titled *Mountain of Truth?*" Colonel Killigrew nervously asked. "It's so dust-laden that I can't discern the precise cover language."

"No Sir," Dr. Heidegger promptly answered in a deep mellow voice. "Its goddamned title is *Fountain of Youth!* I found the almost indecipherable volume while exploring for El Dorado up in the Amos Mountains, which as you might know parallel the Andes. That little vignette I've just mentioned appropriately explains *that* exotic book cover proudly featuring a forgotten range of high mountain peaks."

* * * * * * * * * * * *

While the five senile assholes were gathered around Dr. Ludwig Heidegger's round study table discussing old mutual friends that had died, specifically Sarah Yeahvo, Kenny Bunkport and "Shy Ann" Wyoming, the sunlight again reflected through the south-side window panes, which made the four visiting senior-senior-senior citizens *reflect* on what the hell their demented host was attempting to communicate.

Professor Heidegger, former head of the science department at the famed Driftwood Naval Academy located somewhere on the north bank of the Susquehanna River, commenced with his mind-boggling narrative. "My dear old friends, and I do mean old," the whacky Professor sarcastically emphasized, "first of all you four withered-up itinerants should be wearing name tags so that I could fuckin' remember who the hell I had sent invitations to."

Melvin Melbourne cleared his throat and the bankrupt charlatan rudely interrupted the forgetful host, who was presently suffering from a bad case of exaggerated dementia. "Dr. H., how come there are four empty champagne glasses on the table? Are your four undistinguished guests sitting here going to drink air? On second thought, I think we all badly need oxygen, ha, ha, ha!"

"The four stemmed glasses are on the table so that you dumb-ass wretches can assist me in conducting a very odd-but-phenomenal experiment," Professor H. (who actually felt and looked like H) revealed. "Within the confines of this study/laboratory I wish to learn the outcome of my life's work, that is, before I fuckin' die and go to Heaven, Hell, Purgatory, Limbo or maybe to No-where, except into the goddamned ground!"

"Who gives a royal flying shit!" Melvin Melbourne again gruffly butted-in, trying to steal the now annoyed Professor's verbal thunder. "When you're dead, you don't fuckin' know anything!"

"You might be nimble enough to vault into your vault!" cryptically joked Colonel Kile Killigrew to flabbergasted Melbourne. "That type of amusing endeavor would be quite an undertaking, even without the aid of an undertaker dying from HIV/AIDS, ha, ha, ha!"

"We're all obviously suffering from advanced Iron Deficiency Anemia," objectively jested Miss Wilma Whyknot, "so why not serve us four old farts some delicious Geritol, ha, ha, ha! Especially for my old gaseous lover, Mr. Gascoigne here, who I think eats too much goddamned broccoli!"

"Didn't you use to be a bank teller before you were a teller of tale tales?" Gaston Gascoigne merrily expressed to now-demoralized Dr. Heidegger before egregiously farting a loud gas bomb blast lasting for forty-seven and a half seconds. "Dr., are you going to show us how you can annihilate a defenseless white mouse in an air pump, or are we going to examine one of Methuselah's five thousand year old sperm cells under a microscope?"

The three other jollied guests all laughed, burped, belched and farted in response to Gaston Gascoigne's fairly whimsical remarks. But their all-too-serious host evidently was not in a similar jocular frame of mind.

"You're not too far away from the very essence of my innovative theory," Dr. Heidegger replied before rising-up from the musty round table and then slowly limping across the large neglected room, returning just as deliberately while gingerly carrying the giant black heavy book showing the Amos Mountain peaks on its begrimed cover.

The rather clandestine Professor carefully opened the silver clasp bindings and between the first and second pages, the oddball demonstrator cautiously removed what appeared to be the remnants of a rose, or what appeared to be *that* particular flower variety.

After everyone quieted-down from enjoying the previous ongoing ludicrous conversation, the good Dr. solemnly addressed his cynical doubters. "This half-crumbled rose that I'm now holding in my quivering hand had blossomed fifty some years ago. My lovely fiancee Sylvia Ward had given this flower memento to me to wear in the lapel of my 'tuxedo' on our wedding day."

"Yes Professor, but I suppose the only Tucks any of us now know are the suppositories we use to purify our smelly assholes, ha, ha, ha!" Melvin Melbourne articulated as his three equally asinine associates also simultaneously guffawed.

Ignoring the totally preposterous goof-ball remark and the resulting laughter, undaunted Dr. Ludwig Heidegger proceeded with his esoteric exposition. The four dubious attendees finally fathomed that the profound Professor was deadly serious about further delivering his strange lecture.

"For over half a century this treasured flower I've kept between the pages of the classic old volume, but now tell me. Do any of you Neanderthal knuckle-dragging skeptics believe one iota that this withered flower can be revived back to its glory days' fresh blossom?"

"Horizontal Wilt Chamberlain decaying inside his extra-long grave looks better than *that* thing does!" evaluated and commented Wilma Whyknot. "You must be a blooming idiot Professor, ha, ha, ha! My dried-up pussy will grow thick brown curly hair again before that wilted rose is ever rejuvenated! Ha, ha, ha!"

"Just watch this unique bullshit!" demanded the now-insulted Professor. "That asshole Shakespeare had it all wrong. This rose is more than a mere rose! Your full-of-shit doubting minds are analogous to your shrunken brains being 'skeptic' tanks that are full of diarrhea! You four facetious assholes will soon learn and appreciate the explicit veracity of my sublime words!"

On-a-mission Professor Heidegger then removed a mint-colored vase that had been obscurely covered by a green cloth shroud, the commonplace object being taken from a previously unnoticed bookcase that had been occupying a space on a dusty side wall. The determined demonstrator next meticulously dropped the lifeless rose into the murky water contained inside the magical vase. At first the lifeless flower was simply floating on top of the cloudy-but-mysterious liquid solution.

"Is that water well water or tap water?" Gaston Gascoigne asked the experimenter. "That water must be tap water because it doesn't look too well to me! Ha, ha, ha!" the flamboyant asshole remarked before loudly tooting a large quantity of expendable gas (for thirty seconds) from his erratic asshole.

"Doubting Thomas," Dr. H. caustically criticized gaseous Gaston. "Now I accuse you other three noodle-brained buffoons of also each being a doltish Doubting Thomas. None of you harebrained fools would have believed Jesus at the Biblical Cana Wedding Feast, even if the Lord had changed the wine he had transformed from water back into water again!"

Soon a most incredible alteration in the experimental rose's composition began to occur. The separate petals began assuming a deeper red texture, and the flower itself was emerging from its deathlike state of existence, or non-existence if you prefer the latter terminology. Then suddenly, without any sign or notice, the slender tender stem and leaves mystically turned green and vibrant.

"This is certainly a deception, a flimsy carnival side-show trick I once saw performed on the Coney Island Boardwalk," Colonel Kile Killigrew remembered and orally shared. "Or perhaps it was on the Atlantic City Boardwalk! I can't seem to accurately recall. But you do recollect, don't you Wilma? We were shacked-up in a fleabag hotel screwing-away like minks pleasurably enjoying the female one's heightened estrus; yes Wilma, we were humping and pumping away, just off of Surf Avenue! Then we walked all over the damned place looking for a tree growing in Brooklyn."

"Have you never heard of the exotic Fountain of Youth Colonel?" Dr. H. asked Killigrew. "The Spanish explorer Ponce de Leon searched for the fabled wonder in vain all over Florida, yes, the fabulous 'flower state,' around three centuries ago. But the lost wanderer never searched for the Fountain in the right place," the Professor professed. "However, a dear friend of mine living near Lake Macaco has remarkably discovered the Fount, and this nondescript mint-green vase contains water from the miraculous underground spring. Even though its wonderful spring water, you can drink it summer, fall and winter too! I promise you Folks, this vial is not vile at all!"

"Holy shit!" Melvin Melbourne rather boisterously exclaimed. "I could sprinkle some of that terrific crap on my dick and it'll get hard for the first time in forty years! And my tiny shriveled-up balls could be resuscitated too!"

"I need that magic water applied to my scrawny chest to firm-up my sagging tits!" Wilma Whyknot excitedly yelled. "My flabby nipples will become big suckers once again! And my clit will get hard again and be just as big as Gaston's erection used to be!"

"I'll have more erections than any friggin' builder or architect ever did, including that dead guy Frank Lloyd Wright!" Gaston Gascoigne enthusiastically shouted. "I'll be able to pop semen all over the damned place, even more so than the brawniest seamen out there sailing the oceans! As I used to say before getting laid back in the good old days, 'A little squirt never hurts!' But honestly, too much sex could also fag-out a gay French faggot like me, Gaston Gascoigne!"

Staring curiously at the ordinary-looking vase full of murky Fountain of Youth water, Colonel Kile Killigrew, no longer looking like 'Death Warmed Over', inanely yelled-out an imaginative exclamatory sentence for all present to hear, "Dr. Heidegger, take me to your liter!"

Indeed, the dumb-assed veteran military officer from Western Pennsylvania now sounded very much like a common stereo-typical fucked-up space alien.

* * * * * * * * * * * *

Seeing that his old flame Wilma Whyknot was looking forward to the kinky prospect of having her clitoris perk-up to its former teenage hardness, Dr. Heidegger became inspired to pour the muddy water taken from the purported Fountain of Youth into the four filthy champagne glasses. Tiny bubbles percolated at the glass bottoms and then the little air pockets rose-up to the glasses' surfaces, magnificently exploding in each example into a lustrous silver spray.

"Before you partake of your drink," the absent-minded Professor said to his over-anxious guests, "remember all of the monumental mistakes you've experienced in your lackluster past lives, and then think of constructive ways you can deal with those perils the second time around on life's wondrous carousel."

"Fuck your philosophical bullshit!" demanded Melvin Melbourne. "Pour us the freakin' magic water before it evaporates into useless hydrogen and oxygen molecules! I don't want to be a goddamned model citizen!" the transplanted Australian vehemently yelled. "I just want to screw a few good-looking bitches who are models and who might incidentally be non-model citizens also! I'll even screw some fat ugly illegal Mexican whores if I get horny enough! Si, mucho gorda feo muchachas! Si Senor Heidegger!"

"But Friends," Dr. Heidegger futilely objected, "just consider what a marvelous advantage you're being offered right this moment. It would be a shameful sin if you didn't practice more wisdom and more virtue on your second more opportune tour of human duty, so to speak."

"Cut the silly-assed sanctimonious bullshit and start pouring the goddamned muddy water," Gaston insisted before expelling a devastating blast of gas, this time propelling his ass right off his chair and then his body two feet into the air. "We're too fuckin' old to joyfully sin without the help of the Fountain's magic water!"

"But what about today's vulnerable youth being tempted by drugs, sex, MTV and alcohol?" the benign retired Driftwood Naval

Academy Professor academically challenged his academically challenged listeners. "What about today's endangered youth?"

"Fuck them!" Melvin Melbourne exclaimed. "Shit on the acne-faced shit-heads' heads!"

"But isn't there more to precious human life than a very limited self-centered biological animal-type existence?" the ball-busting water-pourer requested, all the while seeking some semblance of constructive verbal reactions.

"I hope the miraculous water doesn't grow teeth upon Wilma's gums!" Colonel Killigrew contributed to the zany general debacle. "She gave tremendous blow-jobs when the promiscuous bitch had a full set of choppers anchored in her mouth, but with only gums to suck with, holy shit America! My balls are beginning to ache! I think I'm goin' to pop a huge premature load into my clean white underwear even before ever drinking the fine elixir!"

"Drink hardily then and be satisfied to your heart's content!" Dr. Heidegger sternly instructed, bowing his head and waving his right arm like a respectful Indian servant. "And drink to your dicks and tits' content too! The amazing stuff I'm gonna' serve you will work better than testosterone in men and even better than estrogen in a horny woman like Wilma."

"Stop with all of the lousy pedantic profundity!" sex-starved Wilma Whyknot hollered. "This rather stimulating hormone you're suggesting will once again make *this* veteran whore moan, ha, ha, ha!"

Then the all-too-thrilled cantankerous alligator-skinned bitch indulgently imbibed all but a remaining few ounces of her glass of imported Fountain of Youth water.

"This water tastes like cat piss!" Gaston loudly complained before farting a deep hole into his chair's soft upholstery.

"I understand that swallowing-down cat piss could send the dumb-fuck experimental drinker into a suspended catastrophic catatonic state. Now Gaston, have you ever drunk cat piss to ever be able to make that unethical-sounding, totally distasteful statement?" Melvin Melbourne challenged his rival for Miss Whyknot's sexual favors.

"No Melvin, confidentially, I've only smelled cat piss from a distance at the neighborhood kennel, but I do have box wood hedges all around my property, and box wood smells almost identical to cat piss. In fact," Gaston further elaborated on the wholly boring subject, "every day I would see a large family of cats pissing on my cherished hedge. But unlike the bothersome stray cats roaming around, I've perceptively noticed that the more discriminating canines on my block all piss on dogwood trees instead of on my box wood hedges! However, the other less-sophisticated imbecile dogs in my neighborhood are always pissing on and barking up the wrong friggin' trees, that is to say, oak, birch, pine, maple and elm!"

"It's a good thing you all have advanced Parkinson's," Dr. Heidegger observed and mentioned. "The shaking of your hands while gripping your glasses mixes-up and stirs the Fountain formula most excellently. Someday I'll be able to put every fucked-up nursing home and adult diaper company out of business with this wizard-like Florida water!"

Suddenly the flaccid faces of all four invited guests began glowing and brightening, and soon a healthy ruddy color appeared on their formerly pallid cheeks; in fact, on all their faces and the cheeks on all their ancient buttocks too. Mr. Melbourne, Mr. Gascoigne, Colonel Killigrew and Miss Whyknot no longer looked like morbid funeral parlor corpses about to be cremated.

"Give me more damned water!" Melbourne demanded like a bratty toddler in a high chair. "My limp dick has partially erected while I was looking at Wilma's tits firming-up! Hurry-up Heidegger, before I lose my miniature hard-on! And I really don't give a skunk's shit if I damage my brain with all the blood surging down from my head to my throbbing pecker. I gotta' keep the damned thing alive and growing! I want more water Heidegger, and I want it now!"

"Patience! Patience my Man!" counseled the very suave Professor. "Just pretend you're a successful medical doctor and that you have lots of patients, ha ha, ha!"

More supernatural water was being poured from the mint-green vase into the four champagne glasses, and the recipient merry revelers greedily gulped-down the liquid as if it were refreshing cold soda pop on a sultry summer day. The hideous silver hair on the elderly guests' balding heads was slowly losing its boring grayish hue, and when the study's heavy wooden table rose-up six inches off the floor, all because of Melbourne, Gascoigne and Killigrew's new-found erections, all six avaricious eyes quickly turned upon elegant-looking and now-sensuous Wilma Whyknot.

"Wilma, you look absolutely charming!" the disreputable conniver Gaston Gascoigne hungrily declared, just as his next powerful fart nearly obliterated his expensive trousers.

Instead of masturbating in public, the three horny gentlemen quickly stripped-down nude and then immediately began wildly pursuing Wilma Whyknot around the study's table like dizzy sex-starved maniacs.

"No more vicarious sex for me!" screamed a hot-to-trot Colonel Killigrew. "I want the real thing baby! Yes sir, the real thing!"

"No more casino card playing for me! I'm tired of losing at gambling!" Gaston fanatically bellowed. "Now I want the real deal! Yes, I want the real deal and nothing else: The Queen of Hearts and not the Queen of Diamonds!"

"No more me idiotically looking at merino sheep and hairy wallaby assholes!" Melvin Melbourne yelped. "This fuckin' time it's gonna' be boner-fide penetration! Forget Monica doing Clinton! I want to be fucked and not sucked!"

"I want to be screwed badly too!" shouted the already-fatigued racing woman, being relentlessly chased by the lustful male trio, "but I want to be porked by only one horny jerk-off at a time!"

'Holy hormones!' Dr. Heidegger disgustingly thought. 'Those three assholes desiring to rape Miss Whyknot don't give a shit whether or not they have ribbed condoms! And I now understand that *that* Fountain of Youth miracle water is a fantastic aphrodisiac too! Forget me putting the profitable nursing homes and the lucrative adult diaper industry out of business! I'm gonna' go after destroying Viagra, Cialis and Levitra instead!'

"We're gonna' get ya' Wilma and spread those Rockette legs wide open!" Melbourne yelled ahead to the former harlot, sounding a little like Fred Flintstone. "Keep circling the table! But we're gonna' get you good! Your wet pink snatcheroo is gonna' be pumped dry!"

Professor Heidegger simply stood in a far corner of his musty study with his jaws agape, peering incredulously at the naked men's dandy hard-ons, flapping violently up and down during their hot cunt-hunt pursuit.

"Look here you fanatical nutcases!" shrieked Dr. Heidegger above the chaotic din. "Now I know for sure that frivolous self-centered assholes like you four ingrates are rapidly turning the majestic United States of America into a Third World Banana Republic!"

* * * * * * * * * * * *

When Miss Whyknot's lungs finally ran out of breath, the exhausted-and-retired New York City prostitute was immediately gang tackled by the three more-than-eager gigolos, who during the turbulent tumult, hadn't realized that they had lost their impressive erections while grappling and fighting with each other for "first dibs," for "sloppy seconds" and for "who gives a shit thirds."

Miss Wilma Whyknot now also was extremely disappointed at not getting gang-banged into ecstasy upon the immense study's dirty oak-planked floor. And when the four dazed sex-marathon participants rose-up from their knees to their feet, pissed-off Wilma, feeling ignored and abused, swiftly kicked all three disconsolate and sexually frustrated paramours very forcefully into their now-dormant and inert testicles.

But when the four struggling lunatics had been frenetically rolling around on the study's sordid floor, no one except alert Dr. Ludwig Heidegger had comprehended that the extended scuffle and the ensuing fracas had caused the mint-green vase to fall off of the oak table and then completely shatter upon gravity's impact.

Finally realizing what damage had occurred, all four miserable morons got down on their hands and knees and began aggressively licking the dirty planks, their parched tongues in desperate quest of the remaining minuscule droplets and beads of invaluable and indispensable Fountain of Youth water.

The four elderly misguided fools all stared at unfazed Dr. Heidegger, who was then sitting in his favorite red velvet wood-carved armchair. The shrewd scientist was passionately holding the again-withered rose given to him by Miss Sylvia Ward fifty-three years prior, the selfsame flower that Ludwig had recently rescued from the shattered mint-green flower vase.

"My dick is limp!" moaned distressed Melvin Melbourne.

"My balls are shriveled," cried garrulous Gaston Gascoigne. "I think they're disintegrating! I'm so fuckin' pooped I can't even poop or fart!"

"My tits are horribly flabby and sagging again and my lush brown pussy hair has mysteriously disappeared," volatile Miss Wilma Whyknot vehemently bitched. "Somebody must've put vanishing cream in that fucked-up spiked Fountain of Youth water!"

"Yes my old Friends, you're all impotent shit-heads again," Dr. Heidegger verified. "And unfortunately, I've just received word yesterday that my old acquaintance down in Florida has passed away. Leon de Ponce was really and truly the only person who knew exactly where the singular Fountain of Youth is located!"

And then the eccentric Professor casually limped out of the library/study and methodically progressed through the tall thick doors into the red-carpeted foyer. Several moments later distinct clanking sounds were discerned, and after the metal window shutters slammed closed, the four pathetically trapped elders finally reasoned that they had been successfully locked inside the bizarre haunted room.

A dim dull light being emitted from the chamber's four tall candles revealed Sylvia Ward alternating inside the fearful wall portrait from being fully clothed to being totally nude; and then numerous pale-faced dead medical patients were sticking their eerie heads in and out of the room's dreadful wall mirror; and the two male skeletons were again enacting their perverted sodomy; and finally, Hippocrates began dashing around the accursed study wielding two sharp daggers in his massive white marble hands.

Before any of the doomed hostages could scream, shout or even emit gas, a small square trap opened in the side wall and Dr. Ludwig Heidegger's scary voice declared, "Well my former Friends from the distant past, I've decided that you've all lived on this planet for too long a duration. Yes, I am indeed playing God! I've intelligently retained several additional vases of the sensational Fountain of Youth formula down in my dank cellar, so I plan on being around this isolated part of New Hampshire for at least another century or so."

"What's to become of us?" yelled-out a now-hysterical Wilma Whyknot, who had swiftly scurried to a spider web-infested corner to temporarily evade the formidable stalking of Hippocrates's now-living statue.

"My dear Wilma," Dr. Heidegger condescendingly answered and then snickered, "I'm getting overwhelmingly bored being a chemist, a pharmacist, a medical doctor and a college instructor these past seventy years, and so, I'm finally graduating from Mortuary Science School, but in order to be fully certified, I must first dissect four fresh corpses and then write a comprehensive thesis on my results to allow me to finally qualify for receiving my diploma."

"You can't do this unthinkable mortal sin to us!" shrieked a fully delirious Melvin Melbourne, whom Hippocrates was now keenly eyeing. "This travesty you're engaged in is undoubtedly malicious criminal behavior! You'll pay for your dastardly felonies, I'm sure of it! The FBI will eventually track you down!"

"After the four of you foolish nitwits are stone-cold dead," Professor Heidegger's voice calmly informed his prospective victims through the square trap door in the side wall, "I'll have loyal Hippocrates carry each of you one at a time down to my cellar morgue where I'll diligently commence working on my most difficult Mortuary School thesis!"

"Nathaniel Hawthorne" (1804-1864)

For many years Nathaniel Hawthorne attempted to become an established popular fiction writer. After a decent New England college education, Hawthorne soon returned to familiar Salem, Massachusetts where the aspiring author lived with his mother and sisters for twelve years, staying secluded in a lonely room writing short stories and novel manuscripts. In 1837, his first work titled *Twice-Told Tales* was successfully published.

Hawthorne was chummy with some of the more famous New England literary writers of his time including Herman Melville, Henry Wadsworth Longfellow, Ralph Waldo Emerson and Oliver Wendell Holmes.

Two of Hawthorne's better known works are novels *The Scarlet Letter* and *The House of the Seven Gables.* "The Minister's Black Veil" and "Rappaccini's Daughter" are two of the author's best known short stories.

About the Author

Jay Dubya is author John Wiessner's initials (J.W.) and also his pen name. John is a retired New Jersey public school English teacher, having taught the subject for thirty-four years. John lives in southern New Jersey with wife Joanne and the couple has three grown sons.

Jay Dubya has written other adult literature besides *Thirteen Sick Tasteless Classics, Part III*. *So Ya' Wanna' Be A Teacher*, *The Wholly Book of Genesis'*, *Black Leather and Blue Denim, A '50s Novel* and its sequel, *The Great Teen Fruit War, A 1960' Novel* are humorous literary endeavors. *Frat Brats, A '60s Novel* completes Jay Dubya's coming-of-age action/adventure trilogy. *Pieces of Eight*, *Pieces of Eight, Part II*, *Pieces of Eight Part III* and *Pieces of Eight, Part IV* are short story/novella collections featuring science fiction, paranormal and humorous plots and themes. *Nine New Novellas*, *NNN, Part II*, *NNN, Part III* and *NNN, Part IV* are other sci-fi/paranormal story collections. *Two Baker's Dozen* is another collection of short fiction works.

Ron Coyote, Man of La Mangia is adult humor and a satire/parody on Miguel Cervantes' *Don Quixote*, published in 1605. *The Wholly Book of Exodus* is adult satirical humor. *Thirteen Sick Tasteless Classics*, *Thirteen Sick Tasteless Classics, Part II* and *TSTC, Part IV* are adult satirical rewrites of famous literary short fiction. Other satirical works are *Mauled Maimed Mangled Mutilated Mythology*, *Fractured Frazzled Folk Fables and Fairy Farces* and *FFFF & FF, Part II*.

John has also authored a trilogy of young adult fantasy novels, *Enchanta*, *Pot of Gold* and *Space Bugs, Earth Invasion*. *The Eighteen' Story Gingerbread House* is a new collection of eighteen diverse children's stories.

Jay Dubya likes '50s rock and roll music, and he also enjoys pop' songs by the Beach Boys', Fleetwood Mac, the Eagles, the Rolling Stones, *ELO*, John Mellencamp and by John Fogerty. When not writing or listening to music, Jay Dubya likes watching *76ers* basketball and *Phillies* and *Yankees* television baseball games.

Author Biography

Born in Hammonton, NJ in 1942, John Wiessner had attended St. Joseph School up to and including Grade 5. After his family moved from Hammonton to Levittown, Pa in 1954, John attended St. Mark School in Bristol, Pa. for Grade 6, St. Michael the Archangel School in Levittown for Grades 7 and 8 and then Immaculate Conception School, Levittown, Pa. for Grade 9. Bishop Egan High School, Levittown Pa was John's educational base for Grades 10 and 11, and later in 1960, the aspiring author graduated from Edgewood Regional High, Tansboro, NJ. John then next attended Glassboro State College, where he was an announcer for the school's baseball games and also read the nightly news and sports over WGLS, GSC's radio station.

John Wiessner had been primarily an English teacher in the Hammonton Public School System for 34 years, specializing in the instruction of middle school language arts. Mr. Wiessner was quite active in the Hammonton Education Association, serving in the capacities of Vice-President, building representative and finally, teachers' head negotiator for 7 years. During his lengthy teaching career, John had been nominated into "Who's Who Among American Teachers" three times. He also was quite active giving professional workshops at schools around South Jersey on the subjects of creative writing and the use of movie videos to motivate students to organize their classroom theme compositions.

John Wiessner was very active in community service, being a past President of the Hammonton Lions Club, where he also functioned for many years as the club's Tail-Twister, Vice-President and Liontamer. John had been named Hammonton Lion of the Year in 1979 and in 2009 received the prestigious Melvin Jones Fellow Award, the highest honor a Lion can receive.

John also was a successful businessman, starting with being a Philadelphia Bulletin newspaper delivery boy for two years in the late 1950s in Levittown, Pennsylvania. After his family moved back to New Jersey in 1959, John worked at his grandparents and his parents' farm markets, Square Deal Farm (now Ron's Gardens in Hammonton) and Pete's Farm Market in Elm, respectively. He later managed his wife's parents' farm market, White Horse Farms in Elm for three summers.

Also in a business capacity, for 16 summers starting in 1967 John Wiessner had co-owned Dealers Choice Amusement Arcade on the Ocean City, Maryland boardwalk and also co-owned the

New Horizon Tee-Shirt Store for eight summers (1973-'81) on the Rehoboth Beach, Delaware boardwalk. In addition, "Jay Dubya" was a co-owner of Wheel and Deal Amusement Arcade, Missouri Avenue and Boardwalk, Atlantic City. And then, for 18 summers beginning in 1986, John had been the Field Manager in charge of crew-leaders for Atlantic Blueberry Company (the world's largest cultivated blueberry farm), both the Weymouth and Mays Landing Divisions.

After retiring from teaching in 1999, writing under the pen name Jay Dubya (his initials), John Wiessner became the author of 46 books in the genre Action/Adventure Novels, Sci-Fi/Paranormal Story Collections, Adult Satire, Young Adult Fantasy Novels and Non-Fiction Books. His books exist in hardcover, in paperback and in popular Kindle and Nook e-book formats.

www.ingramcontent.com/pod-product-compliance
Lightning Source LLC
Chambersburg PA
CBHW052021070526
44584CB00016B/1848